THE
INDIAN CARD

THE
INDIAN CARD

Who Gets to Be Native in America

CARRIE LOWRY SCHUETTPELZ

FLATIRON
BOOKS
NEW YORK

www.flatironbooks.com

Library of Congress Cataloging-in-Publication Data

Names: Schuettpelz, Carrie Lowry, 1984– author.
Title: The Indian card : who gets to be native in America / Carrie Lowry Schuettpelz.
Other titles: Who gets to be native in America
Description: First edition. | New York : Flatiron Books, 2024. | Includes
    bibliographical references and index.
Identifiers: LCCN 2024020019 | ISBN 9781250903167 (hardcover) |
    ISBN 9781250903174 (ebook)
Subjects: LCSH: Schuettpelz, Carrie Lowry, 1984– | Lumbee Indians—Iowa—
    Biography. | Lumbee Indians—Ethnic identity. | Lumbee Indians—Tribal
    citizenship. | Indians of North America—Tribal citizenship. | Indians of
    North America—Ethnic identity. | Indians of North America—Legal status,
    laws, etc. | Lowry family. | Iowa—Biography.
Classification: LCC E99.C91 S44 2024 | DDC 977.7004/9730092
    [B]—dc23/eng/20240513
LC record available at https://lccn.loc.gov/2024020019

Our books may be purchased in bulk for promotional, educational, or business use. Please contact your local bookseller or the Macmillan Corporate and Premium Sales Department at 1-800-221-7945, extension 5442, or by email at MacmillanSpecialMarkets@macmillan.com.

First Edition: 2024

10 9 8 7 6 5 4 3 2 1

To Annie Pearl Lowry, and all who came before and after

Contents

Introduction   1

1   Membership   7

   Interlude   29

2   Belonging   32

   Interlude   53

3   Counting   55

   Interlude   75

4   Payment   77

5   Remove   99

   Interlude   123

6   Separate   125

   Interlude   147

7   Disconnect   148

   Interlude   171

8   Identity   174

9   Return   195

   Epilogue   213

   About This Project   217

   Acknowledgments   221

   Notes   223

   Index   249

THE
INDIAN CARD

Introduction

About fifteen years ago, I began to observe a trend.

If you, like me, track the results of the U.S. Census because nothing in this cold world makes sense except the hard facts of multivariate data analysis, you've seen it, too: the population of people in this country who self-identify as Native has exploded.

According to the 2000 U.S. Census, about 4.1 million people checked the Indian box, a term I use to describe the carousel of options that have appeared for Native Americans and Alaska Natives over the years. So, in 2000, when asked to select their race from a list of fifteen options (including "Other"), 4.1 million people checked the box labeled "American Indian or Alaska Native." By 2010, that number had increased to 5.2 million. And in 2020, 9.7 million people—more than twice the 2000 count—self-identified as Native.[1]

Certainly, there have been a few changes to the way we count. In 2000, for example, for the first time in census history, people could check more than one box for race.[2] So, if we assume that people were previously choosing between their racial identities, the 2000 census presented an interesting change in methodology. Indeed, the number of people who identified as Native in the 1990 census was just under 2 million, less than half the number in 2000. There has also been a significant push to count more of the Native people living on reservations, a population that has the highest census "undercount" of any population in the United States, at 5.6 percent.[3] That undercount means that census results are significantly lower than other reliable population estimates from vital statistics sources like birth and death certificates. Over the last ten years, increased Tribal consultation has taken place, as have efforts to "get out the count" in Native communities.[4]

But nothing—not a technical change to the way we count, not increased counting initiatives, not birth rates or adoption rates or a sudden parachuting of new humans onto the earth—can explain the astronomical rise in people claiming Native identity over the last two decades. Nothing, of course, aside from the fact that more and more people are feeling compelled to self-identify as Native.

Self-identifying, though, is just one piece of a very convoluted puzzle. In the United States, there are myriad ways a Native person may be required to demonstrate their identity. That list includes Tribal enrollment. Yet, at the same time that the number of people self-identifying as Native in this country has increased to over 9.7 million, the number of people enrolled in Tribes is much, much lower.[5]

This nuance is particularly pronounced among people who identify as Cherokee. As of 2023, just over 450,000 people were formally enrolled members (called citizens) of the Cherokee Nation.[6] That is, 450,000 people have some sort of card, which they applied for and received, through the process the Cherokee Nation determined. Another (approximately) 16,000 people are enrolled in the Eastern Band of Cherokee Indians.[7] An additional (approximately) 14,000 people are enrolled in the United Keetoowah Band of Cherokee Indians in Oklahoma.[8] Together, about 480,000 people in this country are enrolled in one of three federally recognized Cherokee Tribes.

These numbers are in stark contrast to the results of the U.S. Census, to the little blue boxes instructing users to "print the name of enrolled or principal tribe(s)." In 2020, the number of people who wrote some combination of "Cherokee" or "Cherokee Nation" or "Eastern Band of Cherokee Indians" or "United Keetoowah Cherokee Indians of Oklahoma" was over 1.6 million.[9] So, of the people in this country who self-identify as Cherokee, fewer than one-third are enrolled members of a federally recognized Cherokee Tribe.

Scholars have written a lot about this phenomenon—that because of a complex set of issues that includes patterns of disconnection, relocation, and misrepresentation in family lore, the number of people claiming Cherokee heritage is very high.[10] But we see this not just with Cherokee. This same gap, between claiming Native identity and being formally verified as having it, exists for many other Tribes in the United States.[11]

I imagine that the width of the gap feels different for each person who approaches it. Some may not notice its existence at all. They've been told, for example, that their great-great-great-grandmother was a Cherokee princess, and so they dutifully check the Indian box whenever they get the chance.[12] It's a mere transaction. Maybe they don't even know that the concept of enrollment exists.

For others, this gap is probably more akin to a fiery chasm, its flames whipping their face each time they get close enough to peer into it. They've known about this chasm their entire life, and it's one that's difficult to ignore. It's a gap they'll never be able to cross. Maybe they don't meet their Tribe's enrollment criteria. Maybe their so-called blood quantum isn't high enough. Maybe they don't have access to the necessary paperwork.

For me, the gap seems to change shape every time I approach it. Sure, I'm enrolled in my Tribe, the Lumbee Tribe of North Carolina.[13] I have a card, a wallet-size piece of plastic, that proclaims it so. And, yes, ownership of this card makes me feel validated in ways I'm still trying to unpack in therapy. But I did not grow up surrounded by my Lumbee community. I mostly present as white. My surname is an amalgamation of German consonants I'm told translates loosely into English as something about fur. The one-quarter "Indian blood" I possess could just as easily be stated as the reverse equation: I am three-quarters German, too.

Rationally, of course, I know this isn't how it works. Every person holds multiple identities. Some might even hold them like I do, rattling around inside them like breakables on a flimsy shelf. And I know that blood cannot be divided like an apple—clean cut and cored, separate and distinct pieces of a whole. But this fallacy—the idea of blood being divided into fractions—is exactly how the United States has long

governed Native identity. Part of that governing has included validation. Evidence. Proof. It has included certificates and rolls and cards,
pieces of paper that deem a person Indian or not. Hell, it *still* includes
these things. It still includes certificates of the degree of Indian blood
a person possesses.

I couldn't shake the feeling that, at least in the United States, this is
unique to Native people. That we, uniquely, have been forced into a corner of needing to constantly prove our identities to ourselves and others,
to carry around a card in our wallet that provides not just validation but
also protection from those who'd like us to believe we're not Indian *enough*.

So, I set out to better understand the puzzle. That's what this book,
in fact, is all about.

I began by asking for stories of Native identity. I reached out to Native
friends and colleagues. I reached out to *their* friends and colleagues. I
did the thing that statisticians call "snowball sampling"—I used my own
network to build additional connections. I spent a lot of time in coffee
shops and kitchens, in shared spaces and private homes. I heard things I
could never have fathomed. I saw the real modern-day impacts of federal
policymaking conducted over a century ago. I watched as people tried to
make sense of the rules.

With each story, I became more squarely interested in the issue of
Tribal enrollment, of what it meant and what it didn't mean and where
it came from. So, I researched. I worked with research assistants. I was in
near-constant communication with the records acquisition experts at the
National Archives and Records Administration. I checked out every book
I could find. I dug, and I dug, and I dug, and the more I dug, the more
confused I became. The more I started questioning my own identity. The
more times I read *There There*, by Tommy Orange. God, it all became so
complicated. Like the wadded ball of maroon Navajo-Churro yarn that's
been sitting in a dusty corner of my crafts box for fourteen years, disen-
tangling the threads felt daunting.

My gut response was to turn to something that's always been a com-
forting presence in my life, a warm embrace in a world full of cold truths,

a bright beacon in an otherwise dark and stormy sky. I am, of course, talking about Microsoft Excel.

I decided that, in order to better understand the issue of Native identity, I would need to quantify it. Because there are hundreds of Tribes, and because every Tribe is different, the only way to see patterns was to catalogue the rules across all Tribes, to create a giant spreadsheet on which I could identify which Tribe used what guidelines to determine who could enroll. My hope being that, by understanding the forest *and* the trees, perhaps I could make sense of it all.

But here's the thing. Much like humor, analytics can become just another defense against the universe.[14] Yes, the numbers and patterns were a handy reference point. It was important to understand processes and paperwork and documentation.

None of that, though, could prepare me for the stories. The data couldn't shield me from the personal truths, the reckonings, or the emotional mountain climbing of trying to reach the pinnacle of understanding Native Nation citizenship. Of Tribal enrollment. The inspection of my own card; the turning of the small piece of plastic in my hands, over and over.

The continuous and ever-present asking of the question: how, in the hell, did we get here?

1

Membership

I was six years old when I became a card-carrying Indian.

This was 1990: my favorite outfit was a pair of those stirrup leggings with elastic under the heels and neon socks scrunched to mid-calf, matched with a tie-dye T-shirt knotted at the waist. I had a deep and abiding love for the TV series *The Baby-Sitters Club* and, perhaps more inexplicably, for the movie *Pee-wee's Big Adventure*. When I dug through some plastic totes of childhood papers recently, I unearthed what has become my favorite treasure—my report card from that year, which claims that "Carrie doesn't like to let the other children have their own ideas."

I don't have a beautiful, core memory of discovering my Native identity, of growing up with the teachings or traditions of our people. I wish I did. When you look up the route from Cedar Rapids, Iowa (where I was raised), to Pembroke, North Carolina (where my Tribe, the Lumbee Tribe, is headquartered), you will see that the two are 1,055 miles apart. I can tell you that it's possible to feel every single one of those goddamned miles, because I have—on the two-day drives there and back, sitting in the backseat of my dad's Buick LeSabre eating grapes from a Ziploc bag while tightly crossing my legs because we weren't due for another bathroom break for an hour.

Here's a core memory I *do* have. When my Tribal enrollment card—the size of a driver's license—arrived in the mail, my mother made me wash my hands before holding it.

We were standing in the nine-by-nine-foot kitchen of the house where we lived until I turned thirteen. It was an old house, built in 1913 in the Colonial style. Many of the fixtures were original to that period. There was no shower (just a tub), no carpeting, no central AC. The kitchen was one of only two rooms in our house with an air-conditioning unit—a dusty old brick of a thing that sounded like a jackhammer. On the day the card arrived, I'm sure my mother stood in that way she always did, leaned up against our makeshift wooden countertop with one heel propped against the other ankle, facing the AC's noisy breeze. I remember her showing me the crisp white envelope with its clear cellophane address window. Very official.

"It just came in the mail," she said to me as I scrubbed the dirt underneath my nails. "They won't give me another one if you ruin it."

We didn't have any of those school-pictures-through-the-years frames my friends had hanging in the hallways of their homes. We didn't have crayon portraits stuck to the fridge with some sort of hand-thrown magnet sculpted in elementary art class. We had vintage kitchen tools my great-grandmother had passed down to my mother, all carefully lined up above the cabinets. We had tall, oval frames around sepia-tinted ancestors going back a century. We had curated pieces from our family record like museum antiquities.

History surrounded me in that house. I just wasn't allowed to touch it.

When my hands were deemed clean enough to get ahold of the card, I was able to make out my name, my birth date, and my mother's name—in typeset. I have this distinct memory of the line that was supposed to act as a shelf for each word cutting through the bottom of it, and I was proud that I understood it meant the card had been filled out by a typewriter instead of a computer. Mine was the first kindergarten class at Johnson Elementary School to begin using computers—light-brown boxes with rounded screens that briefly turned green when we flicked the power switch to On.

As with any object I wasn't allowed to touch, there grew some mystique around the card. At first, I tried to be subtle. When I was allowed to sit atop the kitchen counter—to crack an egg into Jiffy blueberry muffin mix or fold Cool Whip into the thing we called fruit salad—I'd inch myself close enough to the neatly stacked piles of receipts and papers where

I suspected the card was kept. When my parents went out each Friday and Saturday night, I could (carefully) rifle through the papers so long as I put them back exactly as they had been.

But eventually, the card disappeared from the counter. My mother had moved it to a destination unknown. It'd be years before I'd see it again.

On the occasions when I've dealt with the Tribal enrollment process, it has felt a bit like going to the Department of Motor Vehicles. I present myself at the turtle-shaped building of the Lumbee Tribe's headquarters, show proof of identification, and sign documentation that certifies I am who I say I am. It requires standing in line. There are clipboards involved. And at the end of the process, I receive a laminated card with an unflattering picture of myself in the lower righthand corner.

One of the primary reasons that enrollment, why Tribal membership, exists is because of the underlying principle of Tribal sovereignty. For Native American Tribes, sovereignty is boss. It's king. Sovereignty is the key that opens all the doors. It's the thing upon which all other things rest. Throughout Indian Country, sovereignty is the shared love language. To understand any Native person's story, it's important to understand the concept of sovereignty.

Over the last 250 years, the U.S. government has ping-ponged between full-scale "termination" of Native peoples to (alleged) protectionism of them to everything in between. And often what has been at stake—besides the obvious human lives and land rights—is sovereignty. That is, in losing their land and, often, their lives, Tribes have clung to their rights of self-determination for continued survival.

Look, my friend David Wilkins, a prominent Lumbee scholar, would urge me not to mention sovereignty without a full discussion of its metaphysical roots; or the ways we understand sovereignty relative to other sociopolitical entities; or the unique and important elements of self-identity that Tribes have cultivated over the centuries.[1] He'd tell me not to forget to discuss cultural continuity or the legal basis for sovereignty that Tribes now have with the federal government. Above all, he'd implore me to avoid using a simplified, Western definition of sovereignty.

But here's a simplified Western definition of sovereignty: At its most boiled-down level, sovereignty means that Native American Tribes—or, at least those recognized by the U.S. government—have the legal right to govern themselves. By the letter of the law, federally recognized Tribes have the right to form their own governments, make and enforce laws, levy taxes, license and regulate activities within their jurisdictions, zone their lands, and exclude individuals from their lands.[2] From a practical standpoint, this means that Native American Tribes have any number of institutions that are otherwise reserved for municipalities—things like Tribal courts, Tribal law enforcement, Tribally operated transit systems and social welfare programs, Tribe-levied sales tax. During my brief time as a graduate student working with the Navajo Nation, I met officers from the Navajo Nation Police Department. I drove past the Navajo Nation Supreme Court. I set up my makeshift office in the Navajo Nation Division of Economic Development.

Along with these functions comes a hierarchy of leadership. Often that hierarchy resembles the structure of certain nation-states, many of which were created *after* Native American governments took their own form. The (Haudenosaunee) Iroquois Confederacy, for example, is often described as the oldest living participatory democracy on earth.[3] In fact, it is thought that the structure of government laid out in the U.S. Constitution was based on Iroquois principles.[4]

Other Tribes, too, have developed sophisticated governing structures that support the idea of sovereignty. The president and vice president of the Navajo Nation can serve no more than two four-year terms. The Cherokee Nation has an elected principal chief, who also can serve no more than two consecutive four-year terms. My own Tribe recently held elections for Tribal chairman after the former chair reached his limit of two three-year terms. We have a Lumbee Tribal Council, also an elected body, which is made up of representatives from each of the geographical districts, another common feature of the governments of Native Nations.

Most Tribes have constitutions laying out the rules for everything from land use to child welfare to employment benefits. And as sovereign entities, every federally recognized Tribe has the right to define its membership through its own process of enrollment.[5]

As of 2024, there are 347 federally recognized Native American Tribes in the forty-eight contiguous United States, and the mantra that's often repeated when it comes to issues in Indian Country is that *every Tribe is different*. Treating "Native America" as a monolith is a bit like claiming interest in "Asian culture." There isn't just one.

When it comes to determining membership, the mantra rings true. While some Tribes base enrollment primarily on the fraction of Indian blood you have, others don't consider this at all. Some Tribes use historical rolls they created at the behest of the U.S. government in the early part of the twentieth century, while others have done away with those.

With enrollment comes political identity, which becomes particularly important when considering the ability of Native Nations to engage and negotiate with the U.S. government. It is a critical piece of Tribes' continued survival. Enrollment can also come with more, let's say, *tangible* benefits. Some Tribes take revenue garnered from casinos or other profitable Tribe-owned enterprises and give out monthly "per capita" checks to enrolled members. Some Tribes award scholarships for secondary education, sometimes a full year's tuition. Some Tribes use enrollment as a qualification for housing benefits or land ownership rights; some do the same with health care. Some Tribes offer special assistance to enrolled veterans or older adults; some offer childcare.

The mantra, I'm learning, is true. Every Tribe *is* different.

My mother and father and my aunts and uncles all graduated from Marion High School, home of "the Indians." The image of the teams' mascot—a red profile of an elderly man with a headdress—was emblazoned on my mother's cheerleading sweater, my father's wrestling uniform, my uncle's football jersey. Despite the mascot, I've never heard my mother mention other Native families in her neighborhood or even her town. Her (Lumbee) father was almost always mistaken for a Black man, including by a (white) reporter for the *Cedar Rapids Gazette*, who once wrote proudly about having a Black barber in the American civil rights era.

My grandfather was born to John and Bessie Lowry on Christmas Eve in 1923, in Pembroke, North Carolina. He was raised in Pembroke and graduated from Pembroke High School, part of the campus of North Carolina's first school built for the purpose of educating Indians.[6] During World War II, he was drafted into the U.S. Navy. While on active military duty in California, he met Anna Marie Klenk, a German woman from the Midwest who was visiting family in San Diego. The two married and made their home in Iowa. They had five children, including my mother. It was the early 1950s, when air travel was considered a luxury and a cross-country road trip would have required more time off than either my grandfather (a barber) or my grandmother (a waitress) could afford—so, frequent trips back to North Carolina were simply not possible. My mother estimates that she visited North Carolina a handful of times throughout her childhood.

The next time my mother drove to North Carolina was with me. My first trip was the summer after sixth grade, and it felt like a scene from those TV shows where people who were adopted at birth reconnect with their "long-lost" biological families: I saw strangers who looked like me (that same prominent chin curving downward from those same plump cheeks and thick lips, those same ringlets of hair that would frizz and fuzz if we let them), but whose accents were unlike any I'd ever heard before. I visited the graves of great-great-grand-somethings, drove past the hardware store my grandfather worked in during high school. I was told I reminded people of "Marvin," the name my grandfather grew up with despite his being known in Iowa exclusively as "Jim." It's not an uncommon story, but it is one that has made my life feel profoundly disjointed.

I remember my mother mail-ordering *The History of the Lumbee* on VHS and asking my third-grade teacher if she could show it to the class. I remember her reading from notecards, standing next to the tall metal trolley with a beast of a television strapped to the top. I remember that the video was one of those voice-over deals, with grainy images of historical photos montaged together between reenactments.

When, recently, I asked my mother why she chose to show the film to my class, she told me she knew we had been studying Native Americans in school and that it was hard for the other kids to relate to what they were learning. "They thought Indians should have feathers and headdresses," she said. "You and I didn't look like what they thought we should look like."

For most of my life, I've vacillated between thinking that I do and do not "look Indian," whatever that means. When I was younger, I would try to Indian-ify myself before going to powwows. I'd straighten my hair to the point where I imagined each strand standing up on its own. I'd wear Lumbee shirts I'd collected from my trips to North Carolina, and dangle earrings from a Native art show my mom took me to every year. I wanted to feel I belonged, and to do so, I used images I'd cultivated in my head from stereotypes I'd seen portrayed in movies and on TV.

Several years ago, a friend sent me an article from the *Washington Post* about the Lumbee Tribe. It featured high-resolution photos of Lumbee people of all ages, with all skin tones and hair colors, with freckles and blue eyes and red hair and tight black curls and deep brown skin and dimples and braids. The title of the piece was "What Makes Someone Native American?" It was one of the first times I remember thinking, *Okay. I can be Indian and not look like someone's stereotype of what that means.* I was thirty years old.

I don't recall any conversations on the playground following the showing of *The History of the Lumbee*, but I do wonder what the other children were thinking. Presumably, they would not have assumed I was anything but white. Or maybe, at eight years old, it hadn't fazed them at all.

And that, really, is the heart of the privilege I possess. I usually present as white, while at the same time I can claim Native identity in circles of my choosing. It's a privilege that has undoubtedly benefited me in more ways than I know. It is also something that has made my identity feel dotted with potholes.

I suppose that's what assimilation is all about: in the process of re-moving Native people from their communities, of surrounding them with non-Natives and making their customs feel foreign, the policies and fuckery unleashed upon Native people by the U.S. government have also made them feel supremely disconnected.

I t was by sheer coincidence that I found myself living in the same small college town as my friend Kevin Washburn.

Kevin and I worked together in Washington, D.C., in the Obama administration. While I served as a policy adviser at the U.S. Depart-ment of Housing and Urban Development, Kevin was the head of the Bureau of Indian Affairs, the BIA. We worked collaboratively on ini-tiatives around Native homelessness, specifically for military veterans.

The same year I moved to Iowa City to teach at the University of Iowa, Kevin took a job as dean of the University of Iowa College of Law. We are two of the only Native faculty on campus—Kevin is a citizen of the Chickasaw Nation of Oklahoma—and find ourselves at a lot of the same gatherings.

I ask Kevin about data.

I can't help myself. Years of working in public policy have led me to view the world through the lens of data, both quantitative and qualita-tive. I'll admit that it's not a singularly positive trait. Certainly, there are all kinds of things we can't data-fy. Ironically, that list probably includes some of the very ideas I'm most interested in, like identity and belonging.

But I can't shake the feeling that data on Tribal enrollment might offer

some insights into formalized Native American identity and the ways enrollment rules have been imposed or shaped by federal intrusion. I know
that data, in and of itself, isn't the answer, but if I want to know the *universe*
of ways Tribes determine enrollment, it seems useful to know how *each*
Tribe does. If I want to better grapple with the question of blood quantum,
it seems useful to know how many Tribes use blood quantum in their enrollment process and to what degree.

Kevin tells me that the U.S. government doesn't keep a lot of data
on Native American Tribes. Yes, some data points are necessary for
funding—that is, for Tribes to receive federal aid for things like housing
or education initiatives. But, largely, when it comes to Native American
data, the U.S. government takes a hands-off approach.

Certainly, from the perspective of self-determination, this makes
sense. There is, after all, an entire global movement around indigenous
data sovereignty—the idea that Native nations and Tribes have the
right to govern the collection, ownership, and application of their own
data.[7] But, I wonder if the pendulum of data has swung too far in one
direction. That even Native American leaders often don't have the benefit
of comprehensive data to inform their decision-making.

Let me put it this way. Say the governor of Iowa expresses concern
about the state's sales tax rate—maybe she's inclined to think it's too low;
maybe she thinks the state is not garnering as much revenue from sales
tax as it needs to or expects. It's likely the governor's policy advisers could
gather robust data within a matter of minutes—things like sales tax rates
around the country and where Iowa ranks among all states; changes to Iowa's sales tax rates over time; sales tax revenue as a proportion of all state
revenue and where Iowa ranks among all states. Knowing this information could help the governor better understand the landscape of sales tax
across all states. It could inform her conversations with other states about
lessons learned. It could help her make better data-driven decisions.

If the president of the Navajo Nation expressed concerns about the
Tribe's sales tax rate, policy advisers would probably struggle to find much
data. They certainly wouldn't be able to find anything comparable to what

they'd find for U.S. states. There isn't a lot of robust data broken down by Tribe. If the president of the Navajo Nation wanted to understand where the Tribe fit into the larger universe of sales tax across Indian Country, policy advisers would need to gather and synthesize the data themselves. The process would be onerous. It'd likely take weeks, if not longer.

It strikes me that some of the data points that would be most useful to a Tribe's leaders are those that wouldn't be in the federal government's best interest to gather—things like Tribes' original land masses and the years when they were stolen; Tribes' current land masses and the quality of the soil; federal Native American treaty responsibilities as compared with actual, implemented policies.

The reasons for this lack of data are many, including the fact that many institutions and agencies simply don't collect it. Abigail Echo-Hawk, an enrolled citizen of the Pawnee Nation of Oklahoma, is the director of the Urban Indian Health Institute. She has spent years fighting for access to data to better understand and make better decisions, particularly around Native health disparities and rates of violence. Yes, anecdotes can be important, but for policymakers and funders, she says, data is more difficult to ignore.[8]

I tell Kevin about the kinds of data I'm most interested in, for better understanding Tribal enrollment. Kevin says he's never heard of such a source. He points me toward the one dataset the BIA maintains and publishes on its website. Initially, I am relieved. I take some comfort in knowing that I have a decent starting point.

That's before I lay eyes on it.

The list is spare, to say the least. Called the Tribal Leaders Directory, it includes every federally recognized Tribe, both in the contiguous United States and in Alaska. Next to the name of each Tribe is the contact information for its leader, the address of the Tribe's main offices, the date of the next election, and each Tribe's—and I'm not kidding—geographic longitude and latitude. And that's it.

I begin the work of building a dataset by winnowing the list down from 574 Tribes by taking out Alaska Native communities. The scope of my research is somewhat narrow in that respect—Alaska has its own unique history, and Native communities there are generally very, very small. I settle on the list of 347 federally recognized Native American Tribes residing in the contiguous United States. With the help of four fantastic research assistants, I assemble the database by visiting websites and reading newspaper articles and library volumes. We rely exclusively on publicly available information. The project takes us more than three years to complete.

One of my research assistants, Clara, is a graduate student from southeastern Asia. She is tenacious in her desire to track down data, including for Tribes that none of the rest of us is able to. I am incredibly impressed by Clara, especially her ability to do this work in what is not her first or even second language, but her third—particularly given that the material can be tricky to navigate without a solid understanding of Native America or at least a passing knowledge of how Tribes are organized or what their rights are as they relate to sovereignty. I provide Clara with articles I believe will give her a helpful background. She devours what I send and asks for additional resources; she is perpetually interested in learning more.

I send her to the Bureau of Indian Affairs website to take a look around. I hope that in navigating that agency's various functions, she can begin to better understand the relationship between the U.S. government and Native Nations.

I ask Clara how such a relationship works in other places she's lived, between the government and different ethnic groups or indigenous Tribes. I wonder if there are mechanisms like the Bureau of Indian Affairs, to ensure that the broader engines of public policy include an indigenous voice.

The question confuses her at first. She takes a moment to ponder. When she speaks again, she does so delicately, slowly. She reminds me that, in some areas of this world, colonialism is not the governing philosophy; in some places, settlers aren't the overwhelming majority. In some countries, the people responsible for making policy are also indigenous to the place.

When my mother finally deemed me old enough to take possession of my Indian card, I was thirty years old and living in a five-hundred-square-foot studio apartment in Washington, D.C. The card was part of a larger haul of childhood memorabilia—plastic totes of kindergarten art projects, middle school research papers, swim meet split sheets. My parents had decided that it was time for me to be in charge of my own archives.

I sat on the college-grade rug in my combination living/dining/bed-room, digging through yellowing papers. When I opened the last box—a navy-blue tub with large cracks in the lid—the card was there, right on top, there with my name in that same antiquated typewriter print. I spent a few moments in front of my dusty, boxy television, eating peanut butter straight from the jar and turning the card over and over in my unwashed hands.

Underneath the card was a single sheet of paper on Lumbee Tribe letterhead, a document that had presumably been sent along with the card all those years ago. It congratulated me on receiving my card and encouraged me to participate in Lumbee activities and events. And it reminded me that I needed to renew my enrollment every seven years.

I called my mom in a panic, and she panicked, too. Neither of us had known about the concept of enrollment renewal. We didn't realize our enrollment wasn't permanent. After all, nothing had changed about my ancestry in those twenty-four years since the card arrived in the mail. Aside from the fact that I was now embracing my curls and had, begrudgingly, started liking tomatoes, I hadn't assumed a different identity. Certainly my lineage remained the same.

When I called the Lumbee Tribe headquarters, they confirmed that, yes, I would need to renew my enrollment. It was a rule meant to ensure that people enrolled in the Tribe maintained some sort of connection to it—a rule I now know to be part of a lot of Tribes' enrollment pro-cesses. It's not dissimilar from maintaining U.S. citizenship while living abroad—if you ever intend to return, you must continue to renew your passport.

In order to renew my Tribal enrollment, I would need to present my-self in person in Pembroke and provide the necessary paperwork. And because I'd let my card lapse, I'd be treated as if I were a new enrollee, thereby required to complete the *other* part of the process, too: the test.

During the seven years I lived in D.C., I had made periodic visits to see my family in North Carolina. Every several months, I'd pack my suitcase and stash it in the trunk of my Toyota Corolla and hop on the Beltway, which forms an uneven circle around the city. The drive from Washington, D.C., to Pembroke, North Carolina, is an easy one: straight south down Interstate 95; six hours without traffic—something people in D.C. fancifully say as if that's ever the case. Everything always takes at least an hour longer than it's supposed to.

In 2014, the year I learned about having to renew my Tribal enroll-ment, I'd planned to meet my mom in North Carolina. She'd fly from Iowa, from our hometown of Cedar Rapids, and I'd pick her up along the way. We'd stay with our cousin Joan, our family's matriarch, at her farm outside Pembroke. Joan's mother and my grandfather were brother and sister. I never know what to call Joan—"first cousin once removed" seems too formal, too distant for what we are. In a lot of ways, Joan is a mother figure for me. She cares for and about me in the same ways I imagine any deeply religious, southern-born, devoted mother of four would. She feeds me more than I can eat and doesn't allow me to swear. Before I got married and had babies, she'd pester me about when I was going to get married and have babies.

Cousin Joan's farm feels off the grid in more ways than one. Cell service is spotty, and internet connectivity nonexistent. The first time I visited from D.C., I brought my laptop in the hope that I could finish some work. It was the last time I'd make that mistake. Not only would technological connectivity prevent me from opening my computer, but timing would, too. Joan had us on a schedule. She marched me around Pembroke like a tour guide, walking me through the newest exhibit at the Museum of the Southeast American Indian, on the campus of UNC Pembroke; pointing to the newest restaurant or coffee shop through the windshield of her sedan. During a single meal at Fuller's Old Fashioned BBQ, it wouldn't be unusual to be introduced to Joan's pharmacist, several students from her days as a classroom aide, an ex-girlfriend of her youngest son, and the senior pastor at her church.

Joan also drove me to what she lovingly called "Lowry Circle," the small grouping of houses where most of her siblings and their families lived. It was easy for me to feel deeply loved on those visits, but it was easy to feel like an outsider, too. For one thing, the minute I opened my mouth, anyone could tell I hadn't grown up there. My Iowan accent is peppered with the flat *a*'s and *o*'s prominent in the American Midwest. The Lumbee dialect, for its part, is something others have described as a mix between Appalachian and Highland Scottish.[9] That, plus, the particular intimacy gained from living every single day of one's life in Pembroke was beyond anything I could imitate. I didn't know where everyone worked or played; I wasn't privy to the latest town gossip; I didn't share a church pew with anyone on Sunday.

By the time my mom and I made our way to Lumbee country that summer of 2014, we had already been warned about the test. It was a new addition to the enrollment process and included questions specific to Pembroke, questions that, for anyone who hadn't grown up there, would be difficult to answer without some preparation. So, we spent the night before our enrollment appointments studying. Joan's sons, grown and with families of their own, took turns quizzing us.

The next morning, as we pulled into the parking lot of the Lumbee Tribe Headquarters, on Pembroke's main drag, my heart radiated electricity into my shoulders and neck. I was nervous. Afraid not just of failing the test, but also embarrassing myself in front of my own people, my family. I followed my mom into the building and waited my turn.

In the end, we both passed. But the process had sewn inside me a thick thread of doubt about my identity. It made me question whether I, someone who did not just inherently know the answers on the test, deserved to call myself Lumbee. Whether I, someone who hadn't grown up in this place or surrounded myself with my Lumbee relatives, should even be enrolled at all.

Now, a decade later, I remain uncertain.

Sure, in that time, the Tribe has done away with the test, opting to require a class on Lumbee history and culture instead. And, yes, I have done my best to remain in touch with my Lumbee relatives, periodically reading the local newspaper and visiting Pembroke as often as I can. But it occurs to me that the special relationships I have with my Tribe and that place are ones I've had to work to maintain—and if I were to stop putting in the work, they are ones that would not be passed down to my children or, if they so choose, their children after them.

In that way, the relationships I have cultivated with my Tribe—with its people and history and tradition and place—are ones that might someday cease to exist.

To understand a Tribe's enrollment process, the first place to look is at its constitution. Not every Tribe has a constitution, but for those that do, the section related to enrollment is generally right up front. It's an important element of the systems that Tribes have put into place—the element of defining membership.

Together with my research assistants, I am able to locate 285 Tribal constitutions.[10] That is, for all but 62 federally recognized Native American Tribes in the contiguous United States, we find some sort of official document—called a constitution and outlining its principles and procedures—that was passed by the Tribe's leadership.[11] Some constitutions are relatively recent: the Kiowa Indian Tribe of Oklahoma passed its most recent constitution in 2017.[12] Some date back centuries: the Choctaw Nation first passed its constitution in 1826, although the Tribe currently operates under a constitution ratified in 1983.[13]

For the most part, Tribes without a constitution are pretty small; most have fewer than a thousand members.[14] One notable exception is the Navajo Nation, whose enrolled population hovers around four hundred thousand members. The Navajo Nation is one of the two largest Tribes in the country (the other being the Cherokee Nation), but it famously does not have a constitution.

In the mid-1930s, after the passage of the Indian Reorganization Act, which encouraged Tribes to adopt governance models that mirrored those of the United States, the federal government pressured Tribes to create formal constitutions.[15] In many cases, the government withheld financial aid until the Tribes complied.[16] The Navajo Nation declined, arguing that constitutions were not a Navajo concept.[17] In 2008, the Navajo Nation Constitutional Feasibility and Government Reform Project concluded that "the concepts of Nation-statism and constitutionalism are inappropriate and ineffective as applied to the Navajo Nation."[18] Rather, the Navajo Nation has, over the years, developed a complex legal code.[19]

Regardless of whether a Tribe has a formal constitution or has opted for alternative systems and processes, most have an enrollment office—sometimes a fully staffed organization, sometimes one person located inside the Tribe's government office; sometimes, it's a person who doesn't earn a salary from the Tribe, but who serves in the role as a volunteer or an elected official. It is this person (or office) who is responsible for processing enrollment requests.

The primary trend that I begin to observe in the data is one that others before me have noticed, too.[20] Specifically: with regard to determining membership, Native American Tribes fall into one of two categories. For about 120 Tribes for which I can find information, Tribal enrollment is based on lineage. That is, in order to enroll in the Tribe, an applicant must demonstrate that a direct relative (a parent, grandparent, great-grandparent, etc.) was a member of the Tribe. Tribes use a census or roll particular to their community as the basis for this determination.

So, if someone wants to enroll in the Tulalip Tribes of Washington, they must find a direct ancestor on the 1935 Tribal census rolls. If someone wants to enroll in the Mohegan Tribe of Indians of Connecticut, they must find a direct relative on the 2002 Tribal rolls. If someone wants to enroll in the Passamaquoddy Tribe of Indian Township, they must find a direct ancestor on the 1900 Tribal rolls.

The other main way that Native American Tribes determine membership is by using a calculation of how much ancestry a person has from that particular Tribe. This number is usually represented as a fraction, and usually called blood quantum. For about 170 Tribes for which I find information, Tribal enrollment is based on blood quantum. And for the vast majority of those, the blood quantum calculation is made from one Tribe alone. So, if someone wants to enroll in the Oneida Nation, they must demonstrate that they have one-quarter Oneida blood quantum. If someone wants to enroll in the Tohono O'odham Nation of Arizona, they must demonstrate that they have one-half *Papago-Tohono O'odham Indian* blood quantum.

Sure, they can have a blood quantum from other Tribes, but it won't be factored into the calculation. No Tribes in the contiguous United States, that I can find, have a four-fourths blood quantum requirement; most, or about 60 percent of those that use blood quantum, use one-fourth as their cutoff: you must prove that you have at least one-fourth blood quantum from that Tribe alone.

The requisite blood quantum can be achieved a few different ways. For example, if someone wanted to enroll in the Oneida Nation, whose requirement is one-quarter blood quantum, they would need to demonstrate that amount through one or several ancestors.[21] So, if Jessica has one grandparent who is "full-blooded" Oneida and three grandparents who are non-Native, then she would be considered to have one-quarter Oneida blood quantum. If Terrance has two grandparents who are each "one-half" Oneida and two grandparents who are non-Native, then he would also be considered as having one-quarter Oneida blood quantum.

Both Jessica and Terrance (figments of my imagination, by the way) are right at the cutoff for Oneida membership: they both have one-quarter blood quantum. So, unless they have children with partners who are also at least one-quarter Oneida, their children will not be able to enroll in the Tribe. If Jessica and Terrance have children together, those children will be considered as having one-quarter Oneida blood quantum and *could* enroll.

Blood quantum is an awkward calculation that makes identity seem like math.

In addition to lineage and blood quantum, some Tribes add other criteria to the mix. Some have requirements around culture and tradition—my own Tribe, the Lumbee, for example, now requires completion of that Lumbee history class before someone can enroll. A handful of Tribes take into consideration which side of your family your Native ancestry is on. Some Tribes require applicants to enroll within a certain period after their birth. Some maintain a residency requirement: the applicant must have been born or currently reside on the Tribe's lands.

Every Tribe is different.

In recent years, and with the advent of consumer ancestry tests, a misconception has emerged that DNA spit tests can be used to gain Tribal enrollment. That's not quite true. No federally recognized Tribe in the United States allows someone to apply for enrollment using just their 23andMe report.[22] Tribes that use DNA tests in their enrollment processes generally do so for maternity or paternity purposes—that is, to determine a person's biological parentage.

The ease with which an applicant can get through the Tribal enrollment process varies. Some people are enrolled at birth. In fact, many hospitals run by the federal Indian Health Service include enrollment as part of the standard maternal care. Enrollment paperwork comes in a package with applications for a birth certificate and a social security number. For people who weren't born at or don't reside in their Tribal community, the process can be more complicated. Usually, an extensive family tree must be filled out; usually, historical birth certificates of ancestors must be submitted. Often, the process must be completed in person. So, if an applicant lives far away, they must travel back to their Tribe.

And then there are the phone calls. Oh, the phone calls.

I remember being a junior in high school and getting ready to take the SAT, a standardized test to determine a student's aptitude for college. I'm not great at standardized tests. I get easily confused by lists of similar answers, and I don't have a lot of patience for sitting still. I remember one of my teachers telling me that the SAT wasn't a measure of how smart a person was but, rather, how well they could take the test. That, in fact, is one reason SAT scores tend to get higher the more times a person takes the SAT—with each attempt, the test taker better understands how the test works.

I feel this way about the Tribal enrollment process. Now that I understand how the process works, I am better able to help others through it.

One of the biggest obstacles people face with Tribal enrollment is verifying their ancestry. It is generally the case that Tribes don't release their historical rolls to the public. Certainly, from a sovereignty perspective, this makes sense. After all, the U.S. government doesn't maintain a public-facing list of all its current citizens. I can think of a hundred reasons this sort of public cataloguing would be problematic. The same goes for Tribes.

A key difference, of course, is that for Native American Tribes, citizenship via enrollment is not geographical as it is for the United States. In the United States, the vast majority of citizens—87 percent, by some estimates—acquire their citizenship by virtue of being born in the United States.[23] In fact, the United States is one of only thirty-five countries in the world that maintain this policy, often called birthright citizenship.[24]

For Native American Tribes, citizenship is *never* geographical. No Tribe in the United States confers citizenship to everyone born on its territory or land. Rather, citizenship in Native American Tribes is always *relational*.[25] It's fully dependent on whom a person is related to. The process of verifying those connections is, therefore, a crucial one. It's not enough simply to verify that a direct ancestor was from a particular Tribe; their name must be on a specific roll. And, often, determining whether their name is on that roll requires a phone call to a Tribe's enrollment office.

On the occasions that I've had to make such a call, I can say that I have been greeted with the same amount of enthusiasm as found at any other bureaucratic office I've dealt with in my life. And I get it. I can only imagine the sorts of questions Tribal enrollment offices field. And I'd guess that Tribes using more historical rolls are probably more susceptible to questionable enrollment claims. Just as Tribes vary in the age of their constitutions, so, too, do Tribes vary in the age of their rolls. And, obviously, there's a huge difference between finding your parent's name on a list from 2002 versus locating the name of a generations-old ancestor on a list from the nineteenth century.

Such is the case with the so-called "Five Civilized Tribes," whom I'll choose to refer to as "the Five Tribes" from here on out. In addition to using censuses from the early 1900s, called the Dawes Rolls, these Tribes represent an interesting anomaly in the sense that their rolls *are* public. Anyone with internet access can search the base rolls of the Cherokee Nation, the Chickasaw Nation, the Choctaw Nation of Oklahoma, the Muscogee (Creek) Nation, and the Seminole Nation of Oklahoma.

When I speak with Kyle Key, the executive officer of self-governance for the Chickasaw Nation, he tells me that the farther away from the Dawes Rolls of 1907 they get, the harder the process of Tribal enrollment becomes. He tells me that the Chickasaw Nation receives tenuous enrollment claims on a weekly basis. Because their base rolls are part of the public record—searchable on most online genealogy sites—anyone with access to the internet can dive into the lists.

"Almost weekly, we have someone who has traced themselves to someone on the Dawes Roll," Key says. "But usually they've just found someone who happens to have the same name."

Twelve hours after I'd birthed my daughter via cesarean section, my husband gently informed me that we needed to complete her paperwork. The paperwork would be used to process her birth certificate and Social Security card—documents that carry so much weight that they absolutely should not be presented to a woman who's just had her internal organs ripped out of her body and then shoved back in. I knew that this paperwork would live on in the historical record for time immemorial. It was, after all, in the initial stages of writing this book that I used birth records and U.S. Census records to create my own family tree going back generations.

I've always found it strange to capture my identity in small boxes. The problem being that forms, whether surveys or rolls, don't allow for any nuance. Just as there are never enough tiny squares for all the letters of my last name, there's rarely room for complexity in counting.

The conundrum my husband had—one that I had, too—was whether to check the Indian box on my daughter's forms. My daughter was born in Iowa and will likely be raised there. She'll probably struggle to navigate the same distance I always did: the one between her home and that other home, the home of our Tribe. In some ways, I imagine the distance will be greater for her. She will never get to meet my grandfather or my great-uncle or my cousins Arthur and Calvin or the other relatives who have since passed. The Lumbee elders whom I credit with guiding me on my own journey of identity formation will, for her, exist only in stories.

If we take stock in blood quantum—which I'm pretty sure I don't—my daughter's will be even smaller than mine, her ancestry a more diverse array of geographies and family lore from both mine and my husband's sides. I will, of course, try to pass along the origin story and traditions of our Tribe. I'll try to nurture the connections between my daughter and her larger Lumbee tree. But, in the end, only time will tell whether her Native identity will be salient for her.

From my hospital bed, I asked my husband what we had written for our son, born two years earlier. Neither of us could remember—my excuse being hospital-administered narcotics; my husband's being his height. We always joke that, at six foot ten, the thinner air he breathes up there makes him more absentminded.

Our son was born in April 2020, a few months into the Covid-19 pandemic. It was a time when panic seeped its way into everything—our groceries, our mail, our clothing; the air we breathed. I had terrible depression after my son was born, perhaps as a result of postpartum hormones, perhaps as a result of the terrifying new global reality, perhaps a bit of both. In any event, my memories from that time have become one of those splotch tests psychologists administer: I see something different every time I look.

In some ways, not remembering what I've written on my son's forms feels like a privilege. As someone who considers herself biracial, but who presents mostly as white, I am privileged in the sense that I can choose what boxes to check on forms. I can choose what *not* to check, too. I can do the same for my children.

For my daughter's paperwork, I was relieved to learn that we could check more than one box. We marked both the "White/Caucasian" box and the one called "American Indian/Alaska Native," giving our daughter a laundry list of identities that, I suppose, she can one day learn to navigate herself. But until that time—until she and my son are old enough to make the decisions for themselves—I must navigate those identities for them.

It was this way when, in 2023, I traveled back to North Carolina to visit my family and renew my Tribal enrollment once again. After three years of near-constant surges, Covid-19 had receded enough for me to feel comfortable traveling with my small children. It would be the first time they'd set foot in Pembroke, the first time any of my extended family would have a chance to meet them. And it would be the first time that grappling with questions of Native enrollment and identity, of membership and belonging, would feel so fraught. Because, in the summer of 2023, on our trip to Lumbee country, I'd be faced with the decision of whether to enroll my children in the Lumbee Tribe.

INTERLUDE

There's this story I heard in my early days working in homelessness policy that changed the way I think about solving problems.

It was about a man who had been living on the streets of Phoenix for almost thirty years. He was a veteran of the Vietnam War and had a pretty severe case of post-traumatic stress disorder. His outreach team, including his caseworker, had been engaging with him for a long time, and when funding finally opened up for housing, the team was thrilled. So, the man's caseworker began showing him apartments. They saw apartments all over the city, in every possible quadrant and of every possible configuration. They saw studio apartments, one-bedroom apartments, apartments on the ground floor, walk-ups. But nothing was acceptable to the man. After a full year of searching, his caseworker—at this point, understandably frustrated—finally asked the man why he wouldn't just pick a place.

Reluctantly, the man explained that it was because in order to be comfortable, he needed to see the front door from everywhere in the apartment. And because none of the apartments they'd looked at so far met this requirement, he preferred to stay on the streets, in the open air, where there were no barriers to block his view of the exits. Decades of severe PTSD were preventing him from living inside.

Once the caseworker discovered the root cause of the problem, he was able to narrow the search. Eventually, he found an apartment for the man with an unobstructed view of the exits no matter where he was, and where he could also sleep outside (on a deck) if he wanted to.

I think about this story a lot. In particular, I think about the—pardon my alliteration—power of patience. Had it not been for an extraordinarily patient caseworker who showed up every day for a year, the man would very likely still be living on the streets, or worse. Finding the root cause of the issue—severe PTSD triggered especially by not being able to find an exit—was the only way the problem could be understood and, eventually, solved.

The search for answers to questions of Native identity feels a bit like this. Not that identity is necessarily a problem to be solved; rather, my own understanding of it. That, even with my burgeoning dataset and better understanding of Tribal enrollment processes, to more fully comprehend what it means to check the Indian box, comprehend Tribal membership and belonging, I must work backward to understand how we got where we are today.

The trouble is, the process feels like that old magic trick of pulling scarves out of your sleeve. The more I pull, the more scarves appear. In trying to find the first scarf, all I end up doing is amassing a giant pile of scarves that *aren't* the first one.

So, I buy a whiteboard.

I imagine myself as the main character on one of those shows my husband and I binge-watch, where they solve complex cases in forty-two minutes plus commercials. Where, arguably, the most important piece of solving the mystery is the Board—the Board being the giant whiteboard or chalkboard or clear glass board covered in photos of people connected by string, maps with important places marked with pushpins, scraps of paper with single-word, all-cap callouts to dates and places peppered throughout. *LAKE. SNOWMOBILE? FEBRUARY 18!*

Along the lefthand side of my whiteboard—the y-axis, if you will—I write *NATIVE IDENTITY*, and on the x-axis, *TIME*. I use oversize notecards to create a sort of time line. The righthand side of the board is, obviously, easier for me. It's the side I'm living on, the present tense. I use key words like *BLOOD QUANTUM* and *TRIBAL ENROLLMENT* and *DNA*. On the left side, I rely on research, albeit limited. I write things like *FAMILY, COMMUNITY, LAND*.

In the middle—in the big, intimidatingly open space—I fill in the dates for notable events I've learned about over the course of my research thus far. I try to make connections among events, but a lot of it feels like speculation, conjecture.

I'll admit I'm not much of a history buff. I'm bad at memorizing facts. My brain tends to transpose certain letters and numbers, and I have difficulty making sense of blocks of text. Plus, much of what I was taught in school felt disconnected from anything I knew as real. Learning about British royalty through the centuries didn't do much for me. I don't have a lot of thoughts about the Romanovs. The signers of the Declaration of Independence and the subsequent succession of white men residing in the White House felt far removed from my Native relatives in rural North Carolina struggling to put food on the table, or my German ancestors living in mud soddies on the Dakota prairie.

So, I was intimidated when it came to doing deep research. Because I set out to piece together the story of Native identity and enrollment, of how we got to the point where we carry around Indian cards in our wallets, using not just personal narratives but also historical records and data, I needed to teach myself the facts—facts, I should mention, that were not on the curriculum when I was in school.

Between the hieroglyphs of the U.S. codes; the dates of various, often contradictory, laws passed by the U.S. government; and the names of legislation and rolls and counts—they all begin to form a congealed mess in my mind that I can't make sense of.

So, as a thought exercise, I decide to pick a point in time. Not a specific year or date but, rather, a dot on a time line that would have been different for each Tribe. On my whiteboard, in my best handwriting, cultivated from years of childhood practice at shading in outlines with a marker—the trick is shading in the same direction with each stroke—I write *THE DAY BEFORE.*

I stare at the phrase and let my mind focus on it.

I ask myself: On the day before Europeans settled on their land, what did the world look like to Native American people? How did they think about identity? Did they have rules or systems that governed membership and community? Before enrollment cards and census forms and little checkmarked boxes, how did Native people determine who belonged?

2

Belonging

Tricia Long can't be more than five foot seven, but she somehow stands taller than that. She's trim, but I have full confidence that she could lift a car off a pregnant woman if necessary. It's this combination of fitness and badassness that always tricks me into thinking she's younger than her fifty-five years.

If you ask Tricia whether she considers herself cool, she'll say no—but trust me that she is. She wears the kind of glasses that look both retro and modern—bent outward around her brows and pointed sharply back inward underneath, like a comma on its side. She has a hooped nose ring and sports cuffed T-shirts that say things like "Fuck Colonialism."

It surprises me to learn that Tricia is self-conscious about her appearance. To me, she has a kind of effortless beauty. Like when someone's curls perfectly shape their face? Streaked with a bit of gray that tells the world they've seen some life? When they can throw on any old "Fuck Colonialism" T-shirt and still look beautifully put together?

Yeah, that's Tricia.

But, growing up, she was told she was ugly by the white children around her, and she now bears the indelible marks such tormenting creates. She sees herself as barrel-chested and admits to being fascinated by women with small waists and hourglass figures, society's idea of what she's "supposed" to look like.

"I'll never have that body type," she says. "It's just not the way we were built."

Tricia is Meskwaki. She's spent the majority of her life on or around the Meskwaki Settlement, a twelve-square-mile plot of land in East Central Iowa. First with her mother and father, then with her mother and stepfather, and eventually as a single mother of two boys. Today, Tricia maintains a modest home on the settlement, with a lush garden in the backyard that she sustains year round. She raises goats on a patch of land next to a shed at the top of her gravel driveway. Whenever I pull up to her house, a small pack of dogs greets me with enough enthusiasm that it's difficult to open my car door.

Recently, after a so-called derecho storm caused winds upward of 140 miles per hour, Tricia's house suffered damage that required new windows and siding. The incident presented the perfect chance for her to add a dormer, something she had always wanted to do. So, she built it herself. Little by little, each day—putting on her canvas jumpsuit and her work boots, Tricia lifted the roof of her house and added structural beams and broader window openings. She made it a reality.

By Tricia's own description, the Meskwaki Settlement is "in the sticks." Its remoteness is exactly what she likes about it. The location lends itself to her passion, which is seed keeping. She maintains seed varieties of beans, corn, squash, and other crops—some of which have been grown by her Tribe for over four thousand years. In addition to cultivating and maintaining the garden plots in her own yard, Tricia's work revolves around preserving the traditional foodways of the Meskwaki for future generations.

Tricia talks about seeds the way some people talk about reversing climate change or discovering water on Mars. For her, solving the issue of food sovereignty—the idea that people should be able to produce and eat culturally appropriate food that isn't manufactured by a corporation somewhere—isn't just a matter of pride but of the survival of the human species.

I first met Tricia while preparing for a panel discussion on land acknowledgments. I knew we'd be friends when we both agreed that they were sort of bullshit.

"I only heard of them three years ago," she told me.

I appreciated that we could use a word like *bullshit* to describe something like a land acknowledgment. (I often feel I'm offending other people in the room when I use such language, particularly when I don't act overly reverential about things.) Hearing Tricia speak was a revelation—with her, I didn't need to be polite when talking about "Native issues"—especially when something felt like, well, bullshit.

My senior quote in my high school yearbook was by the comedian/filmmaker Mel Brooks: "Humor is just another defense against the universe." Growing up in Middle America, a thousand miles away from the Lumbee Tribe—sort of feeling Indian, sort of not; raised in a family with, how do I say this, alcoholic tendencies; often left alone; always feeling less beautiful than the other girls in my class, my hair a fuzzy ponytail, theirs smooth and curled inward at the ends and sprayed into place—humor *was* my defense against the universe. The more I get to know Tricia, the more I wonder if the same is true for her.

Tricia and I both know it's important to connect with the land and its history. What we're *not* sure of is who benefits from land acknowledgments, those scripted statements about the Tribal origins of land on which, say, a university or a corporation now sits. We suspect the answer is: the university or corporation. We suspect that, without any real action to support the idea of Native land *sovereignty*, land acknowledgments will continue to be just another tap dance routine people perform to make themselves feel better about history.

Tricia's life seems anything but performative. The summer after we met, she invited me out to a farm in northern Iowa run by Seed Savers, a nonprofit committed to preserving heirloom plants. It was time to harvest the rows of beans she'd planted several months earlier, and Tricia expected to be working in the fields for most of the afternoon. It was a scorching mid-July day, and I was in the first trimester of my pregnancy—the trimester that made me feel like I was permanently hungover aboard a cruise ship—so I declined. She didn't counteroffer by asking me to come take pictures of her doing the work or to drive by the plots of land to watch the harvest. She'd just wanted me to be part of the process.

One of Tricia's passions is helping other Native women learn to grow their own food. Occasionally, she'll post recipes to her social media accounts—one recent post about milkweed included directions on how to prepare it. I found myself fascinated by recent pictures of chicken of the woods mushrooms and Tricia's instructions on how to pan-fry them.

But it's not just Meskwaki foodways that Tricia is passionate about. She knows her Tribe's creation story the way she knows her own full name. The hero Wisakeha shaping the first humans out of red clay; the origins of the Tribe's name for itself, which in English means "the Red Earth People." She can tell you the dates of important Meskwaki events and the names of Meskwaki leaders going back a century; her cousin is, after all, the Tribe's historian. Tricia speaks some Meskwaki and is trying to learn more. Her living room is decorated with posters from Meskwaki festivals going back a decade—looping neon letters advertising a community feast or powwow—some of which she designed herself.

To me, Tricia is the epitome of what it means to be part of a community, part of a culture and, well, a *Tribe*. A bearer of a very important torch. The problem is, she cannot pass that torch on. That's because, in Tricia's Tribe, in order to do almost anything, you must be able to trace your Meskwaki ancestry *patri*lineally—that is, on your father's side.

For Tricia's family, this rule has created an uneven patchwork of "who's in" and "who's out." Tricia, whose mother is white, is an enrolled member of the Meskwaki Tribe because Tricia's *father* was Meskwaki. Tricia's younger son, whose own father is Meskwaki, is also an enrolled Tribal member. But her elder son, whose father is white, cannot enroll.

In Meskwaki terms, the distinction comes down to enrolled *members*, who qualify for all Tribal benefits—be they land rights on the settlement, per capita payments, access to health care, housing assistance, or simply the ability to claim enrolled status—versus *descendants*, who are acknowledged as having Meskwaki ancestry but do not qualify for much else.

For Tricia's elder son, a Meskwaki descendant, this distinction means he'll never be able to fish or hunt, both passions of his, on Meskwaki land; he'll never be able to earn the same per capita revenue as his brother; he'll never be able to maintain a home on the settlement or serve on the Tribal council. He'll always be aware of his status—that he is not an official, enrolled Tribal member. If he decides someday to have children of his own, they will never be able to enroll in the Meskwaki Tribe, either. And there's nothing Tricia can do about it.

"It fucking sucks," she tells me.

When I think about family, when I think about belonging, I think about my Lumbee relatives who live in a circle.

It begins with a turn onto a gravel path. You'd miss it if you didn't know it was there. You first pass by Cousin Mary Beth's modest two-bedroom home, the one where her daughter Jennifer now lives since Mary Beth passed away. A stone's throw from Jennifer's front door is Cousin Hank's house, where he and his wife, Cynthia, have lived for decades. Hank, who is Mary Beth's brother, spent most of his career working at the Nestlé plant in town, and often when I visit, he offers me the latest of the company's products to try.

If you were to drive a little bit farther down the gravel path, the road would curve to the left, into the driveway of Cousin Leo. Leo, who is Mary Beth and Hank's brother, is arguably the quietest of the siblings. I imagine that's partly because of the tragedies that have plagued him— he's lost not one but two sons. If, from Leo's house, you then reversed and continued on the gravel loop back toward the main road, you'd pass the house that Cousin Hugh's family still lives in decades after he passed.

If you stood in the middle of the circle and yelled loud enough, I'm certain you could call everyone to supper. Often, someone in the family is making a bonfire once the sun goes down, or inflating a small swimming pool for the kids to splash around in. The North Carolina summers, in this part of the state, can feel like a thick layer of silk, heat clinging to everything it touches.

Anytime I visit Pembroke, my cousin Joan—one of the few siblings who does not live in the circle—walks me from one relative's house to another. Usually, it doesn't take long before word spreads that I'm in town, before others start showing up in Hank's kitchen or Mary Beth's living room.

Of course, living that close together is not an entirely positive experience. Just as good news spreads quickly (relatives visiting from out of town), so, too, does bad. Someone's broken up with their boyfriend or girlfriend. Someone's lost their job. Someone's had words with someone else. But, largely, I imagine, the benefits outweigh the costs. I imagine that's why this family circle has existed for so many years.

It seems like most analyses of Native American history, of the centuries-old roots of Native American Tribes, begin with a discussion of kinship. It's a vague word, but one we can generally understand to mean family. That kin, people related to one another by blood or otherwise, stick together.

Sure, the reasons that kin stick together have changed over time. I don't imagine, for example, that Hugh or Hank or Leo or Mary Beth created their family circle out of concern for an invasion by another Tribe, or because they needed as many hands as possible to cut wood in preparation for the coming winter, or to form parties to fish or to herd horses in order to survive. That's because survival has evolved to mean other things.

For my relatives in Pembroke, living near one another provides companionship and support. It provides dinner on a night when there's nothing in the fridge, or milk when you run low. It provides a solid sense of social protection: you know someone will always have your back.

What I know from books I've read and VHS tapes my mom played at home and from my own experience of Lumbee culture is that kinship has always been important to us. One of the first questions one Lumbee will ask another is "Who are your people?" I get asked this a lot, especially as someone who did not grow up in North Carolina. I've developed something of a shorthand response, one that seems to work with most folks: my grandfather Marvin Lowry and his brother Henry lived on Normal Street, next to Mount Olive Church; my grandfather's nieces and nephews—the families who live in a circle—are the family we are closest with today. Sometimes it feels like a secret handshake, going through the ritual of who's connected to whom.

Of course, to understand family connections, to understand how any particular issue plays itself out in Indian Country, is to understand that every Tribe is different. When I began to explore the idea of precontact belonging, the ways that Tribes would have thought about identity or "membership" before colonization, I realized I was asking a question that may not have one distinct set of answers.

It's an iterative lesson for me, that every Tribe is different. From a historical standpoint, it's a lesson I'm trying to replace, undoing others I've been taught over the years. That, despite having sung along with Disney's version of Pocahontas, I now know that not every Native person would have "run the hidden pine trails of the forest" or "tasted the sun-sweet berries of the earth."[1] That, despite what I remember learning in school, not every Native American Tribe lived a nomadic life. Not every Tribe herded buffalo. Not every Tribe practiced communal land rights.

Sure, some did. But some Tribes practiced agriculture. The Mandan, Hidatsa, and Arikara people—today organized as the Three Affiliated Tribes of the Fort Berthold Reservation in North Dakota—cultivated crops like beans and squash and developed systems of food storage for surplus harvests.[2] Some Tribes participated in sophisticated market economies, enabling goods to travel hundreds, if not thousands, of miles.[3] The trade routes of pipestone, a soft stone used by Dakota people to make tobacco pipes, spanned half the continental United States.[4] Some Tribes operated under systems of private property. Among the Nuu-chah-nulth people—whose descendants include the Makah Tribe located on the tip of the Olympic Peninsula—fishing spots, hunting and gathering places, houses, and village sites were all considered the property of particular Tribe leaders.[5]

Unfortunately, studying the ways that every Tribe organized itself before colonization is beyond the scope of my research. It sort of kills me that I can't data-fy kinship. I'd love nothing more than to create a massive spreadsheet outlining the precontact practices of every Tribe in the country, the ways each Tribe would have subsisted or organized living arrangements or defined roles in the community. But I can't.

So, instead, I look for patterns.

I learn that at the moment of first contact with white settlers, the Nez Perce people, ancestors of today's Nez Perce Tribe in western Idaho, lived in villages, or bands, comprised of kinship groups.[6] These villages were usually made up of several related extended families, and young people were encouraged to marry someone outside their own group.[7] Villages would have small councils made up of a few elders.[8] The Nez Perce people, who call themselves the Nimíipuu people, often took a communal approach to childcare. In part, it was a way to encourage respect for elders and instill a sense of importance for kinship ties.[9]

I learn that the Quechan people—ancestors of the Fort Yuma Quechan Indian Tribe in Arizona and Southern California—historically lived in small patrilineal bands. Over time, these bands developed into larger groups known as rancherias, comprising as many as five hundred people.[10] The Osage people—ancestors of today's Osage Nation in northern Oklahoma—were also patrilineal. I learn that Osage people would traditionally have organized themselves into twenty-four clans, each with its own symbol, like an animal or a plant or another "natural phenomenon."[11]

I learn that the Cherokee people—ancestors of three federally recognized Tribes in Oklahoma and North Carolina—historically considered women to be heads of the household.[12] Traditionally, there were seven clans among Cherokee people, and an individual belonged to the clan of their mother. For Cherokee people, clan membership would have been central to one's identity; it would have determined their social relationships, friends, enemies, and whom they married.[13] Kinship guided almost every decision a Cherokee person made. The Hopi people—ancestors of the Hopi Tribe in northeastern Arizona—were also matrilineal. I learn that, traditionally, related Hopi women and their families would live in adjacent homes[14] and that even once a man married and moved to a different residence, he would still consider his real home to be with his mother and sisters.[15]

I learn that the Choctaw people—the ancestors of three federally recognized Tribes across the southern United States—divided themselves into two groups, the Inhulata and Kashapa, each of which consisted of six to eight clans.[16] They were further divided into local groups. Membership in these groups was traced through the mother and assigned from birth. Members considered one another family regardless of how distant in relation.[17]

I learn that the Seminole people—ancestors of three federally recognized Tribes in Oklahoma and Florida—would traditionally have organized themselves into clan camps. Each Seminole was born into their mother's clan, and clan membership was the "single most important way in which an individual related to the rest of society."[18] I learn that the Seneca people—ancestors of two federally recognized Tribes in New York—would traditionally have lived in so-called longhouses. Each longhouse was divided into a series of "barracks" where a family unit would have lived, and several families of the same kin would have shared an entire longhouse.[19]

The more I dig, the more I wonder if kinship is the one issue we *can* generalize. Read any account of the history of a Native American Tribe precontact, and you'll come away with a solid sense that kinship was important. Indeed, I can't find any account of a Tribe categorically disavowing kinship as an organizing principle in favor of something else.

What I do find is a lot of jargon. I get stuck on *exogamous* and *moieties* and other words scholars use to describe Native kinship networks. Exogamous societies marry outside their social groups. Systems of moiety divide societies into two equal parts. The words are vaguely familiar to me—an anthropology major in college—but they're ones I have to look up. They're the kind of words someone would never use to describe themselves. I, for example, have never once heard a person classify themselves as a member of "one of two exogamous moieties."

I try to think about how Native people themselves would have described their societies before colonization, before European settlers barged in, imposing their beliefs and ideas of organization. I try to remember that what's being described are people, that we're talking about human beings. That it's human nature to think first about the idea of family, to remain close to the people who are closest to you, to raise children with a strong, solid notion of community; that members of a village or band help one another out.

That creating a family circle—living within shouting distance of your kin—is an instinct as old as time itself.

I imagine it's by design that the main thoroughfare of the Meskwaki Settlement, Meskwaki Road, begins with a pretty spectacular view of the Meskwaki Nation water tower, striped in red and green. Every time I've visited, I swear the paint has been new, bright. And although the tower is one of the only signs of the settlement you can see from Highway 30 West, it stands impressive all the same. "We are still here" is what it always says to me.

From there, the point at which Highway 30 intersects with Red Earth Drive, the brick-and-glass façade of the Tribal health center, a sphere centered by two outstretched corridors, rises up out of the Iowa cornfields like a phoenix.

When I worked in the Obama administration, we were constantly on the lookout for best practice. Something a community was doing that felt like it was really working, something that could be replicated in other communities with similar success, something that could "change the game." This Meskwaki health care center feels like best practice. The modern architecture is paired with a one-stop-shop model of care. Under one (beautifully designed) roof, patients can be seen for everything from diabetes management—Native people are three times more likely to be diagnosed with diabetes than non-Hispanic white people—to podiatry, to dental work, to mental health care.[20] Patients can access their own records through an online portal.

The rest of Meskwaki Road is just as well maintained. A single-story public works building, including the fire department and police headquarters, sits across from a well-equipped park. Since becoming a mom, I've become something of a park connoisseur, so trust me when I say that this one is good: colorful rubber turf, separate plastic toys for infants, two slides, and swings? Hell, yes.

Farther down the road is the Meskwaki Settlement School—home to the Warriors—which boasts just shy of three hundred students in grades K–12. The school, which underwent a substantial renovation in 2009, appears both modern and rooted in tradition. Its upper windows provide natural light to most of the school's interior spaces, and the curved roof lines remind me a bit of those of the National Museum of the American Indian in Washington, D.C., whose own curvature was designed to mimic wind-sculpted rock.[21]

At the end of the stretch of road—where the settlement merges back into U.S. Highway 30, is the Meskwaki Bingo Casino Hotel. Even with its impressive size—including a recent addition to the hotel—the casino looks like, well, a casino: a mostly windowless building with a large enough parking lot to accommodate tour buses, its digital sign advertising any number of upcoming concerts or jackpots.

Beyond the Meskwaki Nation buildings, single-story houses with well-manicured lawns dot the landscape, which, in true midwestern fashion, changes dramatically with every flip of a page of the calendar. Summers are deep green edged by lush forest; winters are bright white, snow spread across the rolling hills like a crisp fitted sheet. Autumn, my favorite Middle America season, is leaves of every color of the spectrum, from yellow to red, and a chill that provides much reprieve from the humidity of July and August.

About nine hundred people live on the settlement, the twelve square miles of land the Meskwaki Nation has slowly purchased over the last 150 years. The Meskwaki are sometimes referred to as the Sac and Fox Tribe of the Mississippi in Iowa. While the Meskwaki and Sac (also spelled "Sauk") form two distinct groups, they have often been associated with each other.[22] Initially, the Meskwaki people were part of the larger "Indian Removal Act" signed in 1830 by U.S. president Andrew Jackson. The act, whose name alone should signal its heinousness, led to the forceful

removal of Native Tribes from their ancestral homelands so the United
States could profit from the sale of their (valuable) land. You may recall
the notorious Trail of Tears as a particularly horrific offshoot of this policy.

In the mid-1840s, the Meskwaki, having historically made their home
in Iowa, were removed to a reservation in Kansas that still exists today.[23]
Many members of the Tribe stayed in Iowa, hidden, and some eventually
returned. Many continued to fight for their right to live in Iowa. In 1857,
the Tribe purchased its first piece of land there and has continued to grow
its settlement since then.[24]

It is this process of purchasing land from surrounding (non-Native)
landowners that differentiates the Meskwaki's *settlement* from other
Tribes' *reservations*. The key difference is that the Meskwaki themselves,
and not the federal government, hold the title to much of their land.

It's an important distinction, given that Tribes with reservations (to
which they do not hold title) do not have full sovereignty over the use
of that land. It's a bit like the difference between renting and owning a
house, if by "house" we mean ancestral land and by "renting" we mean
being held hostage by the U.S. government. Increasingly, more Tribes
are pushing for land ownership. In 2021, two Tribes in Delaware, the
Nanticoke and Lenape, bought back forty acres of their ancestral lands.
But even that transaction required financial assistance from several non-
profits.[25]

The Meskwaki are proud that they own much of their land outright.

Over lunch with Tricia one warm summer Monday, I tell her that I
feel out of place in a lot of Native spaces, that I wish I had a tighter-knit
Native community. I often dreamed of growing up in a small town, surrounded by my people.

"I mean, there's good and bad, right?" she says.

Tricia worries about the teenagers on the settlement. She wonders if
her younger son, who is enrolled in the Meskwaki Nation, will ever feel
he can leave to pursue college or jobs or to travel—or if he'll feel pulled
to stay on the settlement because of peer pressure from others who stay.

Whether growing up in a small Native community means that's all he'll ever feel comfortable with. At the same time, she worries that her elder son, a Meskwaki "descendant" who can never own a home on the settlement, will never feel truly at home in this place.

Tricia grew up with a father whose main goal was for her to "act white"—not because he wasn't proud of his Meskwaki heritage but because he wanted his children to, as Tricia puts it, "win in the white man's world." A fluent Meskwaki speaker, Tricia's father taught her some Meskwaki words, but there was no language immersion. He was a survivor of an Indian boarding school, one of the residential facilities notorious for kidnapping Native children from their families and brutally "assimilating" them to white ways. Recently, such schools became the focus of federal investigations after large burial plots were discovered around boarding schools in Canada and the United States and the remains of hundreds of Native children were unearthed. Like many of the schools' pupils, Tricia's father was beaten for speaking his native tongue. "That kind of stuff stays with you forever," Tricia says.

Because housing on the Meskwaki Settlement was nearly nonexistent in the mid- to late 1970s, the Long family rented a series of drafty and aging farmhouses in the surrounding area. And because they didn't live on the settlement, Tricia and her brothers didn't attend the Settlement School. Instead, they were enrolled in Tama public schools, where most people didn't look like Tricia and where she was bullied relentlessly.

The worst of the harassment Tricia experienced was from school staff. Once, Tricia ended up in the hospital with an impacted bowel because her teacher wouldn't let her be excused to use the restroom. The teacher had announced to the class that Tricia just wanted to leave the classroom so she could go through everyone's lockers.

Like many so-called border towns, Tama, Iowa—three thousand people strong and a stone's throw from the settlement—shares a sometimes uneasy relationship with the Meskwaki Nation. Yes, Tama has a higher population of people who identify as Native than most towns, but that number is still low—estimated at just 10 percent in 2020.

Though I haven't spent much time in Tama, I have in other border towns. Often, they are rife with violence and racism, and at disproportionately higher rates than towns not near a Native reservation or settlement.[26] Often, there are instances of police brutality against Native people—Native people in border towns and across the United States are more likely to be killed by police than any other minority group.[27] Often, discrimination leads to a lack of housing or employment for Native people. Often, Native people are perceived as a threat; that, if allowed to stay, their "Nativeness" will somehow bleed into the adjacent (predominately non-Native) community.

In March 2022, after a shooting at the Grand Gateway Hotel in Rapid City, South Dakota, a border town to some of the country's largest Native Nations, the hotel's owner announced that Native Americans would no longer be allowed on the property. Her main rationale was that "Natives kill Natives."[28]

Here are some facts that absolutely shouldn't matter when considering whether to ban all Indians from an establishment. The Grand Gateway Hotel is within a three-hour radius of four of the country's largest reservations—Standing Rock, Rosebud, Cheyenne River, and Pine Ridge. Rapid City, population seventy-four thousand, is made up of more than 13 percent Native Americans. Archeological sites in the Black Hills suggest an indigenous presence in the area we now call South Dakota going back more than twelve thousand years, or at least until 1876, when the U.S. government ordered all Native Americans in the area to "report to their assigned reservations."[29]

It shouldn't need to be said that the actions of the Grand Gateway Hotel were wrong. But the truth is the mass outrage resulted because people heard about it. It was in the national news. It was on social media. Word spread online. The U.S. Department of Justice got involved. All too often, that's just simply not the case. Native people are harassed, jailed, and even killed every day without cause and without such publicity. And a lot of it happens in the border towns that surround Native Nations.

The sheer size of the problem, together with the underreporting of many cases, has motivated an entire movement around Missing and Murdered Indigenous Women. In the United States, Native women are more than twice as likely to experience sexual violence than any other demographic; more than four in five Native women experience violence in their lifetime; and Native women are murdered at rates ten times the national average.[30] There is no category of violence that Native women are *less* likely to experience than their non-Native counterparts.[31]

Among the many reasons these facts are so striking is that, traditionally, many Native communities considered women to be the heads of families. Upon first contact with settlers, many Native Tribes were matriarchal and matrilineal. As historians have written about extensively, European settlers brought with them "notions of the inferiority of all women in general."[32] In addition to the colonization of land and religion and language, there was a noticeable colonization of gender roles. I wonder if the fact that Native women face such high rates of murder and violence is, at least in part, thanks to the imposition of these beliefs.[33]

In Tama, growing up, Tricia got bullied by more than just her teachers. Some of the other children would taunt her or worse. She remembers being tough as a result of having only brothers, but she is also a human being who would have preferred not to have been pushed and hit and spat on. She wonders what it would have been like to go to school at Meskwaki, where kids "looked like me."

Eventually, Tricia left home and enrolled at a university. It was a less-than-ideal start, given the trauma she'd endured through her middle and high school years. Once on campus—at least initially—things weren't much better. "There wasn't anyone who looked like me at college," she tells me.

After struggling for a couple of years, she eventually found art—painting and drawing, in particular—something she compares to a refuge. She was able to find other so-called outcasts, others who didn't fit into the 1980s version of normal, who wore their colorful hair longer on one side or who had piercings on the parts of their bodies that showed. She found a faculty member, a Black man, who would go on to mentor her throughout her time in college. She suspects he felt a little bit like an outcast, too.

I start to wonder about the idea of being a woman in a patrilineal Tribe. I wonder if it's impacted Tricia's sense of self, the idea that it's not enough to be a Meskwaki woman to pass down Tribal membership; that you need a man to do that. If it has contributed to the violence against women she has both seen and experienced.

When I ask Tricia about this, we are sitting together in a large, airy restaurant eating lunch. She lifts her eyes to the ceiling, contemplating. "If anything," she says, "we should be basing everything on the mothers. Women are at the heart of so many of our origin stories. Women are such a powerful force."

I know she's talking about Meskwaki specifically, but as a Native woman and new mother myself, staring across a restaurant booth at a powerful Native woman and mother whom I'm beginning to call a friend, I can't help but feel she could be talking about everything in life.

Although there isn't one common Native American "origin story," historians seem to agree that before the arrival of European settlers, most Tribes relied on oral traditions as opposed to written ones.[34] (This is, indeed, one of the reasons Native language loss is real—when the last speaker of a Native language passes away, there is a real fear that other parts of a Tribe's culture will be lost with them. What with past federal policies around assimilation and the destruction of Native tradition, the loss of a Tribe's language, too, can be devastating.) In many Tribes, stories were told by designated storytellers. They conveyed myths and ritual and history; they shaped identity and helped give meaning to people's lives. Oral traditions would also have included family histories, what we today might call genealogy.[35] By listening carefully and committing these stories to memory, generations of families would have carried forward the legacy of those who came before.

When I ask Dan Littlefield—whose work on the history of the Cherokee Nation has earned him a place in the Oklahoma Historians Hall of Fame—if he knows of any historical efforts by Tribes to write down their records, he's somewhat stumped. According to Dan, most historians seem to agree that, before contact with white settlers, the only written records Tribes made took the form of pictographs, or images symbolizing ideas. Whether painted on rocks or beaded into elaborate belts, these pictographs would have represented events or cultural practices important to the Tribe. Dan tells me that, in his own research, he has not found any lists of a Tribe's "members" until the early nineteenth century, and even those were made by federal officials.

What I take from the conversations with historians like Dan is that, in large part, before contact with settlers, Native Tribes would not have considered it important to record membership on paper. There wouldn't have been much of a need to maintain written records of who belonged. Rather, particularly in Tribes using kinship as their guiding system of governance, they'd rely on leaders of bands or rancherias or heads of families to keep everyone together.

Written records of membership and enrollment, it seems, were a product of colonization. Mostly, they would have been made by the settlers themselves. In other words, the colonization of this land—of this country—would have also included the colonialization of the historical record. According to Dan, even in the case of Cherokee people, whose Tribes have some of the longest histories of written recordkeeping, it wasn't until they experienced removal pressure from the federal government that their members began making census records.

Dan Littlefield is not Native himself. He is quick to point this out; it is important to him that people know that. Especially since it's a fact not matched by the written historical record.

When Dan was born in May 1939, doctors were responsible for completing a newborn's birth certificate. This included answering the question of color, or race. Because Dan (the child of farmers Daniel and Irene Littlefield) was born on Route 1 in Salina, Oklahoma, deep in Indian Country and with a head of black hair, the doctor assumed he was Native American. So, on his birth certificate, despite having not a trace of Native ancestry, Dan Littlefield is recorded as Cherokee.

Tricia introduces me to her cousin Anthony, a Meskwaki historian. She tells me that Anthony is "a quiet man," but kind and knowledgeable. When I visit him, I immediately understand the preface.

Anthony Long speaks so softly that, when I initially ask to enter his office, I'm not sure what his answer is. I take a risk and walk in, sitting down uneasily in the only other chair among stacks of papers and books. I recognize a floppy disk among the piles of yellowing photocopies of who knows what, and I suspect this office has always looked like this.

From behind the piles of office ephemera, Anthony looks very small—frail, almost. He sits in an aging leather chair that has begun to crack at the seams. He wears his graying hair long, a deep part running straight down the middle, and secured in a ponytail at his neck. I'd guess he's in his mid-sixties, but—especially here, in a space that time seems to have forgotten—he's one of those people who appears to have eluded age.

There are no pleasantries or small talk. I tell Anthony that I'm interested in learning more about the Meskwaki Nation's patrilineal system of enrollment. I haven't come across many other Tribes that determine membership patrilineally, and I'm curious as to why the Meskwaki have chosen to do so.

Anthony tells me that the Tribe was never patrilineal, traditionally. In the early 1900s, many of the men who farmed on the settlement were from other Native Tribes. Meskwaki women were marrying these Native men and setting up house with them. The Meskwaki men did not appreciate this dynamic, and so, when in 1937 the Tribe passed its constitution, which outlined the rules for enrollment, it added patrilineality as a way to counteract what they viewed as a threat.

Anthony seems uninterested in talking any more about patrilineality, and I resign myself to this being the world's shortest interview, clocking in at just under three minutes. I've always had healthy deference for my Native elders, something instilled in me by my Lumbee grandfather, whose daily limit was approximately twenty words. He'd drive fifty miles out of his way to fix my mother's dead car battery; he'd save two-dollar bills for me anytime he came across one; he'd let me get that piece of chocolate ambrosia pie at Bishop's Buffet inside Lindale mall—but he didn't need words to do any of that. In that way, Anthony reminds me a bit of him.

As I'm gathering my things to leave, I ask Anthony if he has seen any issues arise as a result of the current Meskwaki enrollment rules. It's as if I've blasted through the door of a moving airliner: suddenly our conversation is blown wide open.

Anthony, as it turns out, is not an enrolled member of the Meskwaki Nation. I had assumed—given that his last name is the same as Tricia's—that he, too, had a Meskwaki father. However, it was an uncle who reared him in what Anthony calls the "traditional Meskwaki ways," who passed on the surname. Despite his mother's being Meskwaki and raising him on the settlement, because his father was white, Anthony will forever be declared a Meskwaki descendant.

Over the next hour and a half, Anthony recounts stories of spirituality, of Tribal politics, of his own journey through the Meskwaki Settlement School, of feeling like an outsider in the only home he's ever known, of reckoning with the fact that his father—his white father—neither looked nor acted like any of the other adults he knew.

Anthony tells me about arriving to college carrying a single suitcase, and he cracks the first smile I've seen since we began talking. He seems proud to have survived the experience. "My buddy dropped me off the night before classes started," he says. "I'd never been there and didn't know anyone."

Anthony feels lucky that his uncle took him under his wing, offering him an education in Meskwaki tradition that included attending ceremonies. "I was a fetch boy," Anthony says. "Fetch that water. Fetch that wood." Eventually, he became a member of the group; he attends every ceremony. Eventually, he became a fluent speaker of the Meskwaki language—one of the only people alive today for whom this is true. He read every book on the Meskwaki, the Sac and Fox, and every Tribe with any connection to them. Yet he is unable to ever own land on the settlement or receive per capita money. He can't hunt or fish on the land. He can't serve on the Tribal council. He can't pass the torch of enrollment on to his children.

Anthony tells me that while he was growing up, the term for "people like him" was *half-breed*. "*Descendant* is the word of the day," he says. "I'm sure it will change."

I begin to notice that Anthony often uses the word *they*. *They* made him feel unwelcome. *They* told him he needed to leave, albeit not outright, but by *their* actions. *They* don't want him here. If *they* try to force him off the settlement, he supposes that's *their* right.

And though I don't ask him whom he means, I realize it's no one person or group. Rather, it's decades upon decades of institutions, of rules and policies and procedures, that have told Anthony Long he's not enough.

Tricia tells me later that Anthony keeps talking about retirement, but there isn't anyone who could replace him as historian, no one else who has the cultural immersion or the academic study in Meskwaki history and tradition. And yet there are people on the settlement who don't recognize Anthony as Meskwaki at all.

After my initial interview with Anthony, as I wind my car along Meskwaki Road, pointed toward home, it strikes me that the reason our conversation almost ended after only three minutes was because I used the word *patrilineal*. It's so formal. So anthropological. A word like *patrilineal* is one that would show up in a textbook, to describe the marriage or lineage systems of a people from the distant past with whom the reader cannot relate. They're not meant to relate. They're meant to whistle at the page and say, "How *fascinating*."

What routinely fails to show up in the textbooks, though, is the modernity of Indianness. Native people still live and breathe, still belly-laugh and ugly-cry, binge-watch and cosplay, ride in Ubers and Door-Dash sushi. Native people walk over the same bones of settler colonialism as everyone else. We're asked to bring a covered dish to "Friendsgiving" or to go in on a cabin Airbnb over Columbus Day weekend. Native people serve in the military—at rates five times the national average, I should mention—and defend the flag representing a government that for centuries wanted us dead.[36] We still struggle with rules that were created 50, 100, 150 years ago. And because a 1937 Tribal constitution says that only people with Meskwaki fathers can claim Meskwaki membership, there are people today who will never truly feel they belong.

On my first trip to visit our Lumbee relatives in North Carolina, my aunt Darla brought along a notepad and a pen. We had all piled into my dad's blue Buick LeSabre, my mom and dad, my aunt and me. It was 1996, before the invention of handheld streaming TV shows or movies or the internet. Before I owned handheld anythings. I remember packing a book and a pillow and taking a big cooler full of snacks. We drove for sixteen hours straight.

The trip to North Carolina was the first time I'd ever traveled much beyond a single-state radius of Iowa. I'd never been farther east than Ohio, never seen an ocean. I remember trading in the long stretches of Midwest farmland for the peaks and valleys of West Virginia. I remember the handmade signs for boiled peanuts as we drove deeper into the Appalachian Mountains. I remember the interstate turning into a roller coaster as we crossed into North Carolina. I remember my excitement with every state's welcome sign—theirs always better than ours, which proclaimed Iowa as "Fields of Opportunity."

When we finally arrived at Cousin Joan's farmhouse, down the long gravel driveway off an exit of Interstate 95, we were road-worn. We'd gotten a flat tire outside Louisville, among other things, and had to stay an extra night on the road.

Despite our exhaustion, my aunt Darla was determined to take notes.

Every relative she met got a line in her notepad—sons and daughters, mothers and fathers, aunts and uncles—their names recorded in what I could tell was her most careful handwriting. At the end of each day, she'd try to assemble the names into something of a family tree, to make sense of how so-and-so was related to so-and-so.

Certainly, part of the reason my aunt needed to rely on notes was that our family is quite large. When the list is extended to include first and second cousins, it can feel like, in one way or another, we're related to the entire population of Pembroke, North Carolina.

I suppose the desire to understand how everything fits together is a natural instinct, too. One of the first toys my son ever took much interest in was a shape sorter—a round wooden thing with separate openings for triangles and squares and circles and stars. He wanted to master it, to perfect the act of fitting the shapes inside.

It's difficult to know how the traditions of Native people would have evolved in a world free from colonization. If matriarchal lineage or kinship bands would have been more widely maintained. Whether Native Tribes would have written family trees in careful script. Had European settlers not invaded and imposed their own beliefs, it's impossible to know if Native Tribes would have developed their own written systems for determining membership. For recording belonging on lists or rolls.

So, I turn my focus to what happened instead.

3

Counting

I f you opened up the U.S. Constitution for a casual read, one of the first things you'd see would be the requirement to periodically count the population. It's there right up front, in Article I, Section 2, that every ten years, there's to be an enumeration of people living in the United States, "in such manner as [Congress] shall by law direct."[1]

Although we could probably think of a host of reasons the U.S. Census is still conducted today—like monitoring changing demographics, understanding patterns of health or poverty or education, making decisions about federal funding—in 1787, when the Constitution was first drafted, a population count was meant mostly for two purposes: taxation and representation.[2]

Of course, in 1787, the method for counting was pretty fucked up. Article I, Section 2, is notorious in that respect—the total population would comprise the number of free persons plus three-fifths the number of slaves. Not until 1868, when the Fourteenth Amendment was ratified, would every person be counted as an entire person.

At least for the first several decades of the U.S. Census, Native people—called "Indians not taxed" in official documents—were excluded altogether. Presumably because, in the late 1700s and early 1800s, many Tribes would have operated under treaty rights with the federal government. That is, at least on paper, they were considered sovereign Nations.[3] For guidance, Native people looked to their own leaders, their own kin, rather than to the newly formed U.S. government. And, as a result, Native people were not taxed; nor were they given the right to vote in U.S. elections.

In 1790, when the United States undertook its first-ever census, only six questions appeared, head of household's name and the number of people in each of five categories: free white males sixteen years and older, free white males under sixteen, free white females, all other free persons, and slaves.

Ostensibly, the male population was divided by age in order to assess the country's military capabilities, to determine how many men could be called up for service, if necessary. But, largely, anyone other than the free (white) head of household was a simple tally mark, to be counted as either one whole person or three-fifths of one whole person.

And that was that.

I've long been fascinated with the idea of counting. Since 2010, when I began noticing the explosion in the number of people self-identifying as Native, I've become particularly interested in the U.S. Census, in its patterns and trends. It wasn't until I really began to dig into the logistics of the census, though, that I developed a slightly different fascination— with how the process of counting can itself illuminate the priorities of a society. How it thinks of the people, of their value.

A perusal of the instructions given to census enumerators over time is telling.

From 1790 to 1840, the rules of census counting were spare. In just two single-spaced pages from an Act of the First Congress (Chapter 2, Section 1), U.S. Marshals and their assistants are instructed to count the inhabitants of their jurisdictions.[4] In that act, marshals are given the oath they are to take, the categories they are to record, and the time frame in which they are to conduct their work. Most of the section is actually a description of salary for employees and the ramifications of inaccurate or untimely counts.[5]

The penalties were severe. In 1790, an enumerator making false claims, whether knowingly or not, or returning their records late would have been subjected to a fine of $200 (over $6,600 in 2023).[6] If a person gave false information to a census taker or refused to give information altogether, they would be sued for $20, half of which would go back to the census taker himself.

I should pause here to say that U.S. Marshals were not specially trained to do census enumeration. In fact, the primary duty of that law enforcement body was, and continues to be, supporting the work of federal courts.[7]

In 1790, this would have included serving subpoenas, summonses, and warrants and making federal arrests—in other words, dangerous work that could reasonably require force.[8] But from 1790 to 1870, U.S. Marshals were the people on the census front lines, responsible for appointing assistants, conducting counts, and ensuring that they returned to the president of the United States—and I quote—"a just and perfect enumeration."[9]

I would guess that the threat of hefty, game-changing fines, in addition to a day job that regularly required the use of muscle, probably served to incentivize certain behaviors. It wouldn't surprise me, for example, if the marshals and their assistants used, let's just say, *aggressive* tactics to elicit census responses. Intimidation would also probably have factored into the process. And this dynamic, I imagine, would have impacted the way people answered—including whether they were fully truthful.

Trying to make sense of census records from 1790 to 1840 is a bit like trying to crack a cipher. It seems like the count was just that: a count. It's heavy on numbers and light on complexity. It tells us almost nothing about the country's population. Unless you know the name of a free white head of household, it's unlikely you'll find anyone in particular. Searching for Native people is almost a nonstarter.

I say "almost" because exceptions do exist.

Before 1850, when race became a separate question on the U.S. Census, the only options were free white people, "all other free persons," and slaves. As you might imagine, a lot of people did not fit neatly into this paradigm. There are two very interesting and verified examples of this.[10]

In the 1830 U.S. Census, David Tate Moniac is listed as a resident of Baldwin, Alabama. Because Moniac is the head of household, his full name appears, and next to it are several tally marks—three for him, his wife, and his young daughter and ten for enslaved people. Moniac's entire household, then, is comprised of three "Total Free White Persons" and ten "Total Slaves." The other entry of note is for Greenwood LeFlore, a resident of Yazoo, Mississippi. LeFlore is single, according to the 1830 Census, and listed as a "Free White Person" owning twenty enslaved people.

In and of themselves, these entries would be unremarkable. I'm sure we could find thousands, if not hundreds of thousands, just like them. They are the entries of two men, both residents of the United States, both slave-owning and landowning, free white heads of household.

Except, David Moniac and Greenwood LeFlore were both Native American.

Moniac was a member of the Creek Tribe. He was, in fact, the first Native person to graduate from West Point and the only Native American officer in the Second Seminole War. He was descended from a powerful Creek family that included at least one chief.[11]

Greenwood LeFlore was the elected principal chief of the Choctaw Tribe before their 1830 removal west. He was a member, through his mother's kin, of a powerful Choctaw family and was a signatory to the 1830 Treaty of Dancing Rabbit Creek, which ceded Choctaw lands in Mississippi to the federal government.[12] It was a controversial move and one that made him his fair share of enemies.

It would be difficult to definitively say why Moniac or LeFlore was counted as a "Free White Person" by census takers in 1830. Both were from Tribes that based identity on matrilineal lines—that is, their mother's family.[13] Both had Native mothers with influential lineage. Both would have been considered members of their Tribes. And although both were of mixed-race descent, including some European ancestry, neither of them would have been considered a citizen of the United States when the census was conducted in June 1830. It wouldn't be until 1924—almost a full century later—that all Native American people born in the United States were granted U.S. citizenship.

Perhaps it was the two men's status as enslavers and owners of land that qualified them as both free and white—particularly LeFlore, who maintained a large cotton plantation. Maybe it was that they were well known in their communities. Maybe the census takers thought they were white; both men were partly of European descent. Maybe it was simply the fact that there were no other options; there were no write-ins allowed.

Or, maybe, "Free White Persons" was a category meant to convey something else.

As I skim through census records, I can't help but think about assimilation. After all, much of the history of contact between Native people and European settlers is just that, a history of the idea that people who looked and acted white—whether they wore European clothing styles, spoke unaccented English, were involved in farming or slave-owning, or practiced Christianity—were rewarded by the dominant, colonialist society.

I guess the realization, for me, was that being rewarded would have included being counted. Whether for taxation or representation or posterity, recording was important. Having your name listed in records—being the free, white head of household—was a benefit in and of itself.

By the time the U.S. Census added a category for "Color," in 1850, Greenwood Leflore was listed as a white farmer. On a separate slave schedule, he was listed as the owner of fifteen enslaved people between the ages of eleven and fifty. David Moniac died in the Battle of Wahoo Swamp in 1836. His son David A. Moniac can be found in the 1850 U.S. Census, still living in Baldwin, Alabama, the owner of nine enslaved people, eight of whom were under the age of eleven. He is listed as a white student.

At least in the U.S. Census, any traces of their Native identity have been erased.

first meet Kayla Dennis via Zoom, but even then, she's practically bursting out of the three-by-three-inch box on my screen. She has, for lack of a better word, enthusiasm.

Kayla has just finished her first year of law school. She isn't sure what kind of law she wants to practice, but she's excited to tell me about her interests in public defense, in human trafficking, in federal Indian law, in working for the good of the people, in representing the marginalized, in speaking truth to power, in maybe someday becoming a judge.

I am introduced to Kayla by a friend who knows I'm looking for a research assistant to help me build my Tribal enrollment dataset. It will be a huge undertaking. After just one Zoom discussion of the data, Kayla is off and running. She'll spend the summer visiting Tribes' websites, reading scholarly articles, and viewing research databases.

It's the summer of 2021, and Covid-19 restrictions are beginning to be lifted. People are starting to feel more comfortable being in public spaces, and so, eventually, I invite Kayla for coffee. We're about five weeks into the data project, but we are meeting in person for the first time. It's there, at that first coffee meeting, that Kayla tells me why she has taken on this project. Why she is working hard to balance it with her other obligations, including a full-time legal clerking position.

It turns out that Kayla is navigating her own journey of enrollment: in the Wyandotte Nation of Oklahoma. The challenge is that her father isn't cooperating. "He's a fugitive," she tells me matter-of-factly the first time we meet.

Now, maybe you're from one of those families who've never had any run-ins with the law. Or maybe you're from a family like mine, where phrases like "can't leave the state" and "unable to vote" have become code. In any case, when someone tells me their father is a fugitive, my instinct is to ask no further questions.

It takes many months before I begin to untangle Kayla's story. She, like me, grew up in Iowa, hundreds of miles from Oklahoma, where the Wyandotte Nation has its reservation. She's quick to add that her (white) mother tried to instill as much Native culture in her as she could. "My mom would take me to powwows around here," Kayla says, sweeping her hand vaguely to indicate "Midwest."

The challenge is that her mother also had a drug problem—it's how she met Kayla's father—and so Kayla grew up partially in foster care. She didn't meet her father until she was eighteen, despite the fact that he had been living a mere twenty miles from her for her whole life. When she did finally meet him, Kayla was surprised: "He looked homeless," she tells me. She pulls out her phone and scrolls until she finds a picture. What she hands me is the image of a man who has definitely seen some life. He's missing teeth, and his hair is a disheveled salt and pepper. He wears a hoodie that's two sizes too big for his fragile frame. But his eyes look a lot like his daughter's, and for that she is grateful. "I always wondered where I got some of my features." She points especially to her thick dark hair when she says this.

Soon after their first meeting, Kayla had to set some boundaries. Her father was living a life of poverty, mostly working odd jobs and couch-surfing, and she worried that he'd hit her up for money. The life Kayla has built for herself is one of control. Maybe in response to a childhood where she had so little control, she is self-reliant and poised. She arrives to our coffee dates dressed for a law firm, and she speaks with the kind of aspirational confidence that will serve her well in the professional world. In spite of everything the universe has thrown at her, she has kept her shit together. Part of that, for her, is limiting contact with her father.

Kayla has accepted the fact that her father will not be able to help in her Wyandotte enrollment journey. The problem is that no one else in her father's family has responded to her pleas. And, without her father's original birth certificate, she cannot pursue formal enrollment in her Tribe. The Wyandotte Nation, like many others, determines membership based on your ability to prove you are a descendant of someone on the original rolls created by a census of the Tribe in 1937.

It's not a surprise that Kayla's father wouldn't want to release his birth certificate. The fact that his own father, a non-fugitive living on the East Coast, won't answer her phone calls or reply to her emails is more troubling. "I've called and left voicemails," Kayla tells me one rainy afternoon. "He doesn't respond. And now I'm kind of scared of him actually answering the phone."

Kayla's story isn't unique. I've met many Native people who cannot formally enroll in their Tribe because one or another relative won't play ball. A friend of mine has a daughter who's Apache, but she would need paperwork from the girl's father to proceed with enrollment. "My ex is mentally and emotionally unstable," my friend tells me. "I don't want to have that conversation with him."

I never expected my research into Native American identity and enrollment to take me to the thirteenth-century Mongol Empire, but that's exactly where I end up.

Historians cannot say with complete certainty when or where the practice of counting people began. Some point to the Babylonian Empire, which in 3800 BCE took the first-known census, tallying livestock, butter, honey, milk, wool, and vegetables—ostensibly to account for how much food stocks they'd need to maintain.[14] Unfortunately, none of those records has survived.

The oldest census data on people comes from the year 2 CE, from China's Han Dynasty, which recorded 57.7 million people living in 12.4 million households.[15] That count was conducted primarily for tax purposes. So, too, were censuses conducted by the Roman Empire. In one edict from 104 CE, by the prefect responsible for Egypt, all persons were to "return to their own hearths" so that a census could take place.[16]

It is the Mongolian census, though, that most sparks my interest.

The Mongol Empire was, at least geographically, the largest in history. Under the leadership of Genghis Khan, among others, armies invaded and conquered land that, at the empire's height, stretched from modern-day Europe to the Sea of Japan. Between 1250 and 1270, the Mongols took a census of captured territories in Europe and Asia. The counts were used to demand resources from conquered peoples in exchange for peace, resources that funded subsequent conquests.[17] The census was also used to pursue policies of population extermination and deportation, particularly for people in North China.[18]

In at least one version of the census of the Mongol Empire, people were divided into four categories: Mongols, North Chinese, Southern Chinese, and "Miscellaneous Aliens."[19] It is the first instance I can find of a population count that included some notion of what, today, we might call race.

Jane Ferguson, a historical anthropologist who focuses especially on Southeast Asia, calls censuses institutions "rooted in imperialism."[20] Indeed, many historians have observed that colonization and counting went hand in hand. As Ferguson has written, data collection, including censuses, deeply shaped the way colonizers both viewed and exerted power over colonized populations[21]—and part of that included the idea of racial categories. In his work researching the origins of the modern census in Malaysia, sociologist Charles Hirschman reflected that, with British colonization, Malaysia's censuses became more squarely connected to race.[22]

Beyond the obvious problems of an imperial power, a colonizer, using racial categories to separate and enact violence on a population, there is another problem with this kind of data. Censuses operate under the false assumption that people are quantifiable. That a person's identity can be neatly reflected on a form. "The fiction of the census," political scientist and historian Benedict Anderson once wrote, "is that everyone is in it, and that everyone has one—and only one—extremely clear place."[23]

My German grandmother—my father's mother—was fascinated by genealogy. She'd keep thick binders of laminated newspaper articles and photocopied black-and-white photos of our relatives, most long gone. Every few pages, I'd find original photos of myself as a baby—different from the ones my parents had, taken from my grandmother's perspective. Many of the captions were in German, a language I was never taught; nor was my father, born seven years after the end of World War II. English was my grandparents' second language, but the only one that survived.

My grandmother was doing her genealogy work in the 1970s and '80s, before widespread internet access or the advent of websites dedicated to ancestry. She spent a lot of time using the microfilm machines at the public library, looking for old newspaper birth and marriage announcements and obituaries. But she did much of her work from memory, from stories passed down from her parents and grandparents. I'm not sure I ever really appreciated the amount of time she put into her projects. It's one of the many things I wish I could tell her now, over a decade after she passed.

Several summers ago, when I had a few weeks off from teaching, I decided to trace my genealogy. I started with my father's side, the German side, because I had a solid foundation with the work my grandmother had done. I was able to add to that branch of my tree things like christening records and ship passenger manifests. Census records were relatively straightforward and matched my understanding of events.

But the majority of my time that summer was spent on the paternal side of my mother's family, the Lumbee side. It was there that I was starting from scratch, building something none of my immediate family had done before. It was there where I began the process of matching relatives whose names I had heard in stories with tangible documents, with paper and ink. And it was there that I stumbled upon more confusion than I expected, where records didn't exist or didn't match one another, where sometimes they didn't make any sense at all.

If you imagine a family tree with yourself at the bottom and some great-great-great-grand-something at the top, genealogy is like tracing your finger upward, zigzagging through fathers and mothers and daughters and sons. It can be a fascinating process, linking yourself to someone with an old-fashioned name and likeness, maybe finding an image of them and detecting a similarity or two in their facial features. Feeling a sort of kinship with the parallel and perpendicular lines that connect you to so many people who have come before.

At least, that's the beautiful version.

The truth is, in the United States, if you're trying to track down anything *other* than white, male ancestors, tracing your lineage can be convoluted at best. Until 1840, the U.S. Census listed only the names of free heads of household. All free persons were listed by name beginning in the 1850 census, but it would take until 1870 for *all* people of color, including freed slaves and sharecroppers, to have their names recorded.

In 1850, for the first time ever, the U.S. Census also began categorizing people by their perceived race—"perceived" because the answer to the question of "Color" was almost always left to the discretion of the person doing the counting.[24] Often that answer was, as you might imagine, only very loosely connected to what we would consider reality.

In 1850, on the schedule for "Free Inhabitants," the options for "Color" were "White," "Black," and "Mulatto." In 1870, enumerators were instructed to write "Mulatto"—a category they were told to be particularly careful with—for "quadroons, octoroons, and all persons having any perceptible trace of African blood."[25]

For both the 1850 and 1860 censuses, there was a separate "Slave Schedule" for enslaved people. There, people were recorded by their age, gender, race, and owner's name. Interestingly, categories for race on the slave schedules were just "Black" and "Mulatto," despite the fact that enslavement of Native Americans and other people of color certainly existed then.[26] Through searches of the millions of census records, I was able to find just six slaves identified as "Indian" or "Native American" in 1850.

For free persons, the option for "Indian" was added in 1860, though rarely used. In 1880, enumerators were told to use that category if they determined that Native people were found "mingled with the white population," regardless of whether they were "full-bloods or halfbreeds."[27] But, largely, the U.S. Census continued to exclude Native people. It wouldn't be until the 1900 census that a separate "Indian Schedule" was added to enumerate Native people both on and off reservations.

My (Lumbee) great-great-grandmother Annie Pearl Lowry (née Oxendine) offers a good example of the way the U.S. Census changed how it documented and, notoriously, misrepresented race. She was born sometime around 1860 and died in 1940—a lifetime that spanned the U.S. Civil War and two world wars. From what I understand, she spent her entire life in Burnt Swamp, North Carolina, a small town in Robeson County, right in the heart of Lumbee country. She raised eight children, including my great-grandfather John. I remember my grandpa talking about her, his own Grandma Annie, who passed away when he was just sixteen.

In 1880, the first census in which my great-great-grandmother verifiably appears, her race is listed as mulatto. In fact, if you zoom out of the page on which "Ann P. Oxendine" is listed, you'll see an *M* in the "Color" column next to most names for Burnt Swamp on that particular page. Generally, people were grouped together on the census according to the location of their homes; neighbors were listed in order of their house numbers for a particular street. It's likely that Annie and her family lived in a neighborhood made up of many other Lumbee families.

In 1880, for the first time ever, U.S. Marshals were no longer responsible for the census count. Rather, enumerators employed as temporary workers by the U.S. Department of the Interior were chosen based on their "fitness."[28] They were required to be residents of the districts they were assigned to count and would have received a slightly more robust instruction manual than existed for prior censuses.[29]

The census enumerator responsible for my great-great-grandmother Annie's 1880 record was D. A. Buie, a forty-six-year-old farmer. A prominent local white man, he was also a former member of the North Carolina General Assembly and a veteran of the Confederate Army.[30]

Now this is purely conjecture, but I'm going to go out on a limb and guess that, as a poor and illiterate person of color living in the 1880s, my great-great-grandmother would have found a white Confederate Army veteran showing up at her door to collect information on her a bit, you know, stressful.

For my Lumbee relatives, the descendants of several woodland and coastal Tribes who intermarried with both free and enslaved Black people and white settlers, D. A. Buie marked "Mulatto."[31] Perhaps he based that decision on the fact that he could detect some amount of "African blood" in Annie Pearl and her family. More likely, enumerators were given instructions for how to categorize the community. A scan of the records shows that all Lumbees living in Robeson County, North Carolina, were labeled mulatto that year.

We'll never know how my great-great-grandmother Annie was categorized in the following census, in 1890, since most records from that year were lost in a fire. By 1900, the rules for census recording had changed considerably. "Mulatto" was eliminated as a category; choices for the question of color or race were now "White," "Black," "Chinese," "Japanese," and "Indian." Enumerators were given a separate schedule to record "every family composed mainly of Indians."[32]

So, in 1900, Annie P. Lowry—now forty, married to Archie, and, inexplicably, living in a household with twenty-one other people—is listed as Indian. On the "Indian Schedule," in the column prompting "Has this Indian any white blood?," there appears a zero next to her name. By 1910, when the Indian Schedule had once again changed, in the columns for "proportions of Indian blood," Annie P. Lowry is listed as "4/5 Indian" and "1/5 White." By 1920, the Indian Schedule had been done away with altogether. In 1920, 1930, and 1940, the last three censuses in which Annie appears, her color or race is listed as, simply, "Indian."

I guess the subjectivity of the historical record had never smacked me in the face quite the same way it did when I traced my great-great-grandma Annie. In some ways, I suppose the subjectivity is natural. The people who are responsible for making records are, after all, human. They follow misguided orders and make mistakes. They take guesses when the instructions are unclear. They fear the consequences of submitting inaccurate or untimely records.

But when scrolling through the decades and centuries, looking for my Lumbee kin, I detect something else. I guess I'd call it dismissiveness. The haphazard guessing at ages, the misspelled names, the flip-flopping between races. The lack of interest seeps through the hundred-year-old handwriting on the yellowing page scanned onto my laptop. The residents of Burnt Swamp and Pembroke and Lumberton, North Carolina, read like afterthoughts.

I can't help but compare this to my father's side of the family, the German side, the one on which my grandmother had done most of the genealogical legwork. I did make some new discoveries, but there, the secrets were mostly lighthearted ones. I learned that one set of great-grandparents had apparently lied to the entire family and been—gasp!—*un*married while sharing a berth on the ship to America; that my great-grandfather's name, according to his baptismal record, was not actually "August," as we had all thought, but "Carl" (the same as my father's); that our surname, "Schuettpelz," originally had an umlaut over the *u*.

No, I don't think my German ancestors had easy lives. Based on the stories my grandmother used to tell—the famine, the disease, the babies lost—I know that suffering happened there too. It's just that, for my Lumbee kin, the discoveries feel heavier to hold. My great-great-grandmother Janie Jacobs died at age thirty-five of something labeled "acute insanity," as reported by her husband on her death certificate. One great-grandmother married at age sixteen and had her first child at seventeen. Her name was "Nessie" on one census and "Bessie" on another. My great-great-grandfather Archie, Annie Pearl's husband, was the product of an affair, and his biological father never claimed him as his own. It is the reason our family carries the Lowry name—because Archie's mother, Diana, gave him her own.

I suppose an optimistic perspective is that these relatives, whose lives were objectively difficult, are mine. We are there, together on the tree. We dovetail with other Lumbee families and converge on geographies we still call home. We will forever be part of the larger Lumbee story.

Throughout the summer, Kayla and I begin meeting more frequently in person. Each time, she arrives in a state I would call "joyfully frenzied." She smiles and laughs a little when recounting the last meeting from which she's always running. She seems to thrive in an environment where she can keep herself busy. She drops her cross-body satchel on the table at the coffee shop with dramatic flair, as if it's on fire, as if carrying it for another second will cause permanent damage to her spinal cord.

Each time I meet her, I am supremely impressed by Kayla. She was a Fulbright Scholar, she interned with the state's attorney general, and she balances a job with full-time law school studies. She has the kind of zeal I'd like to think I had when I was a student.

Though we usually start on the subject of the enrollment dataset, Kayla and I almost always find ourselves solving mysteries. On one particular day, in what feels like an ominously dark corner of the coffee shop, we're huddled underneath stained-glass table lamps looking for birth records.

Once Kayla was deemed old enough to be told about her father and his whereabouts, it only sparked more intrigue. For one thing, he had left his home state on the East Coast, where the rest of his family remained. Having never been there, Kayla resorted mostly to internet research to connect the dots. She wanted to meet her father's side of the family. Eventually, she was able to track down her aunt, her father's sister.

"She's great," she tells me. "She really wants to help me figure this out." "This" being how Kayla is connected to the Wyandotte Tribe. The challenge, or at least *one* of the challenges, is that the aunt with whom she has reconnected is Kayla's father's half sister. She has a different mother and, therefore, is not Wyandotte herself.

Kayla believes that it is her father's mother who was Wyandotte. However, because she passed away several years ago, the only person who can provide Kayla with her grandmother's records—including the most critical piece, the birth certificate—is her grandfather who will not return her calls. As is the case with census information, there is a "decades rule" for birth certificates: in the state where Kayla's grandmother lived, only birth certificates one hundred years old or older are a matter of public record.

The little that Kayla knows about her grandfather, including his first and last name and his line of work, feels like breadcrumbs: too small to lead us anywhere fruitful. Even my diligent note-taking doesn't seem to help us transform the breadcrumbs into a pathway—so, we eventually make our way to ancestry sites online.

I had, by this point, spent a great deal of time on my own family tree. I was interested in tracing my family's Lumbee lineage farther back than the stories from my grandparents and great-grandparents had led me. It was an often frustrating, but also fulfilling, experience. I enjoyed finding copies of birth certificates, military draft cards, and photographs, in the rare instances that they were available.

I can now admit that it was with an inflated sense of confidence that I offered to help Kayla put together her own family tree—"inflated" because our searches were very different. For one thing, I knew a fair bit about my immediate relatives. I knew my grandfather while he was alive. I had spent a lot of time with him in his small one-bedroom house in the Time Check neighborhood of Cedar Rapids. I had learned how to find the ripest rhubarb in his garden. He had taught me how to decode the numbers at the bottom of the Bingo lottery scratch-off tickets. I knew his birthdate, Christmas Eve—the night we'd always celebrate with his favorite clam chowder served in Styrofoam bowls—and the names of his siblings and parents. I knew where everyone lived and the general time frames of important life events. I'd been to Uncle Henry's house on Pembroke's College Street; I'd seen where my grandpa was born. And when I reached roadblocks in my search, my mother and her sister had helped me through them by telling me the stories they remembered.

But for Kayla, I underestimated just how much we *didn't* know. For one thing, we aren't entirely sure about the spelling of her grandmother's maiden name. Replace an *e* with an *a*, and all of a sudden we're looking at people in Kentucky. Add a *y* to the end of a name, instead of an *-ie*, and we're in Eastern Massachusetts. We know that Kayla's grandmother lived most of her life on the East Coast, but we aren't sure how she got there or what her connection was to Oklahoma.

The Wyandotte Nation, which Kayla identifies with, determines enrollment based on lineage. According to the Wyandotte Constitution, the most recent version of which was passed in 1999, membership in the Tribe is restricted to those who are related by blood to a member of the Tribe who appears on the official "Census Roll of the Nation" as of January 1, 1937.[33] In order for Kayla to formally enroll, she must find the name of a direct ancestor (think: parent, grandparent, great-grandparent) on that list.

I'm becoming increasingly concerned that it's just not going to come together for Kayla, that even if we were to get ahold of the 1937 rolls, she would be unable to connect the dots. There's even a chance that the stories she heard as a child aren't true—that her father is not, in fact, Native.

When I ask her what it was like growing up, her answer is, unsurprisingly, "Hard." In addition to living in foster care for a time, Kayla was separated from one of her brothers at an early age. His father, who was not Kayla's father, got custody of him and raised him apart from Kayla and her other brother. Kayla's mother eventually regained custody of her children and remarried, but Kayla did not get along with her stepfather, and this caused friction in the house.

"My mom wasn't treated well," Kayla says diplomatically.

Kayla has tried to reconnect with her sisters on her father's side, but they, too, grew up in the foster care system and have since spread out. Despite this, Kayla is a proud aunt. She tells me about her nephews' and nieces' latest milestones, showing me photos from Facebook. But her sisters—her father's other daughters—were separated from Kayla until they were all in their early twenties.

When we do, finally, find an obituary for the woman we think is Kayla's grandmother, we are stumped. Nowhere in it is Oklahoma or the Wyandotte Tribe mentioned. Nothing about the way the article reports the woman's death—not the references to her pre-retirement career as a church secretary nor the loving tribute to her husband of fifty years—leads us to believe she was anything but a lifelong East Coast resident. And with Kayla unable to recognize her grandmother, even the obituary's accompanying photo of an elderly woman with a short black bob does us no good.

Still, even without genealogical validation, Kayla continues to maintain confidence—in the search, in her own journey. When we reach a dead end in our online searches, she tries to think of different angles, many of which feel far-fetched. She suggests looking into the Kentucky line of people we've found with a similarly spelled surname. She suggests we check out her grandfather's background—maybe it's actually *he* who is Wyandotte.

I try to remain patient, which isn't easy. Years of watching *Who Do You Think You Are?*–type reality shows have taught me that we should have made some life-altering discoveries within the first hour of our search.

For Kayla, though, it's important to remain calm. To continue the search, to continue compiling the lists of questions she plans to ask her aunt or maybe even her father, if they reconnect once again. For nearly all her life, she's been told by her mother and, eventually, her father that she is Native. She thinks she sees traces of it in the mirror: her dark hair, what she thinks of as broad shoulders and pronounced cheekbones. Those powwows her mother took her to when she was a child are an important memory for her. The fact that she is now her school's Native American Association president is important, too. Being Wyandotte has become part of her identity, of her sense of belonging.

D igging through historical census records begins to affect my mental health. During the day, during my research, I find myself reading, among other things, slave schedules. Lists and lists of people, of children as young as "1/12," or just one month old. There are no names, just persons' races, genders, and ages. In some of the more disturbing of these records, the enslaved people listed are all children. In others, there are only very small children enslaved, all under the age of five.

When I go home at night, it's difficult to look at my fifteen-month-old daughter and three-year-old son and not think about what I've read. I have a series of very vivid nightmares that I can't put the words together to recount.

I try to take a step away from specific records, to dig deeper into the idea of counting more broadly. I want to piece together the story of sorting people, of putting them into categories. I want to better understand how we got where we are today. I come across the work of Melissa Nobles, a political scientist who has written extensively about race and census taking.

I learn that when race first became a question on the U.S. Census, in 1850, the categories were initially supposed to be just "Black" and "White." The category of "Mulatto" was added toward the end of the process, at the request of Josiah Nott, a white, slave-owning anthropologist who posited that Black and white people were two different species of animal.[34] Nott convinced one of his congressmen that, by adding the category of "Mulatto," researchers could better study the impacts of interspecies breeding on things like lifespan and disease.[35]

While 1850 is, at least relatively speaking, recent history, it begins to feel like a million years and a universe ago. I try to imagine the conversation between two white men in some stuffy, smoke-filled chamber of the legislature discussing the idea that Black and white people are two different species. I imagine that Nott would have used some of his previous talking points—that, "the Mongol, the Malay, the Indian, and the Negro, are now and have been in all ages and all places inferior to the Caucasian."[36]

It's difficult to reconcile the fact that the rationale behind certain questions on the U.S. Census would have been to sort the population for purity. To determine who was and was not in the superior class, to measure how much of a certain race a person was. I take some comfort in knowing that the mulatto category lasted only three census cycles, from 1850 to 1880. But I then learn that it was replaced in 1890 with the options "Quadroon" and "Octoroon," to be used for people with one-fourth and one-eighth African blood, respectively, and I have an overwhelming urge to smack my forehead with the palm of my hand.

The fixation on purity in the U.S. Census, on the specific fraction of African or Native blood divided by the more dominant, socially desirable white blood, reminds me of something that would happen a few decades later. According to scholar Robert Miller, a citizen of the Eastern Shawnee Tribe, in the 1920s and '30s, while developing Germany's policies and laws concerning Jews, Adolf Hitler and Nazi officials studied U.S. law involving Native Americans.[37] In a 1928 speech, Hitler seemed inspired to reflect that the United States had "gunned down the millions of Redskins to a few hundred thousand, and now keep the modest remnant under observation in a cage."[38]

The process of gunning down millions of Jews and keeping the modest remnant under observation in a cage began with a census. In order to

achieve their goal, the ethnic cleansing of the Jewish people, Hitler's regime needed first to determine who was Jewish and where they lived. Unfortunately, a traditional census would have taken far too long. Tabulating
the millions of responses by hand was a years-long process. Instead, Nazi
leaders decided to bank on burgeoning technology to help them count.
So, beginning in June 1933, census takers went door-to-door counting
the forty-one million Germans living in Prussia, the nation's largest state.
A sophisticated system of punch cards was used to record each person's
religion and ethnicity.[39] The data was cross-referenced with registers and
lists gathered from other sources to create a "block-by-block" map of
Germany's Jewish residents.[40]

The technology the Nazis used had been invented four decades earlier
by a German American statistician and inventor named Herman Hollerith. Hollerith had begun his career as an employee with the U.S. Census
Bureau; the technology he eventually patented was piloted in the 1890
U.S. Census.[41] It used specialized cards bearing a series of punched holes,
with each hole corresponding to a certain data point: country of origin,
languages spoken in the home, number of children, among others. As
Edwin Black has written, "suddenly the government could profile its
own population."[42] The technology became world-renowned and helped
Hollerith found his own company, which eventually became IBM.

As the Nazi regime became more and more heinous, so, too, did the uses
of its census machines. In one account from a survivor of the Bergen-Belsen
concentration camp in Northern Germany, tens of thousands of prisoners
were catalogued by nationality, age, physical characteristics, and skills.[43] The
corresponding answers were compared to a list of work needs—prisoners
were sent to locations based on the kinds of work they could do, or killed
when they served no purpose to the Nazis overseeing the camps. Each pris-
oner's census punch card was completed only when column 34, "Reason for
Departure" was punched. The reasons given were: "Released," "Transferred,"
"Natural Death," "Suicide," "Execution," and "Special Handling," a category commonly understood to mean extermination.[44]

remember my first trip to the Holocaust Museum in Washington, D.C. One of the first exhibits I saw upon entering the main hall was a pile of shoes. Maybe "pile" isn't sufficient to describe it. It was more like a mountain; a mountain of shoes in all sizes, from well-tread adult loafers all the way down to tiny brown Mary Janes, probably worn only a handful of times. The shoes belonged to those who had died at the hands of the Nazis—in concentration camps, in the notorious gas chambers, in overcrowded bunks from disease. They are some of the only tangible items from the victims that remain.

I remember the aftermath of the deaths of Eric Garner and George Floyd, both African American men killed by police officers for minor alleged offenses. Both killings were caught on video by bystanders wielding cell phone cameras. Both videos were widely circulated online. I remember watching the video of Garner's killing in 2014 and feeling physically ill; it was the first time I'd ever watched someone die. I remember telling myself that I needed to feel the emotions, to feel sick, that it would help me remember the rage. In the summer of 2020, when George Floyd was murdered, I couldn't make myself watch the video. I had read that, in the video, Floyd can be heard calling out for his mother. By then, I was the mother of a months-old infant. I remember feeling a little bit ashamed of my inability to engage with the footage.

I begin to think about historical data—particularly lists of Native people—through the lens of justice.

It's not easy to have an emotional connection to lists. Lists are easy to ignore. It's easy to let our eyes pass over them, to save ourselves from the truths they tell in their columns and rows. But the fact is, sometimes lists are all we have.

No, lists are not always as precise or nuanced as we need them to be, but they can help us understand magnitude. Data, even the kind without a lot of nuance, can help us understand intent. Digging through lists can help us "see" the facts. And yes, of course, those "facts" are often misconstrued or tailored to fit the narrative the dominant power wants to convey. Often, lists are created with the intention of wiping out the very people they were compiled to describe. But without any other form of evidence—without cell phone videos or citizen journalism. Without a mountain of shoes. Maybe lists are the only way we can most fully understand.

4

Payment

To look at the names that scholars use to describe the phases of relations between the U.S. government and Native American Tribes is
to feel ice run down my spine. First, there was "coexistence" (1789–
1828), then "removal and reservations" (1829–1886), then "assimilation"
(1887–1932), then "reorganization" (1932–1945), then "termination"
(1946–1960), and then "self-determination" (1961–1985).[1]

I think about the humans on the receiving end of this historical
shorthand—the humans with whom settlers coexisted; the humans being
removed, assimilated, reorganized, terminated; the humans determined. I
suppose terms like these are de-humanized, separated from any mention
of people, for a reason. In the end, it's easier to call it "removal" and not
to think about the who or the what. To just leave it at that.

I want to understand the ways that each of these phases contributed to
the situation we have now. How today's ideas around Native enrollment
and membership, around identity policing and crises of belonging, have
been shaped by machinations that occurred inside some stale office in
Washington, D.C., in some cases, over two hundred years ago.

I start at the beginning.

If by "coexistence" we mean murder and conquer, capture and pil-
lage, then, yes. The years between the founding of the United States and
the late 1820s meant just that. It was during this time that some of the
bloodiest battles between European settlers and Native American Tribes
were fought. The War of 1812, the First Seminole War, and the Arikara
War all took place in the "coexistence" period.

Of course, most of these battles were fought over land. Colonizers
were determined to take ownership of the land they had "discovered,"

and they knew of two ways to do that. One was through warfare, the other was through what European settlers would have considered the fair and legal process of treaty making.[2]

If treaty making between the U.S. government and Native American Tribes was a game of straws, Native Tribes got the short straw every time. Treaties achieved important goals for the U.S. government, whether it was to control Native land, ensure loyalty, or exchange prisoners. For Tribes, treaties served one purpose: to take things away.[3] There is no treaty between the United States and a Native American Tribe that granted the Tribe more land.[4]

Even before the United States declared its independence, the signing of treaties with Native Tribes was a common occurrence. With the exception of Russia, every European power that settled in North America executed formal agreements with at least some of the Tribes it encountered.[5] After 1763, when the British claimed victory over France in the French and Indian War, treaty making was taken over by the British Crown.[6] After the Revolutionary War began in 1775, treaty making became a project of the revolutionaries and, eventually, the U.S. federal government. I imagine that, for Native Tribes, this felt sort of like a carousel. One foreign power would make them promises or agree to certain terms, only to be replaced by a different foreign power with different promises and terms.

The first written treaty between the United States and a Native Nation was the Treaty with the Delaware—who call themselves Lenape—in 1778. Having just declared its independence in 1776, the United States had vested upon itself a right to negotiate and ratify formal international treaties.[7] In the Treaty with the Delaware, or the Treaty of Fort Pitt, the United States agreed to allow the Tribe to join with other pro-U.S. Tribes to become a fourteenth state in the union—something that, obviously, never happened. In return, the Lenape had to pledge neutrality in the Revolutionary War and guide Continental soldiers through their territory (modern-day Michigan) so the soldiers could attack the British.[8]

In the end, the United States—then a self-appointed government that granted itself treaty power and signed this particular treaty without so much as approval from the Continental Congress—didn't hold up its end of the bargain.[9] Lenape people felt their leaders had been told lies, had been expected to join a battle they never intended to wage.[10] The Lenape chief Koquethagechton (White Eyes) was murdered by the Continental militia just months after the treaty was signed.[11]

And so began a nearly century-long treaty relationship between the United States and Native Nations.

Between the 1778 Treaty with the Delaware and 1871, when Congress added a sneaky line into its annual appropriations bill that effectively ended treaty making with Native Nations, 369 treaties were ratified.[12] Some were outright lies. Some were based on policies on which the United States never intended to follow through. Some were written in a way that purposely misled Native signatories, using language that was not adequately translated or concepts that would not have been comparable with a Tribe's experience.[13]

One famous example of this is the Treaty of 1804, or the Treaty of St. Louis of 1804. In it, Sauk and Fox leaders agreed to sell fifty million acres of their land in return for an annual payment of a thousand dollars—that is, a plot of land the size of modern-day Nebraska for what would have amounted to ten loaves of bread per member of the Tribe.[14] If you're thinking that sounds like a steal, it was. Not only were the Sauk and Fox leaders who signed the treaty not authorized to do so, but it's been said that U.S. officials got them very, very drunk before the deal was struck.[15]

Later, after both the 1804 Treaty and one penned in 1816 that reiterated the terms of the sale of those fifty million acres, Sauk chieftain Black Hawk (Mahkatêwe-meshi-kêhkêhkwa) reflected. "I touched the goose quill to the treaty, not knowing, however, that, by that act, I consented to give away my village."[16]

Taylor Beyal is one of the few people I know who can make a university-appointed office look beautiful. Every time I step into her space at our campus's main hub, I find something new to love. She keeps the overhead fluorescent lighting turned off and uses lamps instead. There's a calming quality to the room. She's hung small shelves on the walls that she uses to showcase a series of succulents and artwork. One gorgeous line drawing of a Native woman always stops me in my tracks.

"That's a Navajo artist," Taylor tells me the first time I visit. "His name's R. C. Gorman."

Taylor is quiet and kind. There's a gentle confidence in her that translates to everything she does, whether decorating her office or otherwise. She describes herself as half Navajo. Her mother, whom Taylor describes as full-blooded Navajo, grew up on and off the Navajo Nation reservation in New Mexico. Taylor's father has been out of the picture for as long as there's been a picture, but Taylor thinks he's mostly white. "I don't exactly know where his ancestors came from," she tells me one night over dinner as my children swarm around her. "He was born and raised in Iowa."

Taylor, too, was born and raised in Iowa. She grew up in Kalona, a town in the eastern part of the state whose population of 2,660 is made up of large Amish and Mennonite communities. For nearly Taylor's entire life, it's mostly been the two of them, her mother and her. Taylor is eight years younger than her next sibling and sixteen years younger than her oldest sibling. Those siblings grew up in New Mexico among her mother's family. Taylor is the only sibling for whom the Navajo Nation has never been home.

"My mom got sober in Iowa," Taylor tells me. "She became a Christian."

It isn't long after I first meet Taylor that I meet her mother, Deb. Both women are part of the Native community in our town, and they often come together to gatherings. Deb stands several inches shorter than her daughter, but she has a presence nonetheless. Over coffee one morning, I ask her about the journey from Navajo Nation to Iowa, a place she's lived for over thirty years.

Deb describes her move to Iowa in 1990 as having been driven largely by desperation. She'd found herself living the same patterns she'd watched many of her family members repeat, including drug addiction and alcoholism. She'd survived several periods of abuse by family members and others. Once she'd reached her breaking point in New Mexico, she made the decision to relocate to Iowa to live with her ex-husband's mother, Connie.

As anyone might look at that choice with hesitation, so, too, did Deb. But she needed a place to stay. "When I first got to Iowa, there wasn't anyone to talk to besides Connie," Deb tells me. She says that she was often lonely, and felt judged by Connie and her family. "They never asked what happened in my relationship with Connie's son," she says. In Deb's eyes, they blamed her for the breakup.

When I ask Deb about the idea of belonging, especially in a place so far away from her home on the Navajo Nation, it doesn't take long for the words to float to the surface.

"I felt like an alien," she says.

Rose Buchanan is an archivist at the National Archives and Records Administration who specializes in Native American records. She's soft-spoken and kind and one of the only people I've met who can follow along with my scattered logic. It is during a Zoom call, as we continue our seemingly endless discussions of Native recordkeeping, that Rose first mentions treaties.

Treaties, mostly, terrify me. I understand their importance, but I find them heavy on minutiae. Often, they're written in legalistic ways that obscure their meaning. Without any legal training, I worry that I'll misunderstand them. Even the guides to federal Indian law that I check out from my university's library don't do me much good in decoding the centuries-old documents.

I tell Rose about a question I'm pondering, about the origins of list making for Native American Tribes. When the idea of recording membership would have first come into widespread use. I've accepted the fact that list making would not have been a Native American pursuit, at least not initially. Before European settlers invaded their communities, Tribes themselves would not have had a reason to make lists of their membership. I wonder aloud when the first of these lists would have been made.

"I'm guessing they were for annuity payments," Rose casually says.

If we think about the word *annuity*—a fixed sum of money paid regularly—then annuity payments are exactly what they sound like. Payments to Native Nations by the U.S. government that were usually made annually. Sometimes, limits were placed on the duration of the payments; sometimes, they weren't. Such annuities were generally laid out in treaties.

The earliest example of a treaty between the United States and a Native Nation that involves an annuity payment was the 1790 Treaty with the Creeks, also known as the Treaty of New York. In it, the United States committed $1,500 to be paid annually to the Creek Nation in return for a strip of land running from modern-day Atlanta to Savannah, Georgia.[17]

One inherent problem with this kind of deal was that, for many Native Nations, land would not have been a commodity they monetized. It wasn't generally something to buy and sell and levy (or pay) taxes on.[18] Treaties took advantage of this idea; they took advantage of the fact that most Tribes did not operate inside the same system of land commodification that settlers did.

In a March 23, 1792, message to the U.S. Senate, President George Washington laid out the case for annuity payments. "In managing the affairs of the Indian Tribes," he said, "it appears proper to teach them to expect annual presents, conditioned on the evidence of their attachment to the interests of the United States."[19] It was, in effect, a way to control and "civilize" Tribes. Annuity payments, whether in the form of cash or goods, became something Tribes depended on.

The problem, of course, is that payment for land isn't a "present." Payment for land is a legal transaction that entitles the seller to the total amount they are owed. When a person sells their home, there's a reason they receive the full amount of money the home is worth. If I want to purchase a new home or make important economic decisions for myself, receiving an annual, (paltry) pro-rated payment is not going to help me achieve my goal. This was the case with Native Nations: the U.S. government kept them on short financial leashes, so they became fully dependent on the annual payments to survive.

In the 1805 Treaty of Fort Industry, the United States stole 1.3 million acres of land in northeastern Ohio from five different Tribes in return for a "present" of one thousand dollars per year.[20] In the 1818 Treaty with the Quapaw, the United States stole 30 million acres of land south of the Arkansas River from the Quapaw Nation in return for a "present" of one thousand dollars per year.[21] In the 1819 Treaty of Saginaw, the United States stole 6 million acres of land in Michigan from the Chippewa Nation in return for a "present" of one thousand dollars per year.[22] The list goes on and on.

It would be difficult to say with complete certainty how much the lands that were stolen from Native Nations were actually worth. It didn't matter. As historian Norman Wilkinson has written, "It never remotely entered the mind of an eighteenth-century speculator to offer the Indians anything approaching the real or potential value of their lands." This was, as Wilkinson says, "an attitude shared fully by the government officials who supervised Indian affairs."[23]

But it wasn't just the fact of annuity payments, the idea of a short leash, that made such payments problematic. Equity, too, was a major challenge. At least for the first several decades that annuity payments were used by the United States, there wasn't any one method of distribution.[24] In the earliest treaties, the language on the subject is vague. As Rose Buchanan confirms, the earliest annuity payments would have been allocated to a Tribe's leaders in a lump sum, to be distributed as they deemed appropriate. When payments were made to the chiefs or headmen, the only record created in the field was a receipt signed by the recipient, the agent, and usually a witness.[25]

We can imagine these payments being made in all kinds of ways, using all kinds of rationales. We can imagine there were instances of fraud. In determining who should get the money, both a Tribe's leaders and federal Indian agents working the field probably influenced the process considerably. In an 1834 congressional report, "Regulating the Indian Department," the U.S. House Committee on Indian Affairs noted that they were "satis-fied that much injustice has been done to the Indians in the payment of their annuities."[26] According to the report, the best solution to the issue of inequity would be to make payments to individuals instead of a Tribe's leaders.[27] The committee, however, decided to take no action.

It is in the closing remarks of the 1834 report that I get a peek into the future. The report concludes that monetary payments to individuals or heads of families would be too difficult, requiring an annual enumer-ation, or census, of a Tribe's members. An adjudication of belonging, of sorts. It would require cumbersome recordkeeping that would need to be regularly updated—something the U.S. government was not equipped to do. Individual annuities would also encourage Native people to emi-grate—to move away from their Tribe.[28]

In 1847, individual payments became law.[29]

On occasion, I've sat with both Deb and Taylor together, and I can only describe them as deeply connected. Often, Taylor finishes Deb's sentences, but in a way that feels almost protective. When Deb tells me stories about growing up on the Navajo Nation, she recounts her mother placing a tissue on her head as she hustled her six children out the door to Catholic Mass.

"Didn't you go for the candy?" Taylor gently asks her mother.

"There was candy and coloring books," Deb says.

When Deb was very young, her parents moved the family from the Navajo Nation to the village of Church Rock, New Mexico, near the far southeastern corner of the rez. It's a place she calls checkerboarded with Tribal land, but one where the only non-Native people were teachers from the local elementary school. In Church Rock, the family lived in former U.S. Army barracks, small connected structures that sat five to a row. As time went on, Deb tells me, her father's alcoholism got worse, and her mother became the family's sole breadwinner. She worked long hours and wasn't home much, leaving Deb and her siblings to their own devices.

Periodically, Deb and her siblings would get to visit their grandparents on the rez. They didn't have electricity or running water but instead used a woodburning stove to cook. "It was fried potatoes and mutton most days," Deb says. She remembers feeding their chickens and goats and spending a lot of time outside.

None of Deb's grandparents spoke English; all were Navajo speakers. Deb's own parents were Indian boarding school survivors, and somewhere along the line, a decision was made not to teach Deb or her siblings the Navajo language. Deb thinks it was a combination of her parents' not wanting the children to understand what they were saying and wanting them to succeed in the white world.

Recently, from her home over 1,200 miles from the Navajo Nation, Taylor has begun looking into Navajo language classes online. When her grandfather was still alive, she would try to write down everything he said. "He was a radio announcer and did some translations for movies," she says. On one trip to New Mexico, Deb bought Taylor a Navajo Code Talker doll that uttered phrases in English and Navajo.

Still, being so disconnected from the Navajo community has made language learning, among other things, difficult. "When my cousin was trying to learn Navajo, the elders would hold her tongue to place it correctly," Taylor tells me. "I don't have that here."

When I ask Deb if she ever considered moving back to New Mexico, she says she never intended to be in Iowa so long. "I've lived here longer than I ever lived there," she tells me over coffee on a snowy morning.

Shortly after moving to Iowa, Deb made the decision to enter rehab. She tells me she felt numb when she first moved to the Midwest. She'd survived so much trauma and describes herself as feeling broken. "I was good at understanding how other people felt," she says, "but I couldn't do the same for myself."

The treatment facility Deb had chosen was one that catered specifically to Native people. There, she reconnected with her sense of spirituality. Because many of the other people at the facility were Yankton Sioux, they would often pray to Tunkashila, the Great Spirit. It became a matter of routine, an important ritual for Deb.

In treatment, Deb also began to understand the benefits of reflection. She was able to talk about what had happened to her. She could finally put labels on the "who" and the "how" of the trauma she'd experienced. "I decided to take my life back," she says. When she graduated from treatment, she returned to Eastern Iowa with a renewed sense of purpose.

It wasn't long after that she met Norma, a woman who worked at the same nursing facility where Deb had recently gotten a job. Slowly, the two coworkers developed a friendship that evolved into something more like family. Deb tells me that Norma never judged her or made her feel lesser than. Over many cups of coffee, Deb was able to share with Norma parts of her story she hadn't shared with anyone else.

Taylor chimes in at this point, telling me that Norma and her husband, Buzz, were like grandparents to her. They'd attend Taylor's school concerts and sporting events; sometimes, if Deb had to work, Norma would come with Taylor to parent-teacher conferences.

"They showed up," Taylor says.

The U.S. National Archives and Records Administration has more than 950 volumes related to Native American annuities.[30] Many are bound books of receipts for payments by the federal government in Indian Country, fragile ledgers buried deep in the stacks. For some, it takes several hours for NARA staff to retrieve. I imagine they aren't records anyone routinely looks at these days.

Digging through the volumes becomes a test of my comprehension of cursive. For the oldest of the receipts, I can usually make out about every fourth word of lavish script. Most are dollar amounts or names of witnesses. Sometimes, the receipts are for a particular activity—a trip to the "seat of government," reads an early one from 1801. Others are for specified amounts of goods, for rations of corn or blankets. Sorting through the ledgers feels overwhelming.

Focusing my search on individual annuity lists—that is, payments to individuals rather than to a Tribe's leaders—limits the sheer quantity of records, but it's still a daunting amount of material. I begin to narrow my search by date. I'm interested in figuring out when some of the earliest of these lists would have been made, *how* they would have been made. What the rationale would have been for deciding who was and was not eligible for annuities. I'm interested in getting a glimpse into whom the federal government considered part of the Tribe.

It is during this narrowed search that I come across the 1832 Creek Census.

On March 24, 1832, the United States signed the Treaty with the Creeks, also called the Third Treaty of Washington, in order to shrink the size of Creek lands and make way for settlers.[31] In the treaty, the Creek Nation ceded to the United States its land east of the Mississippi River, in what today is Alabama, in return for a total of around $310,000.[32] The United States also promised to allot plots of land to male heads of household, which they could either maintain or sell and move west. The Tribe's members who stayed were subjected to violence by settlers, which included invasion of lands, murder, and rape. Some were victims of fraud by both land speculators and the state government; many lost their land outright.[33]

In order to assign land allotments to the Tribe's members, a list of Creek people needed to be assembled. So, in June 1832, Benjamin S. Parsons and Thomas J. Abbott, both employees of the federal government, began walking from village to village, organizing information for 84 Creek towns.[34] On the list, which has come to be known as the Parsons and Abbott Roll, 6,447 households were recorded, with a total of 21,762 individuals.[35] Similar to the way the U.S. Census was conducted at the time, the lists are organized by the name of the head of household, with numbers next to each head for males, females, and slaves.

By all accounts, both Parsons and Abbott were majors in the U.S.

Army, working for the Indian Commission on behalf of the Department of War. We know that Parsons was responsible for the census of the upper towns, and Abbott the lower.[36] In a letter written to the secretary of war, Lewis Cass, in February 1833, Indian commissioner Enoch Parsons noted that "the Indians are hard to collect, or hunt up, which causes great delay."[37]

The Creek Census, which was finalized in May 1833, took nearly twelve months to complete. It is one of the most comprehensive Tribal rolls from that period. Yet, at least at the outset, the two men whose names have become synonymous with the rolls of Creek people were given very little guidance on whom to count.

In a brief letter sent on June 24, 1832, by Secretary Cass, Parsons and Abbott were instructed to allow Creek chiefs to make their selections of land first, followed by all other heads of families.[38] And that was it. Federal agents were deployed into the Creek Nation to make a list of members of the Tribe without so much as a nod to whom that list should include.

For their part, those employed by the federal government to undertake the Creek Census were understandably confused. In a letter dated September 7, 1832, Parsons and Abbott requested from Washington, D.C., more clarity on some of the situations they had come across as they attempted to complete their rolls. Specifically, they asked how they should count: slaves; heads of households in cases where an Indian man had more than one wife; a white man married to an Indian woman; an Indian man married to a "negro slave"; and "Indians and negros [sic] of mixed-blood."[39]

Answers to these questions came relatively quickly. On October 10, 1832, in a letter from Elbert Herring, one of the first commissioners of Indian affairs appointed under President Jackson, the rules were spelled out as follows:[40]

- A white man—who, before the date of the treaty, had married a
  Creek woman and had an Indian family, and who resided in the
  Creek Nation—was considered the head of an Indian family. His

marriage with a Creek woman, and his residence in that nation, constituted him one of their Tribe and entitled him to an allotment.

- An Indian, whether of full or half blood, who had a female slave living with him as his wife, was the head of a family and entitled to an allotment.
- Indian chiefs and warriors who—in the late "unprovoked and inhuman war waged by the Creeks against the United States"—had remained friendly to the United States and taken an active part against their own countrymen were entitled to allotments.
- Indian men with multiple wives—including those living in different houses and having families under their control—were considered the head of their several families and were entitled to one allotment.
- Those Creeks who had been removed to Arkansas in 1826 and 1827 and had since returned were not entitled to allotments.
- Plural wives who were living separately from their husbands were not the head of a family and, so, were not entitled to an allotment.
- An Indian woman who had been married and had children living in her home could not be considered the head of a family unless she was a widow or was "duly separated from her husband, and entirely free from his control." Otherwise, she would not be entitled to an allotment.
- Indians who had no family at the time of the treaty, even if they had since married and had children, were not entitled to allotments.

I become most fascinated by those who *didn't* qualify for an allotment: female-headed households; those who had moved to Arkansas during previous U.S. attempts at removal; those without families. At the same time, even as certain Creek people were categorically excluded from allotments, non-Native people were positioning themselves to receive them. Cases of white men marrying and then divorcing Creek women to qualify for a land allotment were rampant. Neah Micco, a Creek headman, noted that "desperate men are rapidly collecting among us, under color of authority as Indian countrymen, are seizing and occupying our most valuable lands."[41]

When I talk to Christopher Haveman, a scholar who focuses specifically on mid-nineteenth-century Creek history, he tells me the federal government wanted to open as much land to non-Native settlers as possible. And in doing so, it used a method of allotment that flew in the face of how Creek people would have viewed the world. In addition to not operating under a system of individual land ownership and titles, Creek people were traditionally matrilineal. Yet, under the Treaty of 1832, the federal government assigned land to male-headed households. Moreover, the federal government decided that allotments would go to households, as opposed to individuals, to ensure that more land was "left over" to convey to settlers.

In the end, the Treaty of 1832 and the ensuing land allotment policy proved disastrous for the Creek Nation. Pressure by the federal government to move west was compounded by land-hungry settlers inciting threats of violence and making good on them.[42] All this precipitated the Creek War of 1836 (also known as the Second Creek War), between the Creek people and settlers, which gave President Jackson all the rationale he needed to forcefully move the Tribe west.

I ask Christopher if the 1832 Creek Census formed the basis for any future counts. If any other rolls would have used it as a starting point for creating a list of members of the Creek Nation. He tells me that by the time the Tribe was removed, the 1832 counts wouldn't have done them much good. They wouldn't have been very accurate. He tells me that, mostly as a result of disease, over one-third of Creek people died within the first year of removal to Indian Territory.

Of the topics I most enjoy discussing with Deb and Taylor is one they're probably pretty tired of talking about. As a single mother with a very young child, Deb initially struggled to find childcare. She was working long hours as a nursing assistant at a nursing home and couldn't afford much. A relative of Buzz had grown up Amish and connected Deb with an Amish family who agreed to babysit.

Taylor laughs a little when she recounts this part of the story. "I was sort of raised Amish," she says.

On any given day, along the paved and gravel roads that connect Kalona to more rural stretches, you'll find the horse-pulled black buggies characteristic of old-order Amish communities. Small farm stands run by women wearing long, dark dresses and structured bonnets dot the landscape.

Taylor shows me a photo of herself as a child: she is wearing an Amish bonnet and dress. She tells me the family who babysat her didn't want her to stick out in their community, so they dressed her in their traditional attire. She remembers attending quilting circles and church services and playing outdoors with other Amish children. She remembers that her Amish family didn't have electricity, and in the summers, she enjoyed drinking well water. She remembers riding in a buggy and collecting eggs from the henhouses. Her story reminds me a lot of the ways Deb talks about growing up with her grandparents on the rez.

One of Deb's favorite stories from Taylor's childhood is from a time when Taylor was about three. She had come home from her babysitters with one specific, confusing request: "She kept asking for 'dunk oya,'" Deb tells me. As Deb's confusion grew, so, too, did Taylor's frustration. "She wouldn't stop crying," Deb says.

In desperation, Deb called Buzz. She held out the phone for a few moments while Taylor continued her tirade and then placed it back to her ear. Buzz, by this point, was laughing.

"She wants toast dipped in an over-easy egg," he said.

Taylor had been asking for the dish in Pennsylvania Dutch, the primary language spoken in her Amish babysitters' home. Deb estimates that Taylor was bilingual very early on, probably from the first days she could speak.

When I ask if she remembers any Pennsylvania Dutch now, Taylor tells me that sometimes words come to her randomly. She has vague memories of a few songs, but, largely, traces of the language are gone. She regrets this; she wishes she remembered more.

To say that Taylor misses her Amish childhood is probably an over-simplification. Certainly, there are elements of the Amish lifestyle she appreciates. She often calls the Amish genuine and says that, in all the interactions she remembers, they were honest and kind. And certainly, there's an element of nostalgia. From just a few months old to age seven, she spent a great deal of her time with Amish people.

"My mom found comfort being surrounded by the Amish," Taylor tells me one day over coffee. "I think their sense of community felt a lot like the Navajo."

By the time Taylor came along, Deb had begun to create a community for herself in Iowa. She'd begun attending church with Norma and Buzz; she'd gotten close to their sons, whom Deb thought of as siblings. Taylor was six months old when Deb was baptized. Standing in front of the congregation, Deb felt, as she remembers telling everyone, that she'd come home.

Still, being Native in an otherwise very white place was sometimes hard. Mostly, Deb tried to keep her head down and work hard. Despite a newfound community that included Norma and Buzz, people she describes as her chosen family, Deb was still a single mom looking out for herself and Taylor. Often, she'd have to wake up at four in the morning to get herself and Taylor ready, drop Taylor at the babysitter's, and arrive to work on time.

It is on a different occasion, when Taylor and I are eating dinner alone, that she opens up about her sense of belonging. She tells me that, growing up, she felt like an outsider in both worlds. In Iowa, she says, she feels "too dark." "People around here ask me where I'm from, assuming it's not Iowa," she tells me. When she corrects them, they're incredulous. She's not sure what they think she is, but she's sure it's rarely Native.

Taylor's complexion is olive, and her eyes are a beautiful, sharp brown. Her apple cheeks serve as a prelude to a toothy smile, one that is warm and honest. Her septum is pierced with a delicate gold hoop, and her forearms bear tattoos honoring her Tribe and band.

When she's in the Navajo Nation, Taylor tells me, she feels "too white." People there, she thinks, can see some Navajo in her features, but they know it's mixed with something else. Often, she finds herself picking up Navajo slang while on visits. "Rez words," she calls them. When she arrives back in Iowa, she performs the careful dance of code-switching, reverting back to the Iowa way of speaking she grew up around, with all the midwestern politeness she can muster.

Taylor doesn't remember there being many kids of color when she was growing up in Kalona. She remembers some kids making fun of her Nativeness—she particularly remembers kids miming "Indian chops" at her on the playground.

As Taylor got older, particularly when she started high school, her family struggled financially. She shared a one-bedroom basement apartment with her mother, and the two slept in the same bed; she rode the school bus long past the time most of her classmates did. "At sixteen, everyone else magically got a car," she tells me.

Despite their financial struggles, Debbi enrolled Taylor in a private Mennonite high school. It was a small school; Taylor remembers her class having just twenty people in it. She also remembers feeling that this was her lowest point emotionally: she faced significant bullying and exclusion; her grades tanked.

Once Deb could no longer afford the tuition, Taylor was transferred to public school. There, she had the benefit of a clean slate. None of the teachers knew her; she could start over. Eventually, she graduated high school with honors.

I ask Taylor if she ever thought about packing up and moving away from Iowa, maybe to New Mexico, where she still has family. "I used to dream about living in the Southwest," she tells me. "But my support system is here."

That support system includes a network of extended family. While not related to them by blood, they are people both Deb and Taylor consider kin. Over coffee one frigid morning after the holidays, I ask Deb about her Christmas, which has just passed. She tells me she and Taylor attended a family celebration with about twenty-five people.

It's interesting to me when Deb and Taylor compare and contrast Iowa and the Navajo Nation, they both seem to agree that Iowa is a highly individualistic place, one where people are expected to work and get by on their own. They both describe the Navajo Nation as communal, where people are expected to help one another out, where someone will give you their last dollar if you need to pay for gas to get to work. Yet, in a lot of ways, both Deb and Taylor have carved out elements of that communal life for themselves in Iowa.

"Home will always be home," Deb tells me. By home, she means the Navajo Nation, her Navajo family and community. She tells me that a Navajo tradition is to bury a child's umbilical cord in the ground, a custom meant to symbolize a transition—from being nourished by a mother's body to being nourished by the earth, by Mother Nature. It also provides an ever-present reminder of one's roots.

"I'll always know where my home is," she says.

I wonder if Parsons and Abbott, the two men charged with conducting the 1832 Creek Census, knew that the federal government hoped to count as few Creek households as possible. I wonder if, while they were walking around the Creek Nation in all seasons and temperatures, hoofing it for mile after mile, they understood the incentives for a population undercount, an artificially (and inaccurately) low count of Creek people.

Of course, incentives to undercount weren't unique to the 1832 Creek Census. For many Tribes whose land allotments were administered by the U.S. government, a big goal of the process was to end up with "leftover" or "surplus" land for settlers.[43] Those leftovers would have meant not only fewer Native people on the land but also more revenue in federal coffers. In the case of treaty annuity payments, the incentive to undercount was more localized. Divvying up a fixed sum of annuity payments meant that, with each additional recipient, everyone else's sum would decrease. I imagine that, for the earliest treaty annuities, which went first to federal agents and a Tribe's leaders, this would have created a real incentive to undercount.

Even today, these same incentives exist.

Over the last few decades, the issue of Tribal disenrollment has garnered a lot of media attention. David Wilkins estimates that disenrollment, or removing people from a Tribe's rolls, has impacted between four thousand and eight thousand people from eighty Tribes across twenty states.[44]

Particularly in the late 2000s and early 2010s, headlines about disenrollment became more commonplace. In one case, in northern Washington State, the Nooksack Indian Tribe's decision to disenroll 306 members and evict many of them from their homes on the reservation resulted in a call to action from the UN Human Rights Council.[45] Nooksack leaders argued that the 306 disenrolled members had been erroneously granted membership, that they were descendants of one of the Tribe's Canadian bands.[46] That a matriarch from whom they directly descended was not actually on the Tribe's base roll, a 1942 federal census. In practice, the disenrollment led to additional housing being freed up for remaining Nooksack members, a game changer in an affordable housing crisis that's hit the Pacific Northwest especially hard.[47]

Although Tribes cite various reasons for disenrolling members, the "explosion of Native gambling operations" in the 1980s correlated to a huge uptick in the practice.[48] David and Shelly Wilkins estimate that 73 percent of the Tribes actively disenrolling members are gaming communities.[49]

Of the 347 federally recognized Tribes in the contiguous United States, 248—or about 71 percent—run one or more gaming operations.[50] As of 2023, there were 549 Tribal gaming facilities in the continental United States.[51] Of those, 102 were what's called Class II facilities, offering lotteries, Bingo, and other "non-banked" card games. Another 109 were Class III facilities, offering more classic "casino-style" games like slot machines and table games where people bet against the house.[52] The rest included a combination of the two. Class III facilities earn the lion's share of gaming revenue. A few, like the Foxwoods Resort Casino owned by Mashantucket Pequot Tribal Nation in Eastern Connecticut, are highly profitable, bringing in annual sums estimated to be in the mid–eight figures.[53] Many, particularly those located in more remote areas, struggle to earn much revenue at all.[54] Still others sit somewhere in between.

What Tribes do with their gaming revenue is regulated by the federal government. According to the Indian Gaming Regulatory Act, which was enacted in 1988, Tribes can use gaming revenue to: fund Tribal operations, provide for the general welfare of the Tribe and its members, promote Tribal economic development, donate to charitable organizations, and help fund the operations of local government agencies.[55]

Gaming revenue can be hugely beneficial for a Tribe's economic development. In some instances, the creation of a casino provides a reservation with much-needed employment opportunities and an infusion of capital investment.[56] For some Tribes, casino revenues have fueled social programs to fund college scholarships and elder care and to supplement health programs, among other things.[57]

In addition to funding economic and social programs, some Tribes have chosen to distribute a portion of gaming revenue to their members via per capita payments—colloquially known as per caps. Funding received through per caps is taxable as income. Data on per caps is spotty, as Tribes do not have to publicly disclose their existence or amount. According to some researchers, the number of Tribes that use a per cap system is in the ballpark of 130, or just over half of all Tribes that run gaming facilities.[58] Anecdotally, I have heard about per caps ranging from under a thousand dollars per year to sums much, much higher.

Do any casual internet search of terms related to Indian Tribes and casino revenue, and you'll walk away with the impression that Native people are swimming in an endless sea of gold coins. The truth is that only a small proportion of Tribally run casinos are highly profitable. The National Indian Gaming Commission estimates that, among Tribal gaming facilities, just forty-three casinos earn half of the total revenue and that 55 percent of casinos earn less than 5 percent of all revenue.[59] For every Tribe with impressive casino revenues, there are eight others without. Plus, even for Tribes with a large casino presence, the sheer size of their membership means that individual payments would be significantly less than smaller Tribes. The Navajo Nation is a good example of this—the Tribe once estimated that instituting a per cap would result in monthly payments of less than five hundred dollars per person.[60] And that calculation was done when the Tribe had one hundred thousand fewer members than it does today.

On the other end of the spectrum are Tribes with very small memberships and very large revenue streams. For those Tribes, the existence of per caps can create enormous incentives to undercount. Gabe Galanda, an enrolled member of the Round Valley Indian Tribes and an indigenous rights attorney specializing in disenrollment cases, represents the so-called Nooksack 306, among others. He tells me that although mass disenrollment isn't always about money, most often it is. In the cases he's been involved with, "the goal for Tribal politicians is often to concentrate unearned income." The biggest source of that income is from gaming.

In the early 2000s, the Pechanga Band of Indians, a Tribe headquartered in Southern California, disenrolled some 250 members.[61] A few, including a woman who died in 1899, were disenrolled posthumously. By extension, so, too, were all their descendants. The rationale behind the disenrollments was murky, explained vaguely by the Tribe's leaders as a "lineage issue."[62]

In the Pechanga disenrollment case, the issue of money loomed large. The Pechanga Band of Indians operates one of the most lucrative Tribal gaming facilities in the country. The Pechanga Resort and Casino, a two-hundred-thousand-square-foot complex strategically located off Interstate 15, sits halfway between San Diego and Los Angeles.[63] As part of its gaming revenue allocation, the Pechanga Band has a per cap. And because the Tribe's enrolled population is relatively small—in 2023, it was just shy of 1,400 people—the per cap is significant. In one account by a disenrolled Pechanga member, kicking out so many people increased the per cap from $15,000 to $40,000 per month.[64]

When I ask Gabe if disenrollment is as big an issue as the media make it out to be, he tells me that, unfortunately, it is. He gets calls almost weekly from someone who's been disenrolled. "The common denominator in every disenrollment I'm aware of," he says, "is some combination of power and greed."

5

Remove

f you haven't yet settled on a least-favorite U.S. president, might I suggest you consider Andrew Jackson.

It's impossible to know what would have happened had Andrew Jackson *not* been the seventh president of the United States (1829–37). Perhaps the country's second phase of relations with Native Nations, the removal and reservations phase, would never have happened. After all, Presidents Thomas Jefferson and James Monroe had previously argued that the Indian Tribes in the Southeast should exchange their land for lands west of the Mississippi River, but neither of them did anything about it.[1] Jackson, however, had a strategy.

In the last several years, the word *gaslight* has become more and more popular. The term was coined in 1938, in the British play *Gas Light* (later made famous by the 1944 American movie *Gaslight*). It's about a man who wants to steal his wife's money. He decides that the best way to do this is to have her committed to an asylum. So, he makes his wife think she's going insane. His tactics are diverse and many, but the play's title is for the one that finally works. When he slowly dims the gaslight in their home, his wife comments it. But he denies her reality, making his wife feel like she's crazy. Today, *gaslighting* has become colloquial shorthand to describe behavior that causes someone to doubt their experience. Behavior that makes them feel that they're the one in the wrong, that they're the problem.

The events surrounding President Jackson's passage of the Indian Removal Act of 1830 are a master class in gaslighting. In a speech to Congress on December 6, 1830, Jackson gave some insight into what would become a hallmark of his presidency—the removal of Native Nations from their homelands, the forced march of Native people that resulted in thousands of deaths along the way.[2] If we measure the speech by levels of calculated manipulation, President Jackson really hit it out of the park.

First, he framed himself as benevolent and his legislation as protective. By separating Native people from white settlers, he asserted, conflict between them would be reduced. In reality, the conflict that had been happening was mostly one-directional. It was, after all, white settlers who stole livestock, burned entire towns, squatted on land that was not theirs, and cheated Native people out of their landholdings.[3] And it was white settlers who petitioned the U.S. government to remove the Native people so they could more seamlessly settle in the coastal South, in states like Mississippi and Alabama.[4]

Next, Jackson characterized the land to which Native people would be removed as that where their existence "may be prolonged and perhaps made perpetual." The lands west of the Mississippi River, he said, would allow Native people to support themselves the "moment of their arrival." In reality, those lands were undesirable and incompatible with Native ways of life.

Finally—and this really is the pièce de résistance—Jackson proclaimed that Native people had no right to be upset about their removal. That, despite their having to leave the resting places of their ancestors, the land they had called home for generations, moving, Jackson said, was really no big deal. In fact, they should be grateful! The federal government was, after all, giving them land, providing for their relocation expenses, allowing them to travel to new places! To see new things!

At the end of Jackson's speech, he rhetorically asked, "Can it be cruel in this Government when, by events which it cannot control, the Indian is made discontented in his ancient home to purchase his lands, to give him a new and extensive territory, to pay the expense of his removal, and support him a year in his new abode?"[5]

We all know what happened next.

Among other events, Indian removal, the despicable forced march of sixty thousand people from the Five Tribes—the Cherokee, Chickasaw,

Choctaw, Muskogee (Creek), and Seminole—away from their home-lands.[6] The route was long, more than five thousand miles stretching from what is today Kansas to the Carolinas, from Mississippi up to Illinois. Different paths were taken by different Tribes.[7] In the case of the Cherokee, it took over eight months to travel westward, much of it on foot.[8]

Historians don't agree on the number of Native fatalities during the removal process itself. We know that about one in four Cherokee people died during what has come to be known as the Trail of Tears.[9] It would not be overstating Indian removal to call it genocide. That, in placing Native people in stockades (in pens meant for animals) and then marching them across snow and ice without appropriate clothing, often barefoot, without breaks or rest, the intention was clear.[10] Meanwhile, the nearly seven thousand soldiers who implemented the removal were equipped with wagons, heavy coats, and guns, ensuring they would survive. I cannot find a record of a single soldier dying along the way.

It is during this period of ethnic cleansing that the U.S. government's interest in counting Native American people seems to have been piqued. It was, after all, during this time that the government would have had a keen interest in ensuring it got all the Indians out of the way. That every last one was accounted for and removed, making room for settlers and railroads and trade routes. For colonization.

If we look at the records the U.S. government kept during this period, we can see that Indian removal was approached like a calculated military operation. Rather than relying on Indian agents employed by the Bureau of Indian Affairs, who already worked in the field, the U.S. government sent soldiers to oversee the process, perhaps because most Tribes would have resisted removal.[11]

When I track down the lists of Native people removed during this period, the first thing I notice, at the top of each page, is the heading "Indians About to Emigrate West of the Mississippi River."[12] As if it were a choice. As if the Native people were the ones taking the action—"emigrating" rather than being forced from their homes with only a few minutes' warning. As if it were their desire to move to a place they'd never been and never wanted to go; to risk (and lose) their lives along the way.

The lists of Native people being violently removed from their homes are called muster rolls—"muster" as in to gather troops in preparation for battle. The muster rolls include people of every age, from elders in their eighties to newborn infants. Sometimes, when babies were born during the marches, federal agents would write a short note in the column next to the parent's name. Many of the babies did not survive.

In instructions given by the U.S. Army's Commissary General of Subsistence, the "Indian removal agents"—that is, soldiers—were told to include in their muster rolls the heads of Native families and all persons within those families who were being removed. In an appendix to the regulations for Indian removal, soldiers were instructed to follow a template that looks strikingly similar to the way the U.S. Census was structured at the time.[13] The first column lists the name of the head of household, with other columns breaking down males and females into several age categories: under ten, ten to twenty-five, twenty-five to fifty, and over fifty. There are separate columns for slaves, divided only by gender.

Because the rolls were handwritten, often on blank pieces of paper as opposed to a preprinted template, they are a bit of a mixed bag. Sometimes, the age breakdowns are different. Sometimes, there are no separate tally marks for gender. Sometimes, there are no columns for slaves. The more lists I look at, the more I realize that every soldier made his list slightly differently.

I become fascinated by the "Notes" column, on the far-right side of the records. Nowhere in the instructions were soldiers told what to write in this section, so it became something of a catchall. Sometimes, there are notations about a person's political status. One soldier whose lists I find is fond of the phrases "Considered a chief" and "A very influential man among the party."[14] Another soldier notes a "baby girl born on day 17 of the journey." Still another, in lists from the Seneca Nation, notes when families will join at a later date. "Left at Cattaraugus in consequence of inability to dispose of houses in time to go with the party," several say.

As I'm reading through President Jackson's speeches and scrolling through microfilm scans of the muster rolls of "Indians About to Emigrate West of the Mississippi," I can't help but think about the ways the records have been framed, the language that has been chosen. The words that are used—*emigrate, party, journey, abode*—are casual; positive, even. The way that Indian removal was documented made it seem like a pleasant little trip Native people should consider themselves fortunate to embark upon. Even the instructions to soldiers who carried out removal—how many dollars could be spent on a wagon or a pint of corn—seem to be describing something far different from what we know to be true.

I can't stop thinking about that famous quote by the writer and activist Alice Walker. That, if you're silent about your pain, "you will be killed by those who claimed you enjoyed it."[15]

Darlene Wind is quiet, but if you sit next to her long enough, you'll hear her flawless delivery of one-liners.

She jokes about "watching her carbs" as she orders a piece of chocolate cake for breakfast, about the television her grandkids bought her four years ago that's still in the box in her living room. When we bead together, she jokes about the earrings she's "making," despite no notable progress. Every now and then, when someone asks how the earrings are coming along, she smirks and lifts a large piece of oval wire with a single bead dangling from it and says, "Great!"

A small jewelry store in our town hosts a beading circle for indigenous women every month. The first time I attend, I notice Darlene. She is sitting at the end of one of the folding tables fiddling with the drawstrings of her hooded sweatshirt. The sweatshirt, which proudly proclaims "Cass Lake," is, I'll come to learn, part of a larger collection of hoodies emblazoned with the names of places important to her: Cass Lake, Leech Lake, Red Lake. Darlene wears them almost like armor, like oversize cotton shields.

When I first introduced myself, Darlene offered me a delicate handshake and pronounced her name so quietly I had to ask for it again. She wore her dark brown hair short. If she hadn't told me, I wouldn't have believed her eldest granddaughter was twenty-eight.

Darlene retired from a job with the U.S. Forest Service in Albuquerque after spending almost two decades with the Minnesota Chippewa Tribe, working her way up from data entry to director of IT. She identifies as Ojibwe from Minnesota, with relatives from both the Red Lake and Leech Lake Reservations, but she lives full time in Iowa now. That part, the Iowa connection, wouldn't be made clear to me until a few months after we first met.

Darlene was born at the Cass Lake Indian Hospital on the reservation of the Leech Lake Band of Ojibwe. Leech Lake, which is about two hours straight south of the Canadian border, is one of six reservations in Minnesota that together form the Minnesota Chippewa Tribe.

I suppose I should pause to explain that, historically, settlers bestowed different names on the Ojibwe, who are part of a larger group of indigenous people who call themselves Anishinaabe, or "the original people." It's thought that the name "Chippewa" was a mispronunciation of "Ojibwe" by Europeans upon first contact.[16] I've heard it said that "Ojibwe" is used on the Canadian side of the border and "Chippewa" on the U.S. side, but my experience in Minnesota is that both are commonly used.

About two years after Darlene was born, her father died, leaving her mother a single parent of five small children with no job and a tendency toward alcohol. So, Darlene, the youngest of the five, and her four brothers were placed in foster care. The three oldest boys were sent to one home; Darlene and the youngest of the boys, Ron, to another.

Iowa would perhaps never have factored in Darlene's life had it not been for the fact that she and her brother tried to go back home. Within a matter of days of arriving at their first foster home, the siblings, then just two and four, helped each other climb into their snowsuits and began walking in the direction of their mother's house. The walk would have been relatively short—their foster family lived just a few miles from their home—had the weather been better. But as is often the case in Northern Minnesota in winter, a blizzard had overtaken the small town.

Darlene tells me this story at a time when my own son happens to be two years old. Imagining him strapping on his snowsuit and walking for miles through a snowstorm to find me is akin to taking my heart in both hands and wringing it out like a wet rag.

When the authorities found Darlene and Ron wandering around in the snow, they immediately placed them with a different foster family, one even farther away from their mother's home. The rationale being that the more unfamiliar their surroundings, the less likely they'd try to run away. This, in fact, would become a common theme of Darlene's early life—forced movement farther and farther away from home.

Darlene's memories of her second foster home are hazy, but what she's able to piece together from stories she's heard is that her foster parents were good people who would have adopted the Wind children if they'd had the chance. But because Darlene now had a history of running away, the State of Minnesota decided she needed to be adopted by a family outside the area. So, at the age of four, Darlene Wind became Laura Darlene Fountain, adoptive daughter of a white family living on a farm just outside Iowa City. This was 1957, well before the 1978 Indian Child Welfare Act would empower Tribes to govern the adoption of Native children born on reservations and limit the ability of non-Native families to take them away from their communities.

Darlene's brother Ron, just six years old at the time of her adoption, was given a choice of joining his older brothers at their foster home outside Leech Lake or being adopted with Darlene. He chose to go with his brothers. And because anyone who knows six-year-olds knows that they should always be entrusted to make their own decisions, the authorities let him do just that. None of the brothers was ever adopted. Rather, they lived in foster care until they aged out or were kicked out.

It doesn't take long for me to understand how utterly fucked up Darlene's situation in Iowa was. The fact that she was required to call the woman who adopted her "Mother" sends chills down my spine. Inexplicably, despite changing Darlene's name to "Laura" to honor her best friend, Darlene's new mother would yell at anyone who tried to call her that; she made everyone call her Darlene.

When Darlene tells me how isolated she felt from everyone else, including her adoptive siblings, it reminds me of stories I've heard of psychological abuse or even of cults. Of abusers taking away any sense of community from their victims, alienating them from family and friends until the only person they can trust or rely on is their abuser. Darlene recalls a rare attempt she and her adoptive sister—who was also from Leech Lake—made at bonding. They were teenagers by then, talking together in one of their rooms about who knows what. Immediately after the conversation was over, Darlene remembers her adoptive mother interrogating her. She wanted to know exactly what the two had discussed.

The isolation, combined with what seems like a significant amount of post-traumatic stress, has formed large gaps in Darlene's memory of Iowa. She doesn't remember her adoptive brother serving in the army. She remembers almost nothing about her adoptive father. She doesn't remember how she was treated by the predominately white community into which she was adopted.

Not surprisingly, Darlene left her adoptive home as fast as she could. She graduated high school and enrolled at the University of Iowa and stayed with friends during breaks. She decided to study music, then physical education, and then education more broadly.

The summer before her freshman year at Iowa, Darlene drove to Minnesota to, well, she didn't know what; to see if she remembered anything, she guesses. Her adoptive mother had been adamant that Darlene not talk about her life before adoption. Once, on a family road trip to Lake Superior, they passed through Bemidji, and Darlene swore she'd been there before, swore she recognized it. Her adoptive mother snapped at her that she was lying. This, Darlene recalls, was always her adoptive mother's response: that she was lying.

When she returned to Minnesota at age eighteen, Darlene went first to Blackduck, a small town about forty miles north of the Leech Lake reservation, where she was born. She had memories of a statue of a big black duck, wings splayed, ready to take off from its cement base, and she found it in there in the town square. She thought the statue was near where her foster parents lived, so she drove around until she found something that looked familiar.

When she arrived at a faded white farmhouse on a corner lot, a man in his late fifties was working in the yard. His name was Ed Gorman. He took one look at Darlene and simply said, "Olive's in the kitchen; go on back." He had recognized her the moment she pulled into the driveway. This was the foster home where Darlene had lived from the age of two until she was four.

Olive, Darlene's former foster mom, was able to help her piece together the names of her birth family and where they had last lived. She helped Darlene connect the dots between her first foster home, her second foster home, and her adoption. Olive told Darlene that she'd wanted to adopt her and her brothers herself, but the State of Minnesota had rejected the idea. Instead, Olive packed several mementos into Darlene's suitcase, things meant to remind her of her Tribe and of home. Darlene has never seen any of those items, so she suspects that her adoptive mother disposed of them when she unpacked. Any tangible connection to home was thrown away.

It took Darlene a few days to work up the courage to drive to the address Olive had written on a small piece of paper. There, an older woman answered the door. Darlene said, "I'm Carl Wind's daughter," but the woman already knew. She was Darlene's aunt Delma Kingbird, her mother's sister. Darlene says that, within minutes, people were coming from everywhere. They all wanted to see the girl they fondly called Dollyanne.

Eventually that same night, one of Darlene's cousins drove her the fifteen miles to Bemidji, to a bar called the Flame. Darlene remembers walking across the dark room, through a curtain of smoke. She remembers her cousin leading her past the bar, to a tall table where a small group of people sat on stools. She remembers her cousin pointing to a woman in the group and saying, just, "This is your mom." Darlene remembers feeling shock. She remembers crying. By then, they were all crying.

She remembers her mom telling her that no one had expected to see her ever again.

If we believe the muster rolls of "Indians About to Emigrate West of the Mississippi River," then we might imagine a lovely journey that culminated in an all-expenses-paid trip to a wonderful new home. If we believe the facts, we know that this was not the case. Native people, via the Trail of Tears and other forced removals, were sent to plots of land, often called reservations, that were foreign to them and not conducive to their ways of life.

Reservations, though not always called that, had been around for decades before President Jackson's Indian Removal Act was passed. Some point to the Brotherton Indians of New Jersey as the first Indian reservation in the United States, established after the signing of a 1758 treaty.[17] There, a group of about two hundred Lenape people (sometimes called Lenni-Lenape) lived after refusing terms laid out in that treaty with the British to move east.[18] The Brotherton land, which had been set aside by the provincial legislature of New Jersey, was later sold, and members of the community were dispersed.[19]

Some reservations were established by treaty, others by an act of Congress, others by executive order—a practice that ended in 1919.[20] Many sources cite the Indian Appropriations Act of 1851 as the piece of federal legislation that established the modern-day Indian reservation system.

The act is a dense read. I'm not sure what I expected, but upon my fifth attempt, I still can't make any sense of it. It looks like a laundry list of dollar amounts and their purposes—monetary payments, goods, schools, provisions, tobacco. I cannot find any language that would have created something one would call a "reservation system."

When I ask Kevin Washburn for help deciphering the act, he tells me that, by 1851—almost twenty years after Indian removal was put into place—the U.S. government had reframed its Indian policy a bit. Largely, by then, the government had achieved Jackson's goal of removing Tribes from valuable land east of the Mississippi River. By the 1850s, the United States had embarked on a different kind of removal policy, one that involved not removing the Indians from the land but, rather, removing the land from the Indians. In this way, the U.S. government dramatically shrank the size of land that Tribes controlled. Kevin tells me that the Indian Appropriations Act of 1851—the act that's often cited as the one that created reservations—is mostly a list of which Tribes were ceding which of their specific lands in return for what specific "payment." The challenge is that these payments were a far cry from anything we might think of as fair and reasonable.

In return for small payments, Tribes were left to make do with lands that were dramatically smaller than those on which they had previously lived. Many of the new plots weren't suitable for cultivating much more than poverty. The average size of reservations was significantly smaller than the land required for traditional practices like hunting and gathering and fishing.[21] Starvation was common, and living in close quarters hastened the spread of previously unknown diseases introduced by settlers. For some Tribes, the federal government issued food rations, thereby introducing wheat flour, grease, and sugar into their diets.[22]

Certainly, these patterns have continued to have consequences today. I don't want to paint too bleak a picture of modern-day reservations, because there are absolutely Tribes that have done miraculous things with very little. Tribes that have made important development decisions, economic and otherwise; that have used their sovereignty to create infrastructure that best serves their people. Reservations are places where people live and breathe, where they have babies, where they sing and dance, where they celebrate. They are places of sorrow and of joy.

But we cannot ignore the patterns of unemployment, the declining health outcomes, or the structural racism we see on reservations, too. And decisions made by the federal government have played a large role in these patterns. Many Tribes were sent to reservations in remote places that made access to opportunities difficult. Some lack infrastructure, like indoor plumbing or connection to a power grid; many lack access to the internet.[23] Those federal decisions—even those made over a hundred years ago—continue to have real consequences today.

More and more in the United States, we are seeing the increasing importance of wealth gaps. The idea is relatively straightforward: the amount of financial assets is markedly different for different segments of the population. One example is socioeconomic: in 2023, the top 10 percent of American households held 69 percent of the total wealth, while the bottom 50 percent held only 2.4 percent.[24] Another example is generational: in 2023, younger Americans (think Millennials and Gen Zers) owned seventy-two cents for every dollar of wealth owned by Baby Boomers when they were the same age.[25] Another example is racial: in 2023, the average Black family owned about twenty-four cents for every dollar the average white family held. For Hispanic families, that number was twenty-three cents to the dollar.[26]

These gaps often compound—they grow larger with time.

When we think about these gaps, we can think especially about housing and land. After all, for the majority of American families, their home and the land it's on are the sources of most of their wealth. The net worth (the wealth) of a typical homeowner is about forty times the net worth of a renter.[27] For most people, a home is the single largest purchase they will ever make. As a result, it can become their biggest source of wealth.

The problem is that historical events and governmental policies have created a gigantic economic chasm, a monumental wealth gap—specifically along the lines of race. This chasm began centuries ago. For one thing, slavery prevented Black people from owning anything, including homes and land. Post–Civil War violence and intimidation, along with policies like those behind Jim Crow laws, prevented ownership of housing for Black families, too. Racial redlining beginning in the 1930s prevented Black families from securing mortgages, particularly in neighborhoods with more access to opportunity.[28] And those policies have all had domino effects—over time, they have served to compound the racial wealth gap even further.

Think about a (very simplified) example. If Kathrine's (white) grandparents purchased a home in Brooklyn, New York, in 1950 for $28,000 and kept that home in the family, we could reasonably assume her family had access to a significant amount of wealth today. Brooklyn is, after all, one of the highest-priced housing markets in the country. A house valued at $28,000 in 1950 could easily sell for upward of $2.6 million today.[29] Much of that value lies in the land the house sits on. Now let's say that Jackson's (Black) grandparents were unable to purchase a home in Brooklyn, New York, in 1950. Even if they had the down payment and income required, they were prevented from doing so because of racial redlining policies. So, instead, Jackson's family had to rent homes over the years. We can imagine that, today, Jackson's family would not have the same access to wealth. His family would not own a house and a plot of land valued at $2.6 million.

This same kind of scenario has played out for Native American Tribes.

It's estimated that the U.S. government has seized more than 1.5 billion acres of land from Native Nations, much of it during the treaty period from 1776 to 1871.[30] The word *seized* is probably too abstract for what actually happened. Often, Tribes were made to sign treaties that were confusing or written in a language they did not understand or that dramatically undervalued the land they were "ceding."[31]

The 1804 Treaty of St. Louis is a good example of this. In that treaty, the U.S. government shamelessly stole fifty million acres of land belonging to the Sauk and Fox people, agreeing to give them a "present" of $2,234.50 in goods and a payment of $1,000 per year.[32] Let's imagine that, instead, the United States paid the Sauk and Fox people the full amount their land was worth. Let's call that amount $2 per acre—that was, after all, the minimum value of the land as spelled out in the Harrison Land Act of 1800.[33] At $2 per acre, a fifty-million-acre plot of land would have been valued at $100 million. So, a fairer and more reasonable transaction would have been for the U.S. government to pay the Sauk and Fox people a lump sum of $100 million.

We could also imagine another situation, one in which the United States had respected the Sauk and Fox people and their sovereignty and left them in peace. Hadn't overtaken them with disease and warfare and fraudulent land claims. We could imagine the Sauk and Fox people maintaining their traditional homelands today, those fifty million acres still fully in their control. Let's call the fair and reasonable value of that land $6,250 per acre, the average value of farmland across Illinois, Missouri, and Wisconsin, where the Sauk and Fox people traditionally lived.[34] At $6,250 per acre, the value of a fifty-million-acre plot of land is beyond what a simple calculator can compute. It's in the neighborhood of $312 trillion.

Of course, this is an extreme example. Certainly, a lot has changed since 1804. Economic turbulence has come and gone and come again; war has been waged both inside U.S. borders and beyond. It would be impossible to know what would have happened in a counterfactual world in which the Sauk and Fox people were left on their lands and left to their traditions, free from colonization. The point is that they were not, and as a result, Sauk and Fox people today do not have the same economic benefits they could have had under the most equitable and just of circumstances.

Early one winter Tuesday, Darlene and I sit together eating breakfast. As I pick at a lemon poppyseed muffin, Darlene sizes up her breakfast sandwich, eggs over easy running down the side. She pushes up the sleeves of her hoodie so they don't get in the way. When she does this, I notice a small paw tattoo on each of her wrists. She tells me the tattoos represent her family's Bear Clan, one of the five main clans of the Ojibwe people. They are especially known for being strong and steady.

Having gotten my inaugural tattoo just a few months earlier, I'm becoming fascinated with the art. So, I ask if I can look more closely.

When she twists her arms to show me her wrists, I see a trail of scarring down her right forearm, clusters of shallow divots line the skin from her wrist to the crook of her elbow. I can't tell if they're from burns or cuts or something else. I don't ask. I *can't* ask. But she sees me noticing.

"I have no idea where these came from," she says.

Darlene tells me that, several years after reconnecting with her birth family, she brought up the scarring. Her birth mother had passed away by this point, so she asked one of her older brothers if he had any idea where the scars had come from. His theory was that it had happened in a car accident. The whole family had been in the car, and their father had been driving. Darlene would have been just a baby then, less than two years old. Her brother didn't have any other memories from the accident; he couldn't confirm that they went to a hospital or that Darlene had been injured that night.

It's not the lack of memory that strikes me—hell, I can hardly remember what happened to me yesterday—it's more the fact that no one in Darlene's young life could validate her experience. No one could fill in the gaps, help her understand what she didn't remember. Her adoptive mother, in fact, was adamant that Darlene *not* remember anything.

It seems that Darlene's entire life has been like this—a patchwork of memories she's trying, against a significant amount of resistance, to reconstruct.

Darlene describes her time in college as stop-and-start. She'd take classes and study, but whenever she saved enough money from working, she'd take off, travel around with friends or on her own, looking for an-swers to the questions she was beginning to amass.

During her sophomore year, Darlene was approached by the Native student association and asked to join. A small group was trying to build a community at the university, and one of them had spotted Darlene on campus and, as she describes it, "followed me around." Darlene hesi-tantly agreed and began attending meetings at the Chicano and American Indian Student Union, a repurposed old house across from the main campus that had seen better days. There, she cultivated friendships with several other Native students, including one who was active in the American Indian Movement.

This was the early 1970s, when AIM was building momentum. What had begun as a movement highlighting socioeconomic issues facing so-called urban Indians was evolving into more widespread activism around issues plaguing Native communities, things like poverty, environmental degradation, police brutality, and land rights. Often, people associated with AIM would travel from place to place, setting up camp on reservation lands and other spaces.

Darlene credits AIM with helping her figure out who she was. Although she had been visiting Leech Lake as often as she could, getting to know her birth family and the community, she didn't feel entirely comfortable there. She suspects it was a fear of rejection. At this point, she knew nothing about who she was, about her Tribe, the culture. She was afraid that people wouldn't accept someone they perceived as an outsider.

When she tells me this, we're sitting in a coffee shop that's new to both of us, a hip industrial space framed by thirty-foot-tall windows and overlooking an upscale bowling alley. Limited by the length of my computer's charging cord, I'm on the concrete floor, leaning up against the banquette seating running the length of the room. Darlene sits atop a Scandinavian-designed chair, one with a wooden underside, the top covered in black leather. The height differential between us serves to emphasize a feeling I've been having lately, of Darlene as a mentor, and not just to me. I've observed the way that other young Native women in our community view Darlene—with a mixture of deference, deep respect, and love. But, of course, I don't tell her that. In the six months I've known Darlene, I have found her to be a humble person, someone who wouldn't identify herself as the bearer of lessons or some immutable truth, even if that's exactly how she seems to me.

I ask Darlene if she's ever heard the term *imposter syndrome*. I tell her I'm a longtime sufferer of the affliction. Just as she felt about returning to Leech Lake all those years ago, I, too, fear the rejection of my own people and Tribe.

Darlene tells me about one night in particular, when her travels with AIM took her to South Dakota, to the reservation of the Rosebud Sioux Tribe. There, a man whose name she has long since forgotten asked to sit with her. He told her that, in his time observing her, he noticed that she listened too hard. She was constantly watching but not talking. He wanted to know her story. So, she told him about her adoption and how she was raised. By then, Darlene was in her mid-twenties, but it was the first time she had told her whole story, or at least what she remembered of it. She says it was the first time anyone had asked to hear it.

The man gave her some advice. He told her she didn't have to try so hard, that she needed to learn to be comfortable within herself.

As I listen, I type frantically on my computer, trying to get it all down, get it right. She pauses to let me catch up. I finish typing and shift around on the floor to find a more comfortable position. I want to tell her that her story about feeling she didn't fit in is helping me navigate my own feelings of not fitting in. I want to point out that it feels cyclical. That the words of advice given to her all those years ago are giving me comfort, here in this coffee shop a million miles away from the Rosebud Reservation.

I n some ways, post–Jackson era reservation policy represented the first time the U.S. government was able to undertake large-scale Indian containment. Not surpisingly, then, the reservation system also presented an opportunity for the federal government to take its Indian inventorying to scale. On July 4, 1884, the United States declared in an act of Congress that "each Indian agent be required, in his annual report, to submit a census of the Indians at his agency or upon the reservation under his charge."[35]

Let me pause for a moment to say that while, yes, *Indian Agent* would be a fantastic title for a movie about a rogue Native American government employee intent on returning the country to its indigenous roots, the reality of Indian agents is much less exhilarating. Beginning in 1806, with the creation of the federal Office of the Superintendent of Indian Trade, Indian agents were deployed into Indian Country to monitor and control economic activity between Native Nations and the U.S. government.[36] When, in 1824, U.S. secretary of war John C. Calhoun replaced the Indian Trade Office with the Bureau of Indian Affairs, he broadened the scope of Indian agents to include settling disputes between Native Americans and European Americans and, as stated in departmental documents, "acculturating" Natives into European American society.[37]

Let's not be fooled by an ornate word like *acculturating*. Often, it was Indian agents who were responsible for kidnapping Native children, stealing them from their families, homes, and communities and sending them to Indian boarding schools. It is estimated that between 1819 and 1969, the United States operated or supported 408 boarding schools in 37 states.[38] As of its most recent investigative report in May 2022, the Federal Indian Boarding School Initiative had found more than 500 graves of children from these schools, many unmarked.[39] And because the initiative is still early in its process, that number is only expected to grow.

Federal Indian boarding schools were places of corporal punishment (including flogging), solitary confinement, and sexual abuse.[40] The schools were overcrowded and dirty, and the students were usually malnourished. In many cases, children were purposely separated from their siblings or other members of their Tribes. Schools forcibly mixed together children from different Tribes, to prevent their use of Native languages or the practice of cultural traditions.[41]

To more effectively rip Native children from the arms of their parents, the U.S. government often detailed officers from the U.S. Army to act as Indian agents.[42] In one particularly chilling account, Indian agent Fletcher J. Cowart recalled that "it became necessary to visit the [Native American] camps unexpectedly with a detachment of Indian police, and [to] seize such children as were proper and take them away to school, willing or unwilling."[43]

In a 1935 report from Indian agent Charles Berry to the U.S. Department of the Interior headquarters, he writes that although "there seems to be a tendency on the part of the parents to want to keep their children at home," federal agents had determined that there were still plenty of "children who are considered to be of the institutional type and who need to be admitted to the boarding school."[44]

In addition to the heinous acts related to boarding schools, Indian agents were also responsible for keeping tabs on the Tribes in their assigned areas. Beginning with a directive in 1885, Indian agents were instructed to take a census of each Tribe in their jurisdiction, which included each person's "Indian name," English name, relationship to the head of household, sex, and age.[45] Agents were told to retain Native names as much as possible, but not if they were "too difficult to pronounce and remember."[46] Beginning in 1930, censuses conducted by Indian agents were required to include degree of Indian blood.[47]

Few clear directions were given to agents on whom to include in these censuses. The first real set of instructions wasn't distributed until 1919, and even that was vague on implementation.[48] Largely, the decision on whom to include, and not include, on Indian censuses was left to the discretion of each agent.

Many of the Indian census rolls from the 1930s have been uploaded to archival websites from microfilm copies. As a result, most are very darkly tinted; they require a significant amount of lightening of my screen. In one set, from 1930, from the "Eastern Cherokee Reservation of Cherokee North Carolina," I find more than four hundred pages of names.[49] In the headers are the categories that Indian agents were to record, and right up top, in column 7, it's there—degree of blood. As I flip through the pages, I see that, on many, the blood degree is listed as "F."

The censuses from this period included instructions to the field agents. The instructions are brief, with just a few sentences dedicated to each counting category. In the instructions for degree of blood, agents are told to use "F" for full blood, "1/4+" for one-fourth or more Indian blood, and "-1/4" for less than one-fourth Indian blood.[50]

It's strange to see this breakdown, to ponder what the difference was, to federal officials, between a person with "1/4+" or "-1/4" Indian blood. Whether one was more Indian than the other, more deserving of federal benefits or consideration, more likely to succeed, to assimilate into the broader United States. It's also unclear where exactly the one-quarter threshold came from. The number had been used in a few previous documents, including treaties, but never in any federal policies of note. In fact, federal land allotment schemes in the early twentieth century and later policies around Indian "reorganization" had used one-half Indian blood as a cutoff for determining any number of things.

It all feels so random, so haphazardly construed—the perfect precursor to something Vine Deloria Jr. would write many years later. Federal Indian law, Deloria noted, is a series of "vaguely phrased and ill-considered federal statutes . . . which bear little relationship to rational thought."[51] He said that federal Indian law supported a fictional view of American history, one that would have put our country's best novelists to shame.

Darlene and I get stuck on the idea of home. We spend a lot of time talking about what constitutes a home, about where we consider ourselves *at home*. She tells me that, eventually, after years of living and working there, she began to think of Leech Lake as a home. She also considers Albuquerque, where she lived and worked for many years, a home. Iowa, though, is not her home; she doesn't think it has ever been.

In 1972, when she was twenty, Darlene gave birth to her daughter Dawn. Although she and Dawn's father, a non-Native man from Iowa, weren't together, his mother provided a huge amount of help with the baby, so Darlene stayed in Iowa for the support. Eventually, though, being in Iowa was too much for Darlene to handle. Years of emotional abuse and neglect there, along with her experiences in places where she felt more comfortable, made her want to get the hell out. So, she traveled around, searching. She stayed for a while in Lincoln, Nebraska, and then in Rapid City, South Dakota, with friends she'd met in AIM. She told herself she'd try anything for five years. For some reason, that was the period of time she'd always rely on: five years.

In the early 1980s, Darlene made her way back to Leech Lake. It was hard at first. She didn't know her birth family very well, and they didn't know her. But she took a job doing data entry at the Minnesota Chippewa Tribe headquarters, rented an apartment, and made a life for herself. She legally changed her name from "Laura Darlene Fountain" back to "Darlene Wind," the name given to her by her birth parents. She reconnected with her brothers and cousins and their children. Before her mother passed away in 2005, despite the awkwardness of their situation—of not knowing what they were to each other—Darlene tried her best to reconnect with her, too.

During this time, Dawn alternated between living with her paternal grandmother in Iowa and with Darlene. At age sixteen, she moved to Leech Lake to live with her mother full time. She, too, got a job with the Minnesota Chippewa Tribe and came to know the place of her mother's people. Darlene thinks Dawn felt comfortable there, that she felt it was home. By the late 1990s, Dawn had her own children, with a non-Native man who lived at Leech Lake; the eldest of them was born nearby, in Bemidji. But, eventually, Dawn moved back to Iowa, to be closer to her father and paternal grandmother. It was that move that drew Darlene back to Iowa all these years later. Now in her seventies, she wants to be close to her daughter and grandkids.

I feel a little bit nervous asking Darlene if she's enrolled in her Tribe. It's a question I've learned to ask only sparingly, if at all. Asking about someone's enrollment status feels very personal. Plus, I worry that for Darlene, someone adopted out of her Native community, the issue of Tribal enrollment might be particularly sensitive.

Eventually, after lots of conversations about lots of other things, I finally work up the courage to ask. Darlene tells me that, yes, she is an enrolled member of the Leech Lake Band of Ojibwe. At some point when she was in her late twenties, one of her cousins encouraged her to get a copy of her original birth certificate—as an adoptee, she has two—and other documents. Through that process, she discovered that her birth parents had enrolled her at Leech Lake when she was born, a decision for which she is grateful.

Her journey of finding her official paperwork came at a time when Darlene was already a parent; Dawn had been born several years before, but because she was born in Iowa, during a period in which Darlene was still navigating her own Native identity, she was not immediately enrolled. Darlene doesn't remember if she even knew that the concept of Tribal enrollment existed back then.

Once Darlene returned to Leech Lake in the 1980s and developed a stronger sense of community, it became obvious she should enroll Dawn as well. She felt it important that Dawn understand and take ownership of her Native identity, the same way she herself had been doing. Tribal enrollment, Darlene was learning, came with real benefits. Yes, there were education and career programs enrolled members could participate in, but enrollment also offered an important sense of validation. Her own enrollment documents were some of the only remaining tangible mementos of her childhood in Minnesota. Seeing her name, her *birth name*, on the paperwork next to a box checked for "Leech Lake Ojibwe" made her feel she belonged. So, Darlene tracked down the necessary original documents and did a bit of legwork and eventually made sure Dawn was enrolled at Leech Lake, too.

But as Dawn got older and had children of her own, one complexity of Darlene's family tree became of critical importance. Darlene's parents, Carl and Josephine Wind, though both Chippewa from Minnesota, were from two different Tribes. Carl Wind had been born and raised on the Red Lake Reservation. He was an enrolled member of the Red Lake Nation, a sovereign Chippewa Nation. Josephine Wind, née Critt, had been born and raised on the Leech Lake Reservation and was an enrolled member of the Leech Lake Band of Ojibwe, one of the six bands under the umbrella of the Minnesota Chippewa Tribe.

It's a common story among people in the area. Red Lake and Leech

Lake are just eighty miles apart. Red Lake, as a sovereign Nation separate from the Minnesota Chippewa Tribe umbrella, maintains its own rules of enrollment, rules different from those of the other six Tribes. But with seven different Chippewa reservations clustered in Northern Minnesota, the lines between people are much blurrier than those between enrollment rules. People from the area often seek employment in population hubs like Bemidji, or farther away, in Minneapolis and Saint Paul. Like Carl and Josephine Wind, they marry people from different bands and Tribes; they have children with people from different bands and Tribes. They blend their lives together.

To determine if a person can enroll, both Red Lake and Leech Lake use a calculation of blood quantum. And, as with most Tribes in the United States, that blood quantum has to be from *one Tribe alone*. So, to be enrolled at Leech Lake, a person must prove they have the required one-quarter blood quantum from the Minnesota Chippewa Tribe.[52] To enroll at Red Lake, they must prove one-quarter blood quantum from Red Lake Indian Nation.[53] Blood from any other Tribe doesn't count.

This calculation is made from each Tribe's base rolls. So, in order to enroll at Leech Lake, an applicant must find a direct ancestor on the rolls and demonstrate that they, the descendant, have sufficient blood quantum. Darlene's mother, who was born in 1924, is on those base rolls, listed as four-fourths Leech Lake Ojibwe. But because Darlene's father is not from Leech Lake, Darlene's verified Leech Lake blood quantum is only one-half. The Leech Lake blood quantum for Dawn, then, whose father is non-Native, is one-fourth.

As with most every other Tribe in the country, Leech Lake and Red Lake do not allow dual enrollment. You must pick just one Tribe. Of course, navigating the rules can be complicated. Darlene is glad to have succeeded with her own daughter; she's glad Dawn is an enrolled member of the Leech Lake Band. But now, as Darlene watches her grandchildren enter adulthood, sees them graduate college and take jobs and meet partners—eventually, she hopes, to have children of their own—she feels she's grieving a loss. Because they are considered one-eighth Red Lake and one-eighth Leech Lake, they do not meet the blood quantum requirement for either Tribe.

Darlene tries not to think about the what-ifs. That, had the State of Minnesota not relocated her to Iowa, things might have been very different. She tries not to imagine what her life and the lives of her daughter and grandchildren might have looked like were she to have grown up at Leech Lake. Were she to not have been separated from her family and community and everything she had ever known.

remember the first time I read the Declaration of Independence in its entirety. It was 1996, and I was a seventh-grade student at Franklin Middle School, a stately brick building on an otherwise residential street. To honor the 220th anniversary of the year the Declaration was signed, our class was to read aloud from it. We were also honoring one of its most famous signatories: Benjamin Franklin, our school's namesake.

I remember that it was a boring exercise. A lot of the words didn't mean anything to me. A lot of the concepts were too far from my immediate grasp. I remember that we formed a circle with our chairs and took turns reading aloud from handouts our teacher had printed out. I remember a lot of my classmates stumbling over the words just as I did.

The document is relatively short, but as the reading went on, most of us were simply marking time. I usually did this by moving my finger over the words the current reader was about to say, inching myself a few words past their pace. As I did this, I stumbled into a section that took me by surprise. Among the laundry list of grievances against the king of England was the accusation that he had "endeavoured to bring on the inhabitants of our frontiers, the merciless Indian Savages, whose known rule of warfare, is an undistinguished destruction of all ages, sexes and conditions."[1]

Of course, the words *Indian* and *Savages* were what most caught me off guard. They were words I would never have spoken together, words I knew were wrong together—words I was surprised the founding fathers, our own Benjamin Franklin, had signed off on.

I always had a fair amount of school spirit. In middle school, I played a handful of sports and wore my Franklin jersey with pride. I was a tour guide during school orientations. I knew the fight song by heart. I was an enthusiastic member of the school's show choir, its moniker, the "Franklin

Light and Power Company," a nod to Franklin's famous experiment with lightning.

None of that ended after we read the Declaration of Independence in class. I didn't immediately quit show choir. I didn't turn my Franklin Bolts swim cap back in. I didn't stand on my chair and vow to single-handedly rewrite the founding documents of the United States of America with justice and equality more squarely in mind. I simply sat in my seat and stared at the paper in front of me with some difficulty.

It's difficult to look at ugliness and realize that it shares a face with people we've been taught to revere. It's difficult to grapple with the reality that Abraham Lincoln (someone credited, at least in part, with the end of slavery) approved the largest mass execution in U.S. history, of thirty-eight Dakota Sioux warriors;[2] or that Theodore Roosevelt (who imposed restrictions on child labor and championed the National Park system) once said, "I don't go so far as to think that the only good Indians are the dead Indians, but I believe nine out of every ten are";[3] or that George Washington (considered one of the country's most esteemed presidents) called Native people savages who needed to be "extirpated," or destroyed.[4]

And yet, these are realities we all awkwardly shuffle past each and every day. Every school I attended while growing up was named after a notable U.S. leader with a track record for animosity toward Native American people. I was a Johnson Jaguar, a Franklin Thunderbolt, a Washington Warrior. As a federal employee, I got paid vacation days on both Columbus Day and Washington's birthday.

The truth is I'm not exactly sure what to do with any of this. The truth is I'm not so much interested in categorically villainizing people as I am in more fully understanding what happened. The truth is I take a lot of comfort in something writer Clint Smith once said, about there being power in learning. Power in knowing the facts. "Once you are armed with that history and that evidence," he said, "this country can't lie to you anymore about why it looks the way that it does."[5]

6

Separate

I don't have much of a social media presence. Partly, that's to preserve my mental health. Partly, it's because I find it difficult to keep track of all the information the internet tells me I should, and even more difficult to consider all the opinions—all the stances on things, including things I didn't even know *were* things before reading about them on the internet.

Still, I can't help noticing the rise of #LandBack.

The movement is a spin-off from a larger, decades-long movement that has united indigenous people from all around the world to fight for the return of indigenous land and resources. It's a relatively straightforward idea: indigenous people have had their land stolen and their lives taken by settler colonialism, and now that situation should be righted. Billions of acres of land and natural resources have been unjustly removed from indigenous control. In the case of the United States, Native American Tribes should be returned their ancestral homelands, including any natural resources those lands hold. We can think about this argument as an extension of sovereignty—Native people have the right to govern their own lands, including how that land is used.

Certainly, the Indian Removal Act of 1830 was hugely detrimental to Native land sovereignty. Even before that, though, when we look at the last several centuries, we see that much of the history of the Americas has been one of stolen land. Whenever European settlers docked their ships after 1492—after Columbus pilfered, murdered, and sailed the ocean blue—they were looking for new land, "undiscovered" land. Land they could live on, farm on, colonize.

The problem, of course, is that the settlers didn't discover anything.

The land they settled was already home to other people, to people indigenous to that land—Indians, as they were called, thanks to a misguided map reader who told the Europeans they had actually stumbled upon the "Indies."

A papal bull issued by Pope Alexander VI in 1493 provided the validation the European settlers needed. In it, the pope ordered that "the Catholic faith and the Christian religion be exalted and be everywhere increased and spread, that the health of souls be cared for and that barbarous nations be overthrown and brought to the faith itself."[1] That decree, coined the Doctrine of Discovery, formed the basis for what would happen next.

Over the next several centuries, settlers would continue to "discover" lands that were already home to other people. But, *To hell with it*, they thought. *We're more advanced and civilized than these other people, so we shall conquer them. We shall own the land.*

Look, I'm paraphrasing here. But, largely, land has been (and continues to be) at the forefront of so much of American history that it would be a mistake not to emphasize its importance. It would also be a mistake not to acknowledge that a major story from the last several centuries of Native America has been about stolen land.

Arguably, at no point in history was this process—the stealing of land—more accelerated than in the nineteenth century. It was in the early years of that century that Meriwether Lewis and William Clark set off on their famous expedition of the American West, a precursor to increased trade routes and, therefore, increased settlements. It was during this period that the U.S. government, via the Louisiana Purchase, bought land from France that was already home to several Native Tribes. It was during this period that Native people were forcibly marched away from their own land to land that was foreign to them, to reservations. It was during this period that the first railroads were funded and built, that the Oregon Trail was ridden, that the gold rush was sparked, that twenty-nine new states (more than in any other century) were added to the union.

It was, in short, a century of land.

It's perhaps not surprising, then, that in 1862, President Abraham Lincoln signed into law the Homestead Act. As part of that act, the U.S. government awarded 160 acres of land to any adult who could demonstrate they could make the land profitable. And while the act is often associated with a massive movement of settlers westward, it applied to as many as thirty states.[2]

The Homestead Act was an effort not just to spread non-Native people across the land but to incentivize what were considered the ideal uses of the land: farming, herding, agriculture. In order for a homesteader to be successful in their homesteading, they were required to make "significant improvements" upon their plot of land, a vague directive. If, after five years, claimants were successful in their improvements, they would be given full title to the land. That is, they would own it outright.[3]

Now, we can probably all read between the 1862 lines that most of the land granted through the Homestead Act went to white people. Slavery was still in existence when the act was signed into law, and from a practical standpoint, most freed slaves and poor immigrants would have been unable to front enough capital to build a house (required by the act) or purchase the tools and livestock necessary to improve the land (also required by the act).[4] Not to mention the fact that Black people wanting to take advantage of Homestead Act allotments often faced hostility and violence from white settlers.[5]

Moreover, what with the vague language of the act and the severe underfunding of the offices responsible for overseeing its implementation, there was a significant amount of fraud. Historians estimate that most of the land granted through the Homestead Act went to speculators, cattle ranchers, miners, loggers, and railroads. Of the more than five hundred million acres dispersed by the General Land Office between 1862 and 1904, only eighty million acres went to homesteaders.[6]

Still—despite the fraud, despite the fact that the land being granted wasn't the government's to divvy up, despite the inequity of its implementation—the Homestead Act was viewed as a rousing success, something worth celebrating and, eventually, replicating. It was also something that would fundamentally change the way Americans thought about and, indeed, owned land.

Before Marilyn Vann and I talk about her life growing up as a descendant of Cherokee Freedmen—before I marvel at the fact that her father's name appears on the original Dawes Rolls; before we discuss the federal court case in which she was a defendant, the one that ensured Cherokee Freedmen membership in the Tribe—she wants to know how my husband is doing.

He's doing fine, I tell her. He'd been ill several weeks prior, before Marilyn and I first got a chance to talk on the phone. We'd been coordinating a call for what felt like months, but somehow life had just always gotten in the way. Marilyn tells me she was praying for him, and the trace of a southern accent in her voice makes me briefly forget I'm not talking to a member of my own Lumbee family.

It doesn't take long into our conversation for me to notice something else about the way Marilyn speaks. The way she pauses to choose the correct word; the way she starts every answer with "Okay." She carries herself with the precision and conscientiousness of an engineer because, well, that's what she was trained to be. The first woman on her mother's side of her family to graduate from college (from the University of Oklahoma, where she earned a degree in engineering), she spent nearly her entire career as an engineer working for the federal government.

For the first few decades of her adult life, Marilyn focused on checking the same boxes a lot of people do. She achieved her initial goals of earning a degree, landing a job, getting married, raising children, and purchasing a home. She progressed in her career and traveled often. But by 2001, a lot of those boxes had been checked, and Marilyn could take a deep breath. She could reimagine her priorities. She'd done the traditional things she thought she needed to do to have a successful life, and she could shift her focus elsewhere.

It was that year, in 2001, that Marilyn decided to enroll in the Cherokee Nation. Marilyn had always *been* Cherokee, of course, but she tells me that, while she was growing up, there hadn't been much of a push to get people enrolled. "It wasn't until Tribal governments were really exercising sovereignty and taking back the powers that they had in the past," she says. By 2001, Marilyn was seeing that change around her, noticing more and more people getting enrolled.

So, she diligently gathered the paperwork she'd need and mailed her application to the Cherokee Nation. What happened next would ignite a flame of outrage and injustice in her that continues to burn. After submitting her paperwork and waiting for her enrollment to proceed, Marilyn was informed that her application had been rejected. Because her direct ancestor whose name was on the Dawes Rolls, her father, had been categorized as a "Freedman" rather than a Cherokee "by blood," she would be unable to complete the enrollment process. Marilyn was ineligible for membership in the Cherokee Nation.

Although I wasn't in the room when the discussions took place, I imagine that following initial implementation of the Homestead Act of 1862, the country's leaders realized they could use the same concept to solve their "Indian Problem," too. The Indian Problem being several problems, really, but most important—that Native American Tribes were taking up precious land that could otherwise go to settlers.[7] In the government's view, forcing Native people, some of whom lived communally, into individual-plot farming would also force them to assimilate to European American ways. And granting Native people provisional land ownership and provisional U.S. citizenship would serve to wipe out Tribes' authority on the reservations, thereby replacing the authority of the governments of Native Nations with that of the U.S. government.[8]

So, in 1887, the U.S. government passed a law whose language mirrored that of the Homestead Act, the important difference being that it would allot the lands of Native American Tribes. The law was called the

General Allotment Act (known as the Dawes Act), and its official purpose
was to "Provide for the Allotment of Lands in Severalty to Indians on the
Various Reservations." If you had to look up the definition of *severalty*,
you're not alone. It's a somewhat antiquated way of saying "several and
separate," as in, instead of a community of one Tribe, a group of many
individuals.

The Dawes Act's authority was significant. It gave the president the
power to allot the lands of any reservation anytime it was deemed "ad-
vantageous for agricultural and grazing purposes."[9] Plots made available
were generally 160 acres for Indian heads of household and 80 acres for
single adults. The land would be placed in *trust*—the word used to indicate that the government did *not* trust the Indians and would, therefore,
keep the title to their land locked in a drawer in the U.S. Department of
the Interior offices.

Native people who were allotted land were given twenty-five years
to demonstrate that they could succeed at Europeanized agricultural
practices. Then, if deemed worthy, they would receive the title to that
land outright. That is, they would own the land themselves. It should be
noted that this was the same provision found in the Homestead Act—
except there, the waiting period was just five years. It should also be
noted that the land the government was breaking up and allotting to
Native people in the Dawes Act was already controlled by the Tribes.

A lot of unsurprising things happened next.

Much of the land allotted through the Dawes Act was not appropriate
for plot farming—the soils weren't fertile enough, rainfall was insufficient,
and the land area wasn't large enough for proper agricultural practices.[10]
Without sufficient resources to purchase the necessary equipment, Native
people struggled to make the land profitable. Many hadn't wanted to farm
in the first place. Plus, without an actual title to the land, Native people
were skeptical—even if they made their plots successful, they did not fully
trust that they'd get to keep them.

In an oral history of the Dawes Act compiled by anthropologist Peter

Nabokov, Omaha elder Wa'thishnade recounts his experience with allot-ment. "I went on to farm with a certificate," he says. "I believed the land was mine. I have found out the land is not mine; that the Government can take it away."[11]

The U.S. government, as it turns out, did take much of the land away. In addition to selling "leftover" land once a Tribe's members had received their allotments, it levied hefty taxes on the land granted to Native people after the initial twenty-five-year trust period was over. And because many Native landowners could not afford those taxes, their land was often seized by the courts and sold at auction. As Steven Pevar writes, "There were white people literally waiting in line for the land to go into forfei-ture for failure to pay taxes."[12]

The problem was that even if a Native person didn't want to farm, even if they knew they couldn't make their plot successful or profitable, there really was no other option. Once the federal government had allotted a particular Tribe's lands, that was that. Any Native person who was entitled to a plot could either take it or find themselves without a home. Allotment created an inflexible system for Tribes whose traditional practices did not include private land ownership or farming and herding. After Tribal lands were allotted, traditional practices could not be maintained; there was no land on which to maintain them.[13]

All these years later, most scholars would describe the Dawes Act as an abject failure of U.S. policy. Even as early as 1928, the *Meriam Report*, a survey of the conditions of Native people funded by the Rockefeller Foun-dation, concluded that "an overwhelming majority of the Indians are poor, even extremely poor, and they are not adjusted to the economic and social system of the dominant white civilization."[14]

Besides a patent to the land, another of the carrots at the end of the Dawes Act stick was the promise of U.S. citizenship. Only Native people who accepted the allotment scheme would be eligible to become U.S. citizens. This promise had its own—how shall I say this?—utterly fucked-up consequences that are still haunting Native people today. The

Wyandotte Nation, the Tribe with which Kayla Dennis identifies, is a prime example of this.

In 1843, as part of the so-called Ohio Trail of Tears, the Wyandotte were forcibly removed from Ohio to what today is Kansas and promised land by the federal government that never actually existed. They arrived in Kansas to discover that the government had lied to them. So, the Wyandotte purchased their own land—over 23,000 acres from the neighboring Delaware Tribe. The Delaware gave the Wyandotte three additional sections in remembrance of lands the Wyandotte had granted them to live on in Ohio. But the federal government stole that, too, "allotting" it back to individual members of the Tribe. Then, as if that weren't heinous enough, the United States declared in treaties in 1855 and 1867 that the Wyandotte people could either stay in Kansas on their land allotments and be granted U.S. citizenship or be removed to a reservation in Indian Territory (present-day Oklahoma).

That division—between those who remained part of a unified Tribe with communal lands and those who accepted land allotments and received U.S. citizenship—remains today. Those who moved to Oklahoma formed what is now the federally recognized Wyandotte Nation. Those who remained in Kansas, with land allotments and citizenship? They formed the Wyandot Nation of Kansas, which is unrecognized by the U.S. government as a Native American Tribe.

The division wasn't coincidental. One of the primary goals of the Dawes Act—hell, maybe *the* primary goal—was to shrink the size and scope of Indian Country. Once all the eligible Native people had been assigned their allotments, the U.S. government would sell the "leftover" plots to non-Native people. In this way, the total size of Native lands shrank, as did Native influence.

In an 1893 letter, Bureau of Indian Affairs commissioner D. M. Browning instructed that "in your negotiations you shall first endeavor to secure the allotment of the lands . . . and the cession of any surplus remaining to the United States."[15] In a statement by former secretary of the interior and U.S. senator from Colorado Henry M. Teller, he expressed concern that "the real aim [of allotment] is to get at the Indians' lands and open them up for resettlement."[16]

Ironically, it was Indian Territory, or modern-day Oklahoma—to which thirty-four Tribes had been forcibly removed—that the federal government now desperately wanted back.[17] The land was considered valuable, particularly to land speculators, and in the view of the U.S. government, the fertile soils were being completely wasted on the Native people who had been violently forced there.

The problem was that the Dawes Act specifically excluded the territory occupied by the Cherokees, Muscogee (Creeks), Choctaws, Chickasaws, and Seminoles—the Five Tribes that had been removed to Oklahoma as part of the Indian Removal Act. Those Tribes had previously secured treaties with the U.S. government to prevent their land from being divided.

As Vine Deloria Jr. writes, these five Tribes were a threat to the U.S. government not just because of the valuable land they controlled but also because of the success with which they had created their own institutions. Since the 1830s, since being removed to Oklahoma, the Five Tribes had built for themselves "small republics," complete with schools, courts, and businesses.[18] Moreover, leaders of those Tribes had leveraged their people's respect and influence, something that threatened the leadership of the U.S. government.

And so, in 1893, President Grover Cleveland established the Dawes Commission, whose mission—and I'm paraphrasing—was to tear the treaties that had protected the lands of Indian Territory to shreds. As part of the commission, three men were sent to negotiate with the Five Tribes, but the Tribes held their ground and refused. They would not agree with the commission's divide-allot-and-conquer strategy.

The government's response? On June 28, 1898, Congress passed the Curtis Act, which abolished Tribal governments in Indian Territory. It also extended the Dawes Act to these lands—including those of the previously protected Five Tribes. Together, the two acts resulted in the loss of an estimated ninety million acres of land formerly reserved for Native Americans—leaving Native people with less than one-third of their previous land base.[19] The official title of the legislation was an "Act for the Protection of the People of Indian Territory."

The first salient memory that Marilyn has about her Native identity is from kindergarten. She remembers a boy walking up to her on the playground and asking her what kind of Indian she was. "I know you're not colored," he said. Her memory of the boy was that he was white, although she didn't have much concept of race at the time. She imagines that, what with their proximity to so many different reservations and the large population of Native people living in their town, the question was meant as an innocent inquiry more than anything else.

Marilyn was born and raised in Ponca City, Oklahoma, the headquarters of the Ponca Tribe of Indians of Oklahoma. It's a place whose own population, which hovers around 25,000, is a diverse mix of people, about 10 percent of whom are Native. (In comparison, less than 3 percent of the U.S. population identifies as Native.[20]) To drive an hour east or southeast of town is to find yourself squarely in the middle of one of several Tribes' reservations.

On the day of the playground inquiry, Marilyn remembers returning home from school and telling her father what had happened. She remembers passing along the question, asking him what she was. She remembers that he told her they were "Cherokee Indians and that they also had colored ancestry."

As with many Cherokee people, Marilyn's relatives included Black Natives and people enslaved by the Cherokee Nation. It's a common story among the Five Tribes. All five had a significant history of slavery, one that garnered them the name "Five Civilized Tribes" by southern white society.[21] The thinking being that to own slaves qualified them as civilized. It's also a story that hasn't gotten as much attention as it warrants. A story where, sometimes, people enslaved by Tribes were part of those Tribes by blood. Where, sometimes people enslaved by Tribes spoke Native languages and practiced Native traditions; where categories like "Cherokee by blood" and

"Freedmen" and "Black Native" were not distinct but, rather, significantly overlapping. My friend Kendra Taira Field, an African American and Creek scholar, puts it this way: "The North American 'frontier' was far more complicated than my textbooks let on."[22]

Although there is no precise count of the total number of slaves held by the Five Tribes, historians seem to agree that slavery was most prevalent in the Cherokee Nation.[23] Some estimates are that the Cherokees enslaved more than 2,500 people in 1860; in 1867, in a census conducted of the Nation, there were almost 2,500 Freedmen among the 17,000 total Cherokee people.[24]

Although the Cherokee National Council passed legislation in 1863 to free all slaves, it would take until after the Civil War, with passage of the 1866 Treaty of Washington, for all people enslaved by Cherokee to be freed.[25] Often, Cherokee Freedmen remained in the Cherokee Nation, particularly before Oklahoma's statehood was granted in 1907. For many, the decision was pragmatic—that's where their families were; it was the only place they had ever lived. But many Cherokee Freedmen were Cherokee ancestrally, too. As scholars like Tiya Miles have written, the period immediately after slavery in Indian Country was complicated, creating for many Freedmen a legacy of something she calls "in-betweenness."[26]

Marilyn's father was a young child when he was enrolled as a Cherokee Freedman as part of the Dawes Rolls. When Marilyn tells me this, I marvel. I wonder aloud if she is one of the very few people alive today whose own parent was listed there, one of the few people just one generation removed from the Dawes Rolls. Marilyn tells me that by the time he married her mother, her father had already been married and widowed twice before. When she was born, Marilyn was younger than some of her father's grandchildren; she had nieces and nephews who were older than she was. It's a phenomenon I'm familiar with. I tell her I've always called it the missing stair. Because of huge age gaps in his family, my father is about the same age as his niece and nephew. As a result, none of the ages for the rest of the generations of our family line up.

Growing up, Marilyn remembers taking trips a few times per year to the Cherokee Nation, in Eastern Oklahoma, where her father's family lived. She particularly remembers her father, a Baptist deacon, taking her to small country churches there. But as he got older, her father's health began to decline, and the trips became less frequent. Marilyn tried to stay connected as best she could, but information was far less available then. "Nowadays, we have hundreds of books on Native people and identity," she tells me. "Things that are going on now, like culture and language classes, weren't happening then. Tribes were simply trying to survive."

Back in Ponca City, most of Marilyn's neighbors were Ponca. She remembers a lot of Ponca friends from school. She remembers that her parents would occasionally take her to Ponca powwows, and she would try to connect the dots with her own Cherokee family. She'd imagine that they might dance in powwows, too. Despite both her grandparents on her mother's side being on the Dawes Rolls as Chickasaw Freedmen, Marilyn grew up feeling closer to the Cherokee side of her family. She remembers her father telling her that their Indian ancestors were part of the Trail of Tears and that he and his siblings and father received land allotments because they were Tribal members. She is proud of her Cherokee heritage, proud that her ancestors were survivors.

A lot has been written about the impact of the Dawes Act on land and trusts and on the relationship between the U.S. government and Native American Tribes.[27] The consequences for Tribal justice systems, many of which were dismantled through the legislation, and for things like poverty among Native people, were largely a result of forcing them into plot farming without enough fertile land, resources, or tools. The so-called checkerboarding of the land—splitting Native allotments and placing white settlers in between—only further deteriorated Native communities.

But as I sort through congressional records, and historical accounts, and—God help me—law review journals, I remember another fact, too. That, whether by consequence or design, the Dawes Act forever impacted the way we think about Native identity. Although the U.S. government had been dabbling in land allotment policy in Indian Country as early as 1798, the Dawes Act proved to be an important inflection point. It was the start of the turn of the dial from the federal government's reservation policy to its assimilation policy, shifting along with it the government's relationship with Native Americans from one with Tribes to one with individuals.[28] While, previously, the federal government had negotiated mostly with (and defined) Tribes, it was now making a business of adjudicating Indianness, whether in reference to eligibility for land allotments, fitness for plot farming, success at becoming Europeanized, or, as the case eventually became, Tribal "membership."

If we graded the U.S. Congress on how well it thought through this complexity, it would receive a solid F-minus. In fact, nowhere does the Dawes Act define what, exactly, qualified someone to receive an allotment of land. Rather, the original act lists just "Indians." In his 1888 annual report, Bureau of Indian Affairs commissioner John H. Oberly suggested that Congress "confine the benefits arising under Indian treaties to those justly entitled thereto, by excluding Indians by adoption and also the descendants of Whites and Indians beyond a certain degree."[29] In 1891, Congress defined those eligible for land allotments as "All persons who are in whole or in part of Indian blood or descent who are entitled to an allotment of land under any law of Congress."[30]

One of my favorite journalistic phrases is "non-denial denial." I first heard it while watching *All the President's Men*, a movie about the Watergate scandal. It describes a statement that, at the outset, might seem to be a straightforward denial but, upon further inspection, is actually carefully crafted in order to deceive. It does not explicitly deny something; it just makes it seem that way. It's a linguistic workaround so that the person speaking can't be accused of lying.

The Dawes Act allotment feels, to me, like something we might call a "non-process process"—that is, it *seems* like a process to the naked eye but, upon further inspection, is no process at all. Whether this was a choice by the federal government—to write the act vaguely enough so that the people implementing it could do as they pleased—is a matter of my own speculation.

In any event, the process was poorly designed and even more poorly executed.

It began in earnest after Congress created the Dawes Commission in 1893. This three-man task force, chaired by its namesake, U.S. senator Henry L. Dawes of Massachusetts, was authorized to "make correct rolls of the citizens by blood of all the other Tribes, eliminating from the Tribal rolls such names as may have been placed thereon by fraud or without authority of law."[31] In addition to Dawes, the commission initially comprised two other members—U.S. Army major Meredith H. Kidd and former Confederate Army officer Archibald S. McKennon. Neither of the men had any particular expertise in Native policy or Tribes. Both were trained as lawyers, and McKennon, while serving as a prosecutor, had gone to prison for stabbing a judge.[32]

The majority of documentation outlining the work of the Dawes Commission comes from letters and directives sent between Indian Affairs headquarters and commissioners working in the field and from journal entries of the time. In a letter from headquarters to agents in the field dated July 24, 1899, they are given instructions as follows:

> For the purpose of this record you will require all applicants for enrollment to present themselves within the Tribe in which such applicant claims right to enrollment, for examination, under oath, his statements to be taken down by the commission, upon which the commission will determine his right to enrollment, and such record and action of the commission will be preserved and transmitted with the enrollment to be considered by this office and the Department when the rolls made by the commission are submitted for the approval of the secretary of the Interior.[33]

Most of the Dawes Roll cards have been digitized and uploaded to a few of those pay-to-play genealogy websites. After choosing a Tribe from a pull-down menu, I can decide whether to view registration cards from people who were accepted or rejected as "Indian," Freedmen, or "Intermarried White." While the print on the cards has faded over the last 120 years, I can mostly make out the names and ages of those listed, in looping cursive letters, and stamped, red-ink phrases like "citizenship certificate issued" or "dismissed under order of the commission." On many, "REJECTED," in all capital letters, appears to be the only decision given.

If you do enough digging, you can usually find something called an enrollment "jacket," which accompanied most applications. Inside many of these is a transcription of an interview, presumably conducted by a person employed by the Dawes Commission.

In one jacket, I find a list of twenty-six questions, beginning with the most basic ("What is your name?") through those meant to establish biological parentage and whether the applicant had ever received money from the Tribe they identified with (they hadn't). The particular jacket I stumble across is part of a larger series, for a family of sixteen headed by a woman named Caroline Pannell.[34] Ultimately, all the members of the family were rejected.

Reading the enrollment jacket for Caroline Pannell and her family is a confusing experience. According to Mrs. Pannell's written testimony, her maternal grandfather, Peter Harrison, was a full-blooded Creek man. He died at some point during the Civil War. As part of the enrollment jacket are several testimonies on behalf of the Pannell family, including from Wesley Vaden, Mrs. Pannell's father, who was seventy-seven years old at the time. Hardy Vaden, who was eighty-five, testified that he was personally acquainted with Peter Harrison and that he, Harrison, was a full-blooded Creek man. So, too, did Tobe McIntosh, seventy-five, a "full-blooded Creek" who'd lived in the Creek Nation his entire life. Wiley Sooky, another full-blooded Creek man, said the same. Sure, it's impossible to verify the stories from letters on paper, but they seem like credible accounts.

In what feels like serendipity, I find an interview with Caroline Pannell as part of something called the Indian-Pioneer History Project for Oklahoma. It was conducted in 1937, when she was eighty-four years old, more than three decades after the Dawes Rolls were created. In the interview, she recounts being born into slavery in 1853 in Tennessee to a father she describes as Negro and Choctaw and a mother she describes as Negro and Creek Indian.[35]

"My first recollection," Mrs. Pannell says, "was when I was a small child, I—with my parents—were sold at a slave market in Nashville to a plantation owner and slave holder of Texas."[36] She, along with her parents, remained in Texas after they were all set free. Sometime after 1900, the family relocated to Oklahoma, to Checotah, to be nearer to family.

I'll admit that when I first began reading the enrollment materials for Caroline Pannell and her family, it hadn't occurred to me that they presented as Black. The questions answered by family members, the testimony from community members, the lengthy decision given by commissioners—none of them gave me any indication of the color of their skin. Of course, I can't say for certain that the Pannell family was rejected because of their outward appearance, but we know that people who had been enslaved in Native communities faced unique challenges during the non-process process of enrollment. We also know that, in many cases, those freed from slavery lived as "fully incorporated members of Indian Tribes."[37] Yet, when the federal agents responsible for putting together the Dawes Rolls came to town, Freedmen and their families would either be listed on a separate roll or not included at all.[38]

For these decisions, members of the Dawes Commission relied mostly on what scholar Katherine M. B. Osburn calls "eyeballing."[39] In the case of Mississippi Choctaw enrollment, Commissioner McKennon decided that "persons who showed a predominance of Choctaw blood and characteristics should not have to produce evidence of descent," but those who displayed half or less did.[40]

For those whom the Dawes Commission deemed unequivocally Indian—those who, in McKennon's view, showed a predominance of Native blood and characteristics—there was almost no choice but to enroll. Anyone who refused risked jail time or worse. In one of the more notorious of these cases, eight so-called full-blooded Cherokee men—

members of the Keetoowah Nighthawk Society, an organization opposed to enrollment—were arrested and charged with contempt of federal court.[41] Following tradition, the men wore their hair long, considering it an important part of their identity. While in custody, officials threatened to cut the men's hair if they resisted. After officers cut the first man's hair against his will, the other seven submitted.[42] All were forced to enroll.

In the final decision for Caroline Pannell and her family, signed by Acting Commissioner of Indian Affairs C. F. Larrabee, the primary reason for rejection was that the applicants—people who had been enslaved and sold and sent to Texas—hadn't been included on any previous Creek rolls.[43]

When I ask Marilyn if she ever considered enrolling in the Cherokee Nation before 2001, she tells me that the idea of enrollment hadn't garnered much attention while she was growing up. Her father had been enrolled as part of the Dawes Rolls, but he never talked much about it with his family. Until 1970, after passage of the Principal Chiefs Act, the federal government didn't allow Cherokee leaders to be elected by popular vote, so there wasn't a strong council system. When she was young, she says, there wasn't much of a push for people to enroll.

After her enrollment was rejected in 2001, Marilyn felt mostly confused. She hadn't anticipated any problems with her application—after all, her father was on the Dawes Rolls, the Cherokee Nation's only measure of eligibility. When she received her rejection letter in the mail, she immediately called the regional office of the Bureau of Indian Affairs. (As a federal government employee, she had a general understanding of the organizational structure and knew that in addition to a headquarters in Washington, D.C., the BIA had offices around the country, with jurisdiction for Tribes within their regional area.) But the regional office told her the same story the Tribal registrar had, a story that didn't make any sense.

"It felt like a scam," she tells me.

Her next step seemed somewhat natural, like muscle memory. Marilyn's career as an engineer had required a lot of legal research, and although she didn't have particular experience with Tribal law, she knew her way around a law library. She understood the kinds of questions to ask, and from everything she was reading, she found her suspicions confirmed. Legally, she should have been able to enroll.

Among the things Marilyn learned through her research was that, when the Cherokee Nation signed the Treaty of 1866, it agreed to give Freedmen and their descendants "all the rights of native Cherokees."[44] And, despite significant racism and mismanagement, nearly five thousand Cherokee Freedmen were indeed on the Dawes Rolls.[45] She also learned that a 1983 Cherokee Nation ordinance barred all Freedmen from voting in the Tribe's elections.[46] Cherokee Freedmen and their descendants were sent letters informing them that Cherokee Nation would begin requiring citizens to prove their blood quantum via a certificate of Indian blood—a federal document that used the Dawes Rolls as a basis for determining that blood quantum. Even if Freedmen or their descendants had Cherokee ancestry—which many did—it wouldn't have shown up on the Dawes Rolls, anyway. For Freedmen, no blood quantum was listed.

Over the next few years, Marilyn did a significant amount of legwork. She discovered an ongoing lawsuit between the U.S. Department of the Interior and the descendants of Seminole Nation Freedmen, and she reached out to the attorney working the case. He told her that her case would take a lot of time and a lot of money. Marilyn wasn't sure she could afford either, but she told her husband and daughter she wanted to continue the fight. They were both supportive.

For Marilyn, it was important to gain some consensus. She called for a meeting of people who wanted to know more about the Freedmen disenrollment. It was held at a public library in Oklahoma City; she estimates that about thirty-five people showed up.

I imagine that the benefit of retrospect has allowed Marilyn to summarize succinctly the complicated and convoluted series of events that happened next. Of course she remembers the details, but she's gotten good at talking about things more broadly, from a higher elevation. After that first meeting at the public library, she and several other Freedmen descendants formed a board. They held more meetings. They tried to get politicians and newspapers interested, but they were often asked the age-old question "What's in it for us?" The Freedmen group couldn't promise large-scale donations or full-page ads. "No one gave us the time of day," she remembers.

In 2003, together with eight other plaintiffs, Marilyn sued the U.S. Department of the Interior, along with the Cherokee Nation, for failing to protect the citizenship and voting rights of Cherokee Freedmen and their descendants.[47] It was, as the suit stated, a clear violation of the Treaty of 1866.

Over the next several years, the lawsuit would work its way through district and circuit courts and would include lengthy appeals and the overturning of those appeals. In 2009, the Cherokee Nation filed its own federal case against the Department of the Interior and individual Freedmen descendants.[48] Finally, in 2017—a full fourteen years after Marilyn's suit was originally filed—a U.S. district court ruled in favor of the Freedmen. According to Judge Thomas Hogan, "The Cherokee Nation can continue to define itself as it sees fit but must do so equally and evenhandedly with respect to native Cherokees and the descendants of Cherokee freedmen."[49]

Marilyn is proud to tell me that, today, the Cherokee Nation is the only one among the Five Tribes whose Freedmen descendants can exercise their full citizenship rights. Cherokee Freedmen can vote in the Tribe's elections, run for office, serve in the cabinet, and sit on the Tribal council. "I've been in this Freedmen business for twenty-two years," she tells me, "and a lot has changed."

When I ask Marilyn why this work has been so important to her, why she dedicated so much of her life to this cause, she talks about injustice. People enslaved by the Cherokee Nation were also killed in battles; they also walked the Trail of Tears, many of them died along the way. She tells me that Freedmen and their descendants are part of Cherokee Nation.

"The more that there's turmoil between enrolled and unenrolled people," she says, "the less the federal government has to do. They can just let the Indians fight amongst themselves."

Taken together, the Dawes Rolls database is overwhelming. More than one hundred thousand people, all long gone, are listed in what feels like no particular order. Without a kinship connection to anyone on the rolls—my Tribe was not part of them—I decide to do a search of my first name.

Growing up, I hated my name in the same vague way that a lot of people hate their names. "Carrie" didn't feel exciting. Plus, it rhymed with words that made my life difficult: *Hairy. Scary.* For the entirety of first grade, I signed my daily math sheets "Ariel," as in the Little Mermaid. As the years went by, I settled into "Carrie." I began to appreciate its longevity, the fact that there are Carries going back centuries, that the name seems to have withstood the test of time.

According to the ticker at the top of my search bar, 468 people named Carrie were part of the Dawes Rolls from 1898 to 1914.[50] There are Carries represented in every Tribe that's part of the rolls and every category within them: accepted for membership, rejected, Indians by blood, Freedmen. I begin to look for patterns or rationales, but what I find is nothing. It all feels so random.

I begin to fixate on the column labeled "Blood." It's there, on every Dawes Rolls card, listed after the person's name, age, and sex.

Carrie Brookins, age twelve, was three-eighths Mississippi Choctaw and rejected. Carrie Brewer, age eleven, was one-fourth Cherokee and accepted. Carrie Parks, age seven weeks, was three-fourths Cherokee, but she died before a decision could be made. Carrie Bratcher, age thirty-eight, was one-half Delaware Cherokee, but there is no discernable answer for her—simply a large *X* drawn through her entire card.

By the time the Dawes Rolls were being created, the idea of "degree of Indian blood," of blood quantum, had been around for a while. Probably the first legal instance of its use in the United States was in 1785, when Virginia wrote into state law that anyone with one-fourth or more Negro blood would be considered mulatto.[51] In 1866, Virginia expanded its blood laws to define "Indian" as "every person, not a colored person, having one-fourth or more of Indian blood."[52] By that point, North Carolina, Indiana, and California had all done the same. These laws weren't meant as interesting reference points; they were meant to deny rights to certain people. People whose skin was deemed darker, whose traditions deemed uncivilized, whose value was deemed "lesser."

Until the Dawes Act, though, the federal government hadn't really measured Native identity in this way. According to legal scholar Paul Spruhan, in the early years of federal treaty making with Tribes, blood quantum as a linguistic description of ancestry had no real legal significance.[53] Yes, it's true that later treaties included some mention of blood quantum, but only in regard to certain benefits, not for some blanket definition of Tribal membership. Mostly, the federal government had allowed the Tribes to determine their own "membership," a word many Tribes, I dare say, wouldn't have used themselves.

I imagine that many of the Native people faced with the blood quantum question during Dawes enrollment initially scratched their heads and thought, *What the hell does this mean?*

Even today, even looking at the rolls over a century later, I struggle to figure out what the hell it means. Nowhere in the Dawes Act itself, in records from officials and those working in the field, or in historical accounts from observers, was a cutoff for blood quantum stipulated. Rather, the inclusion of blood quantum on the Dawes Rolls has the air of a tracking device, something allowing federal officials to know how many Indians existed and to what degree.

The federal government did, eventually, find a way to weaponize blood quantum. In 1906—just a few years after Dawes enrollment began—Congress passed the Burke Act, which allowed for "competent" Indians to sell, lease, or mortgage their land allotments and gain U.S. citizenship. It was a way to circumvent the twenty-five-year probationary period the Dawes Act had established before Native people could receive title to their land.

As part of the Burke Act, the federal government set up "Competency Commissions" around Indian Country.[54] Bureau of Indian Affairs commissioner Cato Sells ordered Indian agents to submit the names of all Native people in their jurisdiction with less than one-half Indian blood.[55] In 1917, Sells declared the people whose names were listed, along with all Indians with one-half or more Indian blood who passed a commission examination, as "competent."[56] Those deemed competent were awarded certificates of competency and given title to their land, whether they wanted it or not.

The certificates I find are spare.[57] Each forms a half sheet of paper with lines running its width. They are handwritten. At the top is the person's name, and under that are listed the names of their heirs, an allotment number, a description of the plot, and the date it was issued. Gustavus Robertson was deemed competent on January 23, 1910; Mrs. Jennie Blackwood on February 10, 1911; Franklin Haywater on the same date. Nothing on the certificate gives any indication why the person was deemed competent. Nothing in the non-process process alludes to any real method used.

The auspices of the commissions—of the Burke Act's notion of deeming Native people "competent"—was freeing individuals from the restrictions imposed by the Dawes Act.[58] Yet, as Katherine Ellinghaus has written, Native people who were declared competent found themselves prey to "manipulation, deceit, scams, and bad advice."[59] They were also required to pay property taxes, something many couldn't afford. In a 1991 study, scholar Janet McDonnell estimates that the Burke Act was responsible for the loss of 23 million acres (fully one-fourth) of Native land during the period of allotment.[60]

But the Burke Act and its subsequent regulations did something else, too. By pegging competency to blood quantum in official documents—in rules and regulations and instructions to the field—it solidified both in practice and in law the connection between federal policy and the degree of Indian blood.

My former boss and longtime mentor, Jennifer Ho, has a particular pet peeve when it comes to public policy. She calls it false precision, or portraying an issue as overly quantifiable. Making it seem like we can pinpoint or define or count things we cannot.

I am a longtime sufferer of this affliction. After all, I love data—looking at numbers, making hypotheses, quantifying things. When Jennifer would issue gentle warnings to our team about not falling into the trap of false precision, it was usually to me she was directing her comments.

As I read through the Dawes Act and the Curtis Act and the Burke Act—the regulations and policies created to measure Indian people—I can't help but hear Jennifer cautioning me. Telling me to be careful, not to allow false precision to seep into my thoughts about Native identity, what it means to be Indian, to be Indian *enough*. And yet, somewhere in the innermost compartment of my brain, I know it already has.

Despite knowing, rationally, that identity can't be measured in fractions; that the federal project has long been to count Indians only in order to someday assimilate and eliminate us—hell, despite belonging to a Tribe that doesn't use blood quantum for its enrollment process—I have for a long time thought of myself as one-quarter Lumbee.

I wonder if that will ever change.

Disconnect

Karen Diver speaks with what has become my favorite linguistic combination, Minnesotan potty mouth. The way she elongates her *o*'s and *a*'s—which appear in the majority of any given word—is common to people from the upper Midwest. So, too, is the way she inserts question marks at the end of her thoughts. It is the way she peppers her sentences with George Carlin's seven words you can't say on television, though, that most delights me, a fellow midwestern foul mouth.

Once, while telling me about her move from her longtime cabin to an apartment closer to town, she lamented how exhausting transitions can be. When you move, even the little things are challenging. To do something as routine as make dinner, she had to learn a whole new set of patterns. She concluded with optimism, though: she would eventually figure it out. "I'm going to find my fucking spatula, do you know what I mean?" she said.

Karen's never afraid to point a finger at a problem and call it what it is. We both work in higher education now, and we often find ourselves talking about the state of Native student success. Lately, one of her biggest efforts has been advocating for free college tuition for Native students in Minnesota—specifically, at publicly funded institutions sitting on lands that historically belonged to (read: were stolen from) Tribes. It makes sense that members of those Tribes shouldn't have to pay to attend school there.

I had heard about Karen Diver long before we ever met—always in the context of her being someone impressive, someone changing the game. For many years during my time in the federal government, I had heard about her ability to get shit done.

It was 2014 when my boss Jennifer (who is also from Minnesota) invited me on a trip to meet Karen for the first time. We were working in D.C. at the time, but Jennifer had known Karen for years. Karen was her Tribe's highest-ranking official and the first woman to serve in the role of chairperson for the Fond du Lac Band of Lake Superior Chippewa. Fond du Lac is one of six Tribes under the umbrella of the Minnesota Chippewa Tribe, the same umbrella governing the Leech Lake Band of Ojibwe, where Darlene Wind and her daughter are enrolled.

We met up with Karen for lunch at the Black Bear Casino Resort, a Tribally owned enterprise right off Interstate 35, about two hours north of the Twin Cities. The casino was a combination of modern architecture on the outside, dark spaces lit in bright neon on the inside. It reminded me of other casinos I'd been to. The difference was that, there I felt I was part of an entourage. From the moment we walked through the two sets of glass doors, people, individually and in small groups, began to approach Karen.

Karen seemed to understand her celebrity but was not overly affected by it. She remembered people's names—no small feat in a Tribe of more than four thousand members. She gladly shook hands and offered words of encouragement or advice.

The topic that Jennifer had invited Karen to lunch to speak about was housing—specifically, how to support Tribes in their ongoing efforts to provide housing and supportive services to people experiencing homelessness. Native homelessness was a fairly untouched issue, as far as the federal government was concerned, but Native people have some of the highest rates of homelessness among any group and are five times more likely to experience homelessness than the U.S. population overall.[1]

Of course, homelessness is not an isolated problem. It is almost always, including in Native communities, a result of more overarching issues. Poverty, unemployment, mental and physical health crises—all these can lead to periods of homelessness. The difference, for Native people and other marginalized groups in the United States, is that systems of oppression (including racism in employment and the housing market and lack of access to affordable health care) can make these issues feel inescapable.

Native Americans have the highest rates of poverty among any minoritized group in this country.[2] Native children are three times more likely to live in poverty than white children—a pattern that is often weaponized by agencies like Child Protective Services:[3] Native children are four times more likely than non-Native children to be placed in foster care.[4] Native people are also twice as likely to be unemployed.[5] These trends pile onto one another as the generations go by. It's estimated that Native people have an average wealth accumulation of just $5,700, compared with an average of $65,000 for the U.S. population as a whole.[6]

It doesn't help that the solutions to these challenges are not made holistically.

During my time with the federal government, "Native American issues" were often relegated to offices with the words *Native* or *Indian* in their titles. At the Department of Housing and Urban Development, for example, there was an Office of Native American Policy. At the Department of Health and Human Services, it was the Administration for Native Americans; at the Department of Education, the Office of Indian Education. The list goes on and on.

The challenge with this structure is that Native program offices often feel disconnected from the broader engines of change making. Large programs that run homelessness funding, for example, would not routinely (or ever) communicate with the folks running Native programs. Often, we refer to this problem as one of silos, with each office (whether it ran programs for homelessness, affordable housing, or economic development) operating apart from the others. My experience was that many of the people working in the Native American Office at HUD, for example, had never even met the people running some of the department's largest programs.

What Karen had figured out how to do at Fond du Lac was, therefore, somewhat revolutionary. It started with a very specific problem statement: the Fond du Lac Tribe was seeing too many of its elders, especially military veterans, suffering from a lack of stable and affordable housing. Often, when veterans return home from service, there are no adequate support systems in place to transition them back into civilian life. And, often, this issue is exacerbated by mental health challenges like post-traumatic stress disorder. If left untreated for long enough—what we've seen with veterans of the Vietnam and Gulf Wars—this problem can lead to prolonged periods of poverty and chronic homelessness.

So, Karen figured out a way to weave together funding from different federal, state, and local sources to provide supportive housing for her community's veterans experiencing homelessness. The "weaving" part was crucial—it is very rare for one source of funding to be enough to build a building, let alone fund sustainable services or repairs. The challenge is that finding, not to mention being awarded, funding from different sources can be difficult, requiring excellent grant-writing skills, a thoughtful proposal, and, usually, a proven track record. Karen had all three.

After lunch at the casino, Karen took us on a tour of Fond du Lac Veterans Supportive Housing, a ten-unit apartment complex in Cloquet, Minnesota, in the heart of the Fond du Lac Reservation. We pulled into a small parking lot in front of a one-story, two-toned building whose only real signage was a collection of military flags. This was by design, the idea being that supportive housing shouldn't look any different from any other kind of housing. It shouldn't make the residents feel lesser than or different from anyone living in housing that's not supportive or subsidized.

Karen walked us through the building's common room, a well-appointed space with several couches and a big-screen TV. We toured the laundry facilities and met a few of the staff who worked on-site. We were careful not to invade the privacy of the building's residents. Often, while traveling as part of my work on homelessness, I hesitated to take tours of residences. I was keenly aware of my status as a bureaucrat, and the last thing I wanted to do was make people feel uncomfortable—particularly people cast into society's margins. But everyone there knew Karen and seemed happy to see her. They were proud of the building, proud of the accomplishments they had all made together.

It wasn't long after that trip to Minnesota that I heard the good news: Karen had been named President Obama's special assistant for Native American affairs. It felt like a huge victory, having someone in the White House with such a deep understanding of and experience in Native communities. A person whose own family had both benefited and suffered from federal policymaking in Indian Country.

It was soon after Karen arrived in D.C. that a joint program between the Departments of Veteran Affairs and Housing and Urban Development, along with the Bureau of Indian Affairs, dedicated almost six million dollars to tackling homelessness among Native veterans.

Tracing federal Indian policy through the twentieth century is like watching a tennis ball fly between rackets. As fast as I can track the ball in one direction, it quickly reverses course and bounces back to the other.

In the aftermath of the Dawes Act, a flaming garbage fire of policy failure, Native people were struggling. In dividing and allotting Native lands and stealing much of that land through selling "leftovers" and through "forced fee" schemes; in kidnapping Native children and sending them to boarding schools; in taking away the powers and rights of Native Nation governments—the U.S. federal government had pushed Native communities to crisis (or, rather, *crises* plural). These crises were laid bare in the Meriam Report: allotted lands were proving unsuitable for agriculture, levels of poverty were extremely high, and diseases like tuberculosis were widespread.[7] In short, the government's allotment scheme had failed.

The U.S. government—now under the leadership of Franklin Delano Roosevelt—considered the Indian Reorganization Act of 1934 a way to, at least in part, right these wrongs. The act, which has been called the Indian New Deal, was an about-face in the sense that it attempted to undo policies enacted as part of the Dawes Act.[8] Among other provisions, it discontinued the policy of allotment in severalty and returned so-called surplus lands to the Tribes rather than giving them to homesteaders. It granted federal resources for health care and education on reservations and allowed Tribes to practice self-government under federal supervision.[9]

On the surface, the IRA appeared to be pumping the brakes on assimilation—the idea that it was inherently desirable to force upon Native people Europeanized ways of life. Some scholars partially credit Bureau of Indian Affairs commissioner John Collier for this change.[10] Collier had founded the American Indian Defense Association in the 1920s and was one of the people who called for reform, including the study of the conditions on Indian reservations that became the Meriam Report.[11] In his time with the BIA, including during the creation of the IRA, Collier urged the federal government to undo allotment and to provide more resources for Native employment and education.[12]

The challenge was that by the time the Indian Reorganization Act was passed, a lot of damage had been done. For one thing, the U.S. government had already sold a lot of land to non-Native settlers as part of the Dawes Act. The IRA didn't undo those transactions—in fact, to this day, many reservations are checkerboarded, the Tribe's land dotted with non-Native plots.[13] Some critics of the IRA point out that the act did very little for sustainable economic growth.[14]

Plus, although the IRA contained certain provisions for self-governance, its stipulation of federal supervision wasn't completely in line with the idea of sovereignty. Yes, Tribes could adopt a constitution and pass bylaws, but those had to be reviewed and approved by the Department of the Interior. For many Tribes, this was an unwelcome change.[15] Indeed, in some cases, the so-called IRA constitutions reduced the autonomy Tribes had given themselves in their previous constitutions.[16] The ramifications for not accepting federal intervention were real. Tribes that did not adopt a constitution under the IRA lost out on some of the financial benefits of the act.[17]

As part of the federal government's urging of Tribes to adopt formal constitutions, a model constitution was drafted, though it remains unclear how widely it was disseminated.[18] We know that the model was sent to at least some BIA officials responsible for working with Tribes on drafting their constitutions.[19] The model included a "Membership" section with several examples suggesting a blood quantum requirement for Tribal enrollment.[20]

In 1947, Theodore Haas, chief counsel for the Bureau of Indian Affairs, penned an article titled "Ten Years of Tribal Government Under I.R.A." In it, he listed the 110 Tribes in the continental United States that had adopted constitutions under the act.[21] When I cross-reference them with my enrollment database, I find that the majority of those Tribes still use blood quantum requirements for enrollment.[22]

Even today, even on the website of the Bureau of Indian Affairs, a federal agency, the "Sample Constitution" lists as its suggestion for Tribal enrollment one-quarter blood quantum.[23]

If we consider the period before the Indian Reorganization Act (particularly during the Dawes Act) as being guided by the idea of assimilation, we can view the IRA as an experiment in reversing that course, an experiment with the idea that perhaps Native people didn't need to become fully Europeanized. That although, yes, the IRA still placed a lot of restrictions on the sovereignty of Tribes, maybe they could be left to maintain a modicum of their own traditions and cultures and lifestyles.

The experiment was short-lived.

In 1953, just nineteen years after the IRA was approved, Congress passed a resolution to, "as rapidly as possible, make the Indians within the territorial limits of the United States subject to the same laws and entitled to the same privileges and responsibilities as are applicable to other citizens of the United States, to end their status as wards of the United States."[24] This resolution served as a pseudo-official beginning of a phase of federal policy known as termination: by revoking federal recognition and ending federal aid and trust status, the U.S. government would be terminating the distinct relationship it had with Tribes. And, in doing so, it would begin a decades-long process of forcefully assimilating Native people once again.

The mechanisms of termination included dissolving treaties, dismantling Tribal governments, eliminating reservations, and eliminating federal benefits. As part of termination, Public Law 280, for example, allowed state governments to assume criminal and civil jurisdiction over Indian reservations in Alaska, California, Minnesota, Nebraska, Oregon, and Wisconsin.[25] Some Tribes were ordered to distribute their land and properties to their members and dissolve their governments.[26] In Roberta Ulrich's study of termination's impacts, she writes that, in many cases, termination "destroyed the tribal members' sense of identity."[27]

I think about the fact that a Native person born at the turn of the century would have lived in what felt like several different universes. Say this person—let's call him Michael—was born around 1910. Michael would have grown up during the Dawes Act era, so his family would likely have been the victims of allotment, theft of land, and forced assimilation. In 1934, when Michael was twenty-four and perhaps starting a family of his own, he would have found himself in a regime of what we might call *anti*-assimilation, of increased Tribal self-governance and at least some steps toward #LandBack. Perhaps this period inspired hope in Michael, the idea that his community could finally begin to make real economic progress while maintaining its sovereignty. Then, just nineteen years later, the year he turned forty-three, Michael would have found himself once again in the throes of assimilation, in a regime of termination from federal recognition and all the resources that came with it.

It's easy to imagine that making meaningful long-term decisions becomes difficult when you don't know which universe you're living in. If you have no idea which reality you will wake up to the following day. Will the federal government force you to enroll in your Tribe and accept a land allotment? Will you suddenly be expected to farm when you've spent exactly zero days of your life farming? Will the federal government suddenly deem you "competent" because of your blood quantum, thereby charging you a tax to keep that land you never intended to own? Will the federal government grant your Tribe the power of self-rule and give you the right to vote? Will the federal government strip your Tribe of the power of self-rule and rescind any and all resources you need to be successful?

I think particularly about my friends who are Menominee from

Wisconsin. In 1961, the U.S. government terminated the Menominee Indian Tribe. Its rationale was that the Tribe was economically prosperous and could sustain itself without any federal resources.[28] In the end, the Menominee termination was, as some have put it, an "unmitigated disaster."[29] Poverty increased, in part because the newly established Menominee County lacked a sufficient tax base to provide basic services. The reservation's hospital was forced to close. The Tribe's cash assets (valued at ten million dollars in 1954) were largely depleted by 1960.[30] It wasn't until 1974 that the Tribe finally had its federal recognition restored, but by then, a lot of damage had already been done.

From 1953, the time of the congressional resolution outlining termination, to 1970, when the practice (at least officially) ended, 109 Tribes in this country were terminated, losing their status of federal recognition.[31] In a press release from the Department of the Interior dated January 21, 1954, the Bureau of Indian Affairs proposed beginning termination with Tribes from ten different states, representing 66,000 Indian people— roughly one-seventh of the country's entire Native population.[32] As of 2024, 12 Tribes that were terminated—all located in California—still have not had their federal recognition restored.[33]

It takes my computer a full three minutes to download the 1,809-page volume of House Reports from the Second Session of the Eighty-Second Congress in 1952, including everything related to the Bureau of Indian Affairs. I've downloaded it not because I'm in need of a good beach read but because I'm curious about a line I keep seeing in various scholarly articles, about a notorious list of Tribes deemed suitable for termination. It's this list that would have begun the process of termination for those 109 Tribes. I've been told the list appears in this volume. Eventually I find it. It's somewhat unremarkable, in the sense that it's very similar to those I've seen among other materials.

As I continue to scroll through the pages and pages of the report somewhat aimlessly, I find myself gravitating to the data, to the tables and charts, the numbers, the counts. In one section, I find a list of rankings called "States in the Degree of Indian Acculturation." With a surprising amount of precision, the list informs me that, as of 1930, Kansas had the highest amount of acculturation, with just 16.22 percent of Indian culture retained.[34] Lowest on the list is New Mexico, with 69.3 percent of Indian culture retained. In another table, I'm informed that, as of 1910, the Navajo Tribe had the lowest level of acculturation of any Tribe in the country—with 92.55 percent of Indian culture remaining among Navajo people. Its "amount of advancement" is deemed "little." A small note at the bottom of the chart tells me that these figures are based on the proportion of full-bloods, of those able to speak English and read and write, and those of school age who were in school. In the following table, from 1930, the Navajos' number for retained Indian culture had decreased to 80.99 percent, which still made it the Tribe with the highest amount of "culture resistance."

In an accompanying testimony from 1947, William Zimmerman Jr., the assistant commissioner of the Bureau of Indian Affairs, outlines the factors he takes into account when determining which Tribe to terminate and when. Perhaps not surprisingly, the first factor he lists is degree of acculturation.[35]

I realize that these lists were part of a report compiled in the summer of 1952, just a few months before my mother was born. I think about *her* mother, pregnant with a baby who'd surprise everyone with a head full of white hair—a towhead was what my grandmother always called her. I think, too, about my grandfather, a "full-blooded" Lumbee man who had found himself in the Midwest, which probably felt like a million miles away from where he'd grown up in Lumbee country. I think about the fact that, decades later, as he lay dying of lung cancer on a hospice bed in the middle of his living room in the Time Check neighborhood of Cedar Rapids, Iowa, the only consistent thing he seemed to talk about was the idea of going back home.

Before I knew Karen Diver as President Obama's special assistant for Native American affairs, and therefore one of the highest-ranking Native people in the federal government; before she was the chairwoman of the Fond du Lac Band of Lake Superior Chippewa, the first woman to serve in that role; before she was a Harvard graduate or a full-time resident of the Fond du Lac Reservation, she was a kid growing up in Cleveland, Ohio.

I am surprised the first time Karen tells me this. I'm confused why her hometown is a city nearly nine hundred miles from her Tribe's reservation, in a state whose Native population is one of the lowest in the country.

Karen can trace her Cleveland roots to exactly no one. She has no Cleveland roots.

After her parents were married, they made their home on the Fond du Lac Reservation in Northern Minnesota. In order to get work, Karen's father, a dark-skinned Chippewa man, had to drive the thirty-five minutes to Duluth, a city that, in the 1950s, boasted a population of about 150,000. But even there—even in a place with considerably more jobs than on the reservation—he suffered significant hurdles. Duluth, like other reservation border towns, was not particularly welcoming to Native people. The only jobs he could get were dangerous ones that no one else wanted. He was a grave digger, he unpacked trains, he steamed ore. But he desperately wanted work he could rely on, work that would allow him to support his family.

It's humbling to think about what the world would have looked like for Karen's parents in the 1950s. The Indian Citizenship Act of 1924— the first piece of federal legislation to grant Native people the right to vote—was still fresh in the minds of many. Segregation of just about everything was still legal. The Montgomery Bus Boycott, the March on Selma and then on Washington, the passage of the Civil Rights Act of 1964—all these events we now consider turning points in the American civil rights movement were still years away. So, when the Bureau of Indian Affairs approached Chuck and Faye Diver about the new "Indian Relocation Program," they listened.

The Indian Relocation Act was intended to—and I quote—"encourage young employable Indians and the better cultured families" to "leave the reservations."[36] Relocation officers were given quotas for different cities participating in the program, including Cleveland.

When the Divers relocated there in 1960, they had a small child (Karen's older sister, Cheryl) and not much in the way of possessions. Karen tells me that, as part of the move, the family was given vouchers from the Salvation Army to purchase furniture and other household items. Once, while digging through boxes, Karen's mother showed her photos from that time, from shortly after they moved to Cleveland. They were professional portraits, staged photos of Chuck and Faye and their child that would later be used in advertising the Indian Relocation Act to other Native people. When Karen squinted at the photo, which by then was fragile and cracked, she noticed that the child in it was not her sister but, rather, a small boy. When she asked who the child was, her mother told her that because Cheryl had been asleep when the photographer arrived, they borrowed their (Native) neighbor's son. "To the government, it didn't matter," Karen says. "A brown kid was a brown kid."

Over the next several years, Chuck and Faye would have three more children, Karen and her two brothers. Chuck's first job after relocation was on the shipping docks for a garment company. When friends told him about an opportunity with the Yellow Freight Company—a job that could eventually get him into the Teamsters—he jumped at it. He spent the rest of his career there, as a union dockworker, loading and unloading trucks. Karen tells me that, although the work was physically grueling, her father was proud that he could send his four kids to Catholic school, proud he achieved some sense of economic self-sufficiency.

The Divers made a concerted effort to build a community in Cleveland. After finishing his military service, Chuck's brother Don relocated there, and then Chuck's niece. Faye's younger siblings joined them there, too. "We rez'ed up in Cleveland," Karen tells me with a laugh. "A lot of people followed us there." Karen has fond memories of her parents' friends coming over to the house for parties; she remembers one man who'd always bring his guitar.

It was the late 1960s, and pan-Indian communities were sprouting up in urban areas around the country. In 1969, the Cleveland American Indian Center opened, which created even more momentum. Karen remembers that, when she was nine years old, a van from the center showed up in her neighborhood. "My mom grabbed me and told me to go with them," she says. At the center, Karen met Native kids from all over the country. They formed a dance troupe and learned how to make their own costumes. They'd charge people to come to their performances, using the money later to travel the powwow circuit. She remembers going to Michigan, New York, South Dakota, and Sundance.

I tell Karen I'm glad her family has some good memories of that time. For the Divers, the experience of relocation was not as difficult as it was for many others whose stories I've heard. She tells me that, yes, although Indian relocation was a dispossession strategy, her parents were happy to be working and to have good friends. "They were glass-half-full people," she says.

It is an incredible trait, given how Chuck Diver, in particular, grew up. Karen's father had been stolen from his family at the age of six and sent to Wahpeton Indian School, a boarding school more than two hundred miles from his home. It wouldn't be until he was in high school—until Indian Agents transferred him to Flandreau Indian School—that he'd get to return home for a visit. Indian boarding school students had to earn their own money for travel. Karen tells me she has never seen a photo of her father before the age of sixteen, before that first visit home.

At Wahpeton, Chuck tried to look out for his younger brother, Don. Karen tells me that her father would take the blame for his little brother's bed-wetting. That he'd receive the beatings instead. Eventually, Karen came to understand the origins of behavior patterns in her father and uncle that she'd always thought of as strange. They'd shower their children with fruit and treats—a response to having grown up with no food security. They were obsessed with buying new coats, with collecting them—at Wahpeton, the two brothers had had to share one.

It strikes me that because of federal government policies meant to assimilate Native people, Chuck Diver spent very little of his life on his reservation. He was born in 1938, forcibly sent to boarding school from 1944 to 1956, and relocated to Cleveland in 1960. By the time he retired in 1998, he'd lived the majority of his life away from Fond du Lac.

Karen tells me her parents had always intended to return to Minnesota once they retired. For her father, it was especially important that all his children get through school before they made the move. Karen says she could see a lot of pressure lift once her youngest brother graduated from high school.

By then, Karen had moved from Cleveland to Minnesota for college. The journey back to Fond du Lac was neither straightforward nor easy. At fourteen, she got pregnant with her daughter. The baby's father was a youth worker at the Indian center, an adult who'd taken advantage of a teenage girl. "He was a grown-ass man," Karen tells me. She'd just turned fifteen when she gave birth. She describes herself as stubborn; she was going to find a way to figure it out.

Karen remembers calling her parents and asking if they were still planning to come back home to Minnesota. Karen was at a crossroads in her own life, balancing her studies and being a single mother. She knew she needed a support system that included her parents. She even contemplated moving back to Cleveland to be closer to them. Her mother said that, yes, their plan was to move back. That one phone call, Karen tells me, changed the course of her life. That phone call prompted her to remain there, in Minnesota, at Fond du Lac, the place she still calls home.

After the Indian Removal Act and the Dawes Act ("the Allotment of Lands in Severalty to Indians on the Various Reservations"), after the Indian Reorganization Act and the Indian Termination Act, the federal government decided it wasn't finished quite yet. So, in 1956, under the unassuming title of Public Law 959, Congress passed what became known as the Indian Relocation Act. It was designed, at least in part, to "help adult Indians who reside on or near reservations to gain reasonable and satisfactory employment."[37]

There's this quote my dad always gravitates to: "History never repeats itself, but it often does rhyme." No one's sure whom to give credit for the quote—some say it was Mark Twain, but there's no evidence of that in the historical record. In any event, growing up, I remember my dad reciting it often. Language like "transportation to the place of training" and "satisfactory employment" might have been new to the federal Indian policy lexicon, but it sure seems to rhyme with words like "removal" and "assimilation."

The Indian Relocation Act was a kind of culmination of relocation efforts. To more fully terminate the relationship between the federal government and Native Nations, to further assimilate Indians into American society, the so-called Voluntary Relocation Program began in 1952.[38] As part of the educational and vocational training, Native people were relocated to urban cores in cities like Chicago, St. Louis, Denver, Los Angeles, and, in the case of Karen Diver's family, Cleveland. They were given no more than twenty-four months of assistance that purported to include relocation expenses, vocational training, and some housing aid.[39] Native people who relocated through the program often struggled to adjust to their new reality. Many faced unemployment and substandard housing. Many were promised jobs that didn't exist or ended up with jobs that were insecure. In a paper from 1983, Philleo Nash, Bureau of Indian Affairs commissioner from 1961 to 1966, called Indian relocation underfunded and ill-conceived. It was, in his words, "essentially a one-way bus ticket from rural to urban poverty."[40]

The idea of Indian relocation was, at least in part, the brainchild of Dillon S. Myer, a predecessor of Nash's at the BIA. Myer took the position as commissioner in 1950 with a goal of eliminating the "privileges" Tribes received from the government.[41] He proposed legislation that would have permitted employees of the BIA to carry firearms and make arrests for violations of regulations without the benefit of a warrant.[42] Fortunately, the bill failed. In a 1951 article, former interior secretary Harold Ickes called Myer—and I'm not kidding—"Hitler and Mussolini rolled into one."[43]

According to Nash, it was one of Myer's former gigs that perhaps most inspired him in coming up with the Voluntary Relocation Program. From 1942 to 1946, he ran the War Relocation Authority, which was responsible for, among other things, the forcing of Japanese American citizens to concentration camps,[44] called "relocation centers."[45]

Between 1952 and 1972, more than one hundred thousand Native people migrated to urban centers as part of the Voluntary Relocation Program.[46] By 1956, some of the relocation offices had reported that as many as 60 percent of people who relocated ended up returning home.[47] Former deputy commissioner of the BIA and a member of the Oneida Nation Robert L. Bennet later wrote about the high return rate of people back to reservations. "The greatest reason for returning was lonesomeness," he writes.[48] "People who had lived in an extended family relationship were isolated in a nuclear family."[49] The Indian Relocation Act aid did not include resources for getting back home.

Beyond the government-imposed poverty and the disconnection from family, the Indian Relocation Act programs had profound impacts on patterns of residency. In 1970, for the first time ever, the population of Native Americans in cities surpassed that in rural areas.[50] Whereas just 8 percent of Native people lived in cities in 1940, in 1960 that number had grown to almost 30 percent.[51] By 2023, nearly 67 percent of all Native people in the United States lived in urban areas.

As they'd been doing for decades, Native people who were relocated from reservations did miraculous things with very little. Once in urban centers, they formed communities that transcended identification with any one Tribe, but were instead pan-Indian.[52] They came together to create Indian cultural centers, organize powwows, and start networks for activism. Together, they fought against relocation, a policy that, as Vine Deloria writes, "was meant to get Indians off the reservation and into the city slums where they could fade away."[53]

I can best describe the feeling I have while digging through historical records on Indian relocation as cognitive dissonance. What I know to be true—from accounts by former federal officials, patterns borne out in the data, and stories of lived experience—doesn't match the pages and pages of historical records I find in the archives. One brochure, titled *More Jobs for Chicagoland Indians*, is clearly meant for public consumption.[54] It's an advertisement, of sorts. Underneath small, square black-and-white photos of Native people doing different jobs—one person answers a telephone, another types on a typewriter, yet another organizes tools—are several columns of names, Tribe affiliations, and job titles. Lists of Native people who'd been relocated: "Juan, Pueblo, stock helper"; "Mary, Chippewa, maid"; "Richard, Cherokee, shipping helper."

In a binder put together by the BIA's Chicago Relocation Office, I find bright Kodachrome photos of city landmarks: Wrigley Field (home to the Chicago Cubs)! Midway Airport![55] There are scrapbook pages with scallop-edged photos of the seemingly everyday life of relocated Native people. In one, a Native woman stands over a stove while her small son tugs on her apron. In another, an Indian man punches in to work as a smiling security guard looks on. Yet another shows two Native families sitting together in a living room, a Christmas tree in the background, a boxy television blinking in one corner. *American Indians Find Gary, Indiana a Good Place to Live, Work, and Play!* one brochure promises.[56]

I begin to wonder what such materials would have looked like during President Jackson's Indian Removal Act. What if, rather than formal speeches or proclamations, federal officials had made brochures instead? Would those muster rolls of "Indians About to Emigrate West" have included the names of fancified professions? Would there have been bright photos of landmarks that Native people were never, really, going to visit? Promises of modern amenities they'd never own? Would there have been—in all the publications meant to convince Native people to pack up and leave their homes and families and everything they'd ever known—any truth at all?

K aren thinks her uncle, her father's brother, will probably always live in the Cleveland area—this despite Chuck and Faye's moving back to Fond du Lac, despite Karen and other family members moving back, too. Uncle Don will remain where he is.

Karen tells me her father and uncle had very different responses to the trauma of boarding school. For her father, his reservation was where his people were. It would always be his home, no matter where he lived. For her uncle, though, Karen thinks there was a significant amount of dissociation. Being stolen from his home and sent to boarding school at the age of five made him, she feels, disconnect from his family, his people, and his home.

I begin to think about the geographic patterns of Karen's family as deeply connected to trauma responses. That, because Chuck Diver viewed Fond du Lac as home; because he retained a sense of longing for his community, he also retained the hope of someday returning. He and his wife probably conveyed that hope to their children. Though Karen's older sister, Cheryl, passed away in 2002, several of Cheryl's children have returned to Fond du Lac. Karen imagines that their brother will return after he retires. She wouldn't be surprised to see some of her nieces and nephews come back, too.

When I talk to Don Diver, I'm struck by how much he reminds me of Karen. There's a simple honesty about the way he speaks: he's blunt when he needs to be. When I ask what line of work he was in before retiring, he tells me that when he arrived in Cleveland, he applied for every job he could find. Eventually, he took work as a hospital shipping clerk. "I had no idea what the hell they did," he says. Karen later tells me that her uncle retired as a procurement director for the Cleveland Clinic, one of the top hospitals in the country.

Don tells me that, after more than sixty years there, he considers himself a Clevelander. He's been back to Minnesota, of course, but he doesn't remember the last time he lived there. Despite being born on the Fond du Lac Reservation, despite having spent the first five years of his life there, the place is unfamiliar to him.

What Don does remember is the day a black sedan pulled up to his family's home when he was five years old. "I was so excited to go for a ride," he says. Of course, all these decades later, he understands that the sedan was driven by a county worker who was there to steal him and his brother,

Chuck, from their family and take them to Wahpeton Indian School over two hundred miles away. Initially, though, he had no idea what was happening. He tells me that once he got to the school, he cried for a week straight.

It would be years before Don was allowed to return to his family for a visit. The schools did not pay for trips home, and the Diver family was struggling financially. Don and Chuck's mother was ill and spending a lot of time in the hospital. Don tells me that the thing he remembers most from those days is the feeling of complete isolation. "I was so lonesome there," he says. He tells me that by the time he returned home for a visit, he couldn't remember what his mother and father looked like.

Don credits his brother Chuck for his survival. It was natural, then, once Don graduated from high school at Flandreau Indian School and finished his time in the military, that he'd join his brother in Cleveland. He tells me that the adjustment was initially very hard. When I ask him what, in particular, felt difficult, he tells me "everything"—the way people talked, the way people lived.

I gently press him, asking him if there was anything in particular. He considers the question for a few moments. "Would you believe that I'd never attended a wedding or a funeral?" he says. "Those were some of the things that I missed when I was younger." He tells me that, until he moved to Cleveland in his early twenties, he'd never celebrated a birthday. "At boarding school, they didn't teach me that there was any life outside."

Fifteen years after Chuck and Faye Diver moved to Cleveland—after being relocated from their Tribe's reservation by the federal government—the tennis ball of federal policy in Indian Country took a dramatic bounce in the opposite direction, away from forced assimilation once again.

On January 4, 1975, President Gerald Ford signed the Indian Self-Determination and Education Assistance Act to, among other things, "provide maximum Indian participation in the Government and education of the Indian people."[57] The act acknowledged that "the Indian people will never surrender their desire to control their relationships both among themselves and with non-Indian governments, organizations, and persons," something that took the federal government only 199 years to figure out.

The act was penned mostly during the administration of Richard Nixon, who, under pressure from the Watergate scandal, resigned from the presidency just five months before it was signed into law.[58] Nixon spent time during his five-and-a-half-year presidency advocating for Native American issues. He was the first president to return sacred lands to Tribes, he dramatically increased the budget of the Bureau of Indian Affairs, and he worked to end the termination policy that had been put into place by his predecessors.[59]

The work of ending termination was heavily influenced by the Native activism that had been gaining momentum across the country throughout the latter part of the 1960s. Native Americans and their allies, particularly young people, had found inspiration in the Red Power movement. The overarching mission of Red Power and, later, the American Indian Movement was to fight for Native sovereignty.[60] And although controversies certainly arose from AIM and its sister organizations, for people like Darlene Wind, these groups helped instill a sense of Native pride that she carries with her to this day.

Practically speaking, the Self-Determination Act provided Tribes with an opportunity to contract with the federal government to run programs funded by (and on behalf of) the Department of the Interior, gave Tribes increased consultation rights, and provided resources for government capacity and training.[61]

Despite the importance of self-determination, the act was not a slam dunk. For one thing, Tribes that had been terminated did not automatically get back their previous status. Rather, they had to spend a lot of time and money to have it "restored" by the U.S. Congress. In some cases—like for the Koi Nation of the Lower Lake Rancheria, in California—restoration took nearly fifty years.[62] The Self-Determination Act was passed before most terminated Tribes were restored.[63] And because only federally recognized

Tribes are eligible for the provisions of the Self-Determination Act, many Tribes are excluded even today.

Without falling too far down the rabbit hole of legalese, federal recognition grants Native American Tribes all sorts of things, including certain amounts of self-governance, certain legal protections, better access to health care and education, and federal aid.[64] It's an official designation that comes with real, tangible benefits. Tribes that are federally recognized qualify for funding opportunities that non-recognized Tribes do not.

Once the federal government ended the practice of treaty making with Native Nations in 1871, the decision whether to recognize Tribes has been made by Congress and the Bureau of Indian Affairs.[65] It is a controversial process that has left legitimate Tribes on the outside looking in.

The challenge is that the line of federal recognition is not a tidy one. It's not a clear-cut demarcation, with legitimate, deserving Tribes on one side and frauds on the other. Federal recognition can take decades and is often complicated by political machinations. The Chinook Indian Nation was federally recognized in 2001, at the end of the Clinton administration, only to see that decision rescinded by the Bush administration eighteen months later.[66] In 1924, six Tribes in Virginia were stripped of their Native identity on all official governmental documents as a result of the state's "Racial Integrity Act."[67] It would be ninety-four years before the Chickahominy, the Eastern Chickahominy, the Upper Mattaponi, the Rappahannock, the Monacan, and the Nansemond finally gained federal recognition in 2018.[68]

One way some states have combated this problem is by offering their own recognition to Tribes within their borders. As of 2013, there were seventy-three state-recognized Tribes in twenty-one states.[69] When it comes to state recognition, there is a range of formality. Some states have a special commission that hears recognition applications; some have state Tribal reservations; some require municipal consultation with state Tribes.[70] Every state recognition process is different. Unfortunately, state recognition does not grant Native Tribes the same rights or access to resources as the federal recognition.

It's a somewhat ironic idea that in order to practice "self-determination," Native Nations must receive specific permission from the U.S. government. That, in order for Tribes to have legal determination of themselves, the United States must first determine it for them.[71]

I t occurs to me that the life of someone like Chuck Diver, who was born in 1938, would have been perfectly timed for the federal project of Native American assimilation. By the time Chuck graduated, in 1956, from the Indian boarding school where he'd been forcibly sent as a child, the Indian relocation program had just begun. When he moved to Cleveland in 1960, he would have been exactly the kind of person the federal government would have envisioned when it set out to relocate "young employable Indians" from the "better cultured families." And by the time the Indian Self-Determination Act was passed in 1975, he would have come into his job with the Teamsters and made a life for himself and his family in Cleveland, hundreds of miles away from his Tribe.

But Chuck and Faye Diver defied the federal assimilation project. They returned home.

Karen tells me that, particularly when she was chairwoman of the Fond du Lac Band of Lake Superior Chippewa, she saw a lot of people of her parents' generation returning to the community—whether to be closer to family or for better access to health care (at the reservation's Indian Health Service facility) or for other reasons. She tells me she has continued to see a movement of people back home.

Despite the fact that Karen's parents were glass-half-full people; despite the fact that they were able to make community in Cleveland, where they'd been relocated, Karen understands the negative consequences of federal policy. She tells me it's difficult for her to look at federal Indian policy and not see patterns of displacement. After all, many of the people she saw returning to the reservation had left because they'd been taken or coerced; they hadn't left of their own accord.

At least in part because of these patterns, Karen has always been very mindful of how her Tribe's policies affect citizens who don't live in the Fond du Lac community. As the Tribe's leader, she says that it was an intentional question she'd ask: What about the people who aren't on the rez?

At the same time, she has enough experience with tenuous identity claims to know that people are not always well-intentioned. She tells me that in the eight years she served as her Tribe's chairwoman, she received calls almost daily from people who had taken DNA tests that showed they were Native American and who now wanted to enroll. "They'd ask what they could get," she says.

Karen and I have found ourselves on the topic of enrollment because I have posed a question to her that I continue to grapple with: the question of Native identity. The question of who belongs. Karen tells me she tries to think about enrollment through the lens of values; of traditions. She tells me she thinks about it through a series of questions. What are you claiming, and why? What is your motivation? What do you hope to achieve?

"None of this has an easy answer," she says.

My first visit to the Research Room of the National Archives in Washington, D.C., is an overwhelming experience. Past the security desk and the ID check, past the metal detector and the marble columns, long hallways extend into dark horizons. I had read that the National Archives is home to over 187 million pages of records relating to the Bureau of Indian Affairs, some of them located down these seemingly never-ending corridors.[1]

Once I receive my "Researcher" badge and figure out the system of document retrieval, once I write down my records requests on so-called pull slips and find my way to the second floor, I wait. On average, it takes one to two hours for staff to gather requested material. Once collected, the material is wheeled into the Research Room on a metal cart and signed out in a ledger. Any delicate archival material requires gloves.

I have only a few hours on my first visit, so I limit my requests to Indian Relocation Act materials. I'm interested in finding anything related to Karen's family—specifically to Chuck or Faye Diver. I have brought with me my friend Amy, who has very kindly agreed to help me in my search.

It feels a bit like a needle-in-a-haystack situation—if by "needle" we mean a single sheet of paper and by "haystack" we mean 187 million pages of material. Eventually, a National Archives staff member in a navy coat (something that looks almost medical) enters the Research Room with our cart. After signing for it, Amy and I eye the gray cardboard file boxes with some skepticism.

Together, we murmur a word of gratitude that the boxes are arranged by city and year. We know the Divers relocated to Cleveland sometime between 1958 and 1960, so we disregard the files outside that range and begin pulling out thick binders.

Inside each binder, the pages are arranged by month, with one page per week of the year. The information on each sheet is spare. There is a table with a few columns running vertically. Each row lists an entire family, with just the head of household's name, Tribe affiliation, and the number of people in the family. In a lot of ways, it reminds me of the lists of people during Indian removal, during the Dawes Act and land allotment and the early Indian censuses.

As I flip through the binders, I pause briefly on each page to scan the names of people and Tribes, the number of family members. I'm looking specifically for the Diver family, but there are thousands of other families here, their names also listed in these thick binders stored in these never-ending stacks.

Amy and I get to the end of the last binder, the one labeled "Cleveland 1960." We look at each other with dread, noticing the shrinking number of pages left to review. And then, on the third-to-last page, we find the name we've been looking for.

Charles Diver, Chippewa, relocated to Cleveland, Ohio, on July 28, 1960. There were a total of three people in his household, whom we know to be his wife, Faye, and their young daughter Cheryl. They were the only family relocated to Cleveland that particular week, so their information stands alone on the sheet; bold black type on an otherwise yellowing page.

I snap a picture of the record and text it to Karen. "I can't believe we found it," I write.

She responds immediately. She tells me she has tears in her eyes, that she never knew the exact date of her family's move. I suppose it's also emotional for her to see her father's name on the page just a few years after he has passed. The next day, she sends a longer text, a note of thanks from her entire family. She says that the photo of the record is a treasure, a fundamental part of their history.

I am, of course, happy to have found it. I'm glad the Diver family has been given at least a photo of such a meaningful document. But I'm also deeply saddened by the thousands of pages here representing people whose cell phone numbers I don't have. People whose names (whose records) don't belong in some dark corridor of a federal building but in the hands and homes of their families. Their communities. Their Tribes.

Identity

There was this show that aired from 2012 to 2017 called *Longmire*. In it, Walt Longmire, a rough-and-tumble sheriff, solves crimes in present-day Buffalo, a fictional Wyoming town that borders a Cheyenne reservation (also fictionalized). In one episode, Jacob Nighthorse, a local Cheyenne businessman, is attempting to explain the intricacies of Tribal enrollment. Nighthorse tells Sheriff Longmire that "the U.S. government only quantifies three things by blood: dogs, horses, and Indians."[1]

And while the show is a work of fiction, the statement is very much true.

A keen ear will notice that Jacob Nighthorse speaks in the present tense: "the U.S. government *quantifies*"—as in *still, today*. Looking past the centuries-old practices of dividing Indians into fractions and putting them on rolls, past the modern-day consequences of those policies, the federal government is still actively tugging at the puppet strings of Native identity.

Perhaps the strangest example of this is the Certificate of Degree of Indian Blood, or CDIB. I say "strangest" because no one knows where the hell the CDIB came from. Only a handful of scholars have written much about it, and even they must rely mostly on conjecture. Paul Spruhan is one of those scholars. An attorney for the Navajo Nation, he has carved out a niche for himself as a CDIB expert. When I ask him about its origins, he doesn't mince words. "There's no smoking gun," he tells me. "This mystical thing just sort of appeared."

There are no laws or regulations governing the CDIB. There is no uniform procedure for its use, no rules controlling its implementation. The certificate is not mandated by the U.S. Congress. In fact, there is only one reference to it in the entire U.S. Code, in a section concerning proof of citizenship for Medicaid eligibility.[2] As far as anyone can tell, the certificate just sort of appeared one day in the late 1970s, in an internal publication written for employees of the Bureau of Indian Affairs.[3]

I've read that publication. Called the *Bureau of Indian Affairs Manual*, or BIAM, it is written with all the nuance and thoughtfulness expected from a federal handbook. In a section titled, "How to Compute," it instructs that the degree of Indian blood is one-half the combined degree of Indian blood possessed by a person's parents. Because it was written before the existence of DNA technology for paternity testing, the manual also includes a section on children of single mothers: "Degree of Indian blood possessed by children born out of wedlock," it instructs, "shall be determined by taking 1/2 the degree of Indian blood possessed by the mother, unless paternity has been established by the courts."[4]

In a handy appendix, a grid measuring thirty-two squares by eighteen guides me through each possible fraction of a person's Indian blood, depending on the fraction of Indian blood their parents possess.[5] I am told, for example, that if one parent is eleven-sixteenth Indian and the other parent is five-eighths Indian, then their children will be twenty-one-thirty-second Indian. It reads like a recipe card. *Mix together 7/16th Indian with 3/16th Indian and—voila!—you'll have 5/16th Indian!*

This would all seem like a silly little example of federal government folly if it weren't for the fact that CDIBs actually mean something. They carry weight. In some cases, they spell the difference between being able to access education or housing or health care programs and going without.

Scholars like Kirsty Gover have posited that the CDIB, at least in its initial implementation, was probably the by-product of the Indian Reorganization Act.[6] In that law, passed in 1934, Indians were defined (in addition to being members of a federally recognized Tribe) as those with "one-half or more Indian blood."[7]

Focus, especially, on the word *blood*. Let your mind wander to other U.S. policies that granted the federal government the power to quantify people by blood that remain in place today. Let yourself realize that there aren't any. That nowhere else does the federal government quantify people like this.

If asked why this certificate still exists, I'm certain the federal government would point to this line from the BIA manual: "The Secretary of the Interior is responsible for determining who shall be classified as members when the roll is prepared for the distribution of assets which are held in trust for the Tribe by the Government of the United States."[8]

If this language sounds familiar, it's because it is. From the earliest days of treaties between the U.S. government and Native Nations—when annuities were paid to a Tribe's leaders and then to individuals—the distribution of assets has been at the forefront of determining Native identity by federal agents. Somewhere along the way, the CDIB, a document that purports to support the division of federal assets in Indian Country, became about so much more.

For one thing, the CDIB has become a critical gateway to important services. It is often used to apply for federal jobs that have an Indian preference; to access educational benefits, like federal grants reserved for Native people; and to receive care from the Indian Health Service. And, sure, I suppose we could very loosely call these programs "federal assets in Indian Country." But I can't help but get lost in the minutiae, in the overwhelming weight of federal oversight. I feel this way as I peruse the IHS's *Indian Health Manual*, which outlines who is eligible for IHS services. According to one section, the IHS grants medical care to "a non-Indian woman pregnant with an eligible Indian's child for the duration of her pregnancy, and through post-partum (usually 6 weeks after delivery)."[9]

I can't shake the feeling that the CDIB wasn't built for this. (Hell, it was never really built at all—there remain no rules guiding its use.) According to a letter written by the U.S. Department of the Interior on September 10, 2018, the lack of rules around the CDIB has led to its "inconsistent issuance."[10]

The challenge is that the CDIB has become, in many cases, inextricably linked to the processes of Tribal enrollment. It is this way for Tribes like the Navajo Nation—where Paul Spruhan's children are enrolled. There, the CDIB is the only form of enrollment documentation a member receives.[11] That is, possession of a CDIB and enrollment in the Navajo Nation are one and the same. Partly, I imagine, the Tribe has made this decision based on some difficult facts. The Navajo Nation is one of the poorest communities in the country—up to 40 percent of its households lack running water and over 35 percent of its families live below the federal poverty line.[12] And because the Tribe receives federal funding to operate the CDIB program, it can offer this documentation at little to no cost to its members.

For other Tribes, a CDIB is the first step in the enrollment process. In order to apply for enrollment in the Chickasaw Nation, for example, an applicant must first obtain a CDIB.[13] It's not that the CDIB establishes membership in the Tribe; rather, it is a necessary prerequisite.

Generally, where the CDIB and Tribal enrollment are coupled, the Tribe has been contracted by the federal government to process the CDIB. It is this way for both the Navajo and Chickasaw Nations, among others. It's a complexity that makes untangling the roots of the CDIB much more complicated.

I, myself, don't possess a CDIB. While my Tribe offers one, it does not require one.

When I visit the Bureau of Indian Affairs website to determine the criteria for obtaining a CDIB, I am presented with a paragraphs-long list of documentation, including birth and death certificates, a family tree template going back three generations, and a signed statement of identity from the applicant. The website—the *federal government* website—instructs that "your degree of Indian blood is computed from lineal ancestors of Indian blood who were enrolled with a federally recognized Indian Tribe or whose names appear on the designated base rolls of a federally recognized Indian Tribe."[14] Yet, when I go back to the *Bureau of Indian Affairs Manual*—to the publication that first established the

CDIB—I see that it simply states, "There is no definite criteria for determining the most reliable records."[15]

alking into Chase Timmons's house in mid-September is like walking into an autumnal wonderland. The smell of cinnamon hits me from directions I can't pinpoint. A tall wooden hutch in Chase's dining area is filled with signs of autumn, including small gourds and strands of artificial flowers in the fiery oranges and yellows and reds most associated with the season.

Chase and I sit down together at her dining table, which is covered with a whimsical Halloween tablecloth. A seasonal candle—something pumpkin—sits in the middle, on a metal sculpture of a ghost.

"I love this time of year," Chase says.

I can't help but comment on the décor, telling her that I, too, find myself pulled toward autumn in a way I can't explain. It feels like a nostalgic season for me, despite the fact that I can attach almost zero nostalgia to it. Ours wasn't a pumpkin patch family. I don't remember snuggling up in flannel blankets while I was growing up, or sipping hot anything by the fire. We almost never *had* a fire.

I've arrived at Chase's house after a long drive that took me past cornfields and cow pastures, down gravel roads and along precarious one-lane stretches. She lives in a part of the Midwest that's unfamiliar to me; I've never been here before. She thanks me for making the trek. She tells me she relishes rural life. She enjoys the quiet of it.

A mutual friend introduced me to Chase via email. She didn't tell me much more than "You've got to meet Chase," an introduction I can rarely ignore. I've walked into Chase's festively decorated home somewhat blindly. When we meet this first time, in her home, I know almost nothing about her.

After a bit of small talk—or whatever we might call two forty-something Native women chatting about beadwork—our conversation finally settles into a comfortable rhythm. Chase is easy to talk to. We discover that we're just one year apart in age, and there's a certain familiarity of both vocabulary and experience in that alone. Plus, Chase is a natural storyteller. She understands how to build tension, the value of plot.

What I do know about Chase is that her Tribe is located in Canada and that she is not. So, we begin there.

Whether intentional or not, the isolation of Chase's present home seems to mirror the isolation she's always felt. Although she's an enrolled member of the Mi'kmaq First Nations community in Canada, she's spent most of her life in the United States, in the Midwest, where her mother is from. She's been to visit her community in Canada only a handful of times—thanks to the prohibitive length and cost of the trip—but the place has always felt more like home to her than the Midwest. She describes herself as a bit of a black sheep, especially while growing up in a family of blond-haired, blue-eyed relatives. "My mother and I don't look anything alike," she says.

Chase describes herself as one of the only Native people in her small town and says she was thrilled when, recently, she discovered another. "Someone told me about this other First Nations woman here," she says. "I was so stoked." Chase immediately reached out to the woman, and the two have since developed something of a friendship.

Chase's father's entire family lives on the Mi'kmaq First Nation's federal Indian reserve in Southeastern Quebec. It's there where her father grew up and lived nearly his whole life before traveling the United States as an ironworker. After years in Catholic schools that Chase compares to Indian boarding schools, her father was ready to get the hell out. On one of his cross-country tours, he found himself in the Midwest for a longer stretch than he was used to. He began frequenting a local bar and soon made friends with an older woman. She was kind to him. She also pestered him about dating—specifically, dating her daughter—but he'd always balk. "I don't think my dad thought he'd be a good partner or husband," Chase says.

Eventually, despite his misgivings, Chase's father ended up dating the older woman's daughter. ("That was my grandmother," Chase tells me. She has a way of revealing these details slowly, building her tale to a crescendo.) After they'd been dating for a while, Chase's mother got pregnant unexpectedly, with Chase. Chase doesn't say how her parents felt about the pregnancy, and I don't ask, but she does tell me her mother probably wasn't prepared to be a mother—especially given the circumstances that would befall her.

Chase tells me her father's name was also "Chase." She was named after him, in his memory. She knows she would have been named Chase regardless of whether she was born a boy or a girl, but she's not sure what she would have been named had the terrible thing not happened—the thing she alludes to and talks about right up to its edges. She tells me eventually, of course, but this is a story she's both tired of telling and has not figured out *how* to tell.

"My dad and I missed each other by a matter of months," she says. "He was murdered right before I was born."

It's the fall of 2023, and the full 2020 Census dataset on race has just been made available. I can't help myself: I go back to the data.

It might not be surprising to know that processing data for nearly 130 million households takes a lot of time. Usually, the data from one census become publicly available roughly twelve months after completion of the count. For write-in answers, the process takes even longer. For these, U.S. Census Bureau workers must sort responses ranging from the misspelled to the incomprehensible. Write-in data from the 2020 U.S. Census did not become publicly available until more than three years after the count was taken.

For several decades now, the U.S. Census has included write-in options related to a person's race. For those of us checking the Indian box, we are given an option to write in the name of our primary Tribe or Tribes. We can list up to six.

In 1970, such write-ins were unique to Native people—we were the only group listed in the race category asked to take this additional step.

Since then, the U.S. Census has added additional racial write-ins, including for people checking the boxes of "White," "Black or African American," and "Asian," among others. In 2020, there were six race-related write-ins in the census.

The ability to report multiple racial identities only adds to the complexity in how the U.S. Census counts race. In 2000, for the first time ever, census respondents were allowed to identify as more than one race. So, instead of checking just one box—identifying solely as white or Black or Asian, for example—respondents could select as many races as they felt compelled to.

In the data, this change prompted another—the separation of people by those who chose just one race and those who chose several. As one example, in 2000, 36.4 million people checked the "Black or African American" box alone, and 1.8 million people checked that box in combination with others. So, in 2000, a total of 38.2 million Americans identified as Black or African American, a considerable increase over 1990, when 30.5 million Americans checked the "Black or African American" box alone. This same pattern can be seen within all other race categories. The U.S. Census reports that between 2010 and 2020, the multiracial population—defined as people checking two or more races—increased by 276 percent.[16]

From a strict data standpoint, the "American Indian and Alaska Native" category has been by far the one most impacted by this change. In 1990, 1.96 million Americans checked the Indian box. In 2000, when respondents could suddenly check more than one racial category, 4.1 million people checked the Indian box—more than twice the number just ten years before. By 2020, that number had skyrocketed to 9.7 million people.

Circe Sturm is an anthropologist who popularized the term *race shifting*—which means exactly what it sounds like, in the sense that it involves a person shifting from one race to another, but it's specific to Native identity. According to Sturm, race shifters include those who have changed their self-identification from non-Native to Native, including on official documents like the U.S. Census.[17]

Certainly, from a data standpoint, race shifting as a culprit for the change between the 2000 and 2020 data makes a lot of sense. The 87 percent increase in the number of people checking the Indian box can't be explained by much else.

Because the "American Indian or Alaska Native" box is accompanied by write-in space, I become interested in how this change has been borne out in the data, whether I can see any interesting patterns in the write-in responses.

When I speak with someone in the Census Bureau—a very polite and diplomatic official whom I'll call Melissa—I'm told that write-in answers require a significant amount of processing. Census Bureau staff must perform what they call "internal edits." If a respondent writes just "Indian" as their Tribal affiliation, for example, staff will attempt to make that answer more specific by looking at the rest of the respondent's survey along with other individuals from the same household. Melissa tells me there are also what she calls "un-codable" responses: some answers they routinely see for write-in race questions include the names of people's dogs and "None of your business." She tells me that while, in 2010, there were around 50 million write-in answers, by 2020 that number had increased to over 350 million.

According to the 2020 Census, just over 9.7 million people checked the box for "American Indian or Alaska Native." Underneath that box, those same 9.7 million people had an opportunity to write in up to six Tribal affiliations. These could include any number of Tribes—federally recognized or not. I'm told that once more than ten people write in the name of a certain Tribe, that Tribe's name gets added to the next census. Until that point, write-ins go into a catchall category called "Tribes not elsewhere classified."

As I scroll through the list of Tribes and the number of responses for each, I arrive at the end of the spreadsheet, to a different sort of row. It's labeled "American Indian and Alaska Native alone or in any combination, not specified," and next to it appears the number 1.78 million. When I ask Alicia, a statistician with the Census Bureau, about this row, she tells me it's the number of generic, non-Tribe-specific responses. This includes the response "American Indian or Alaska Native" in the write-in space or a check made in the "American Indian/Alaska Native" box, with no Tribe specified.

Farther down the spreadsheet is a similarly titled row, called "American Indian alone or in any combination, not specified," which includes 1.71 million responses. This one confuses me, because if someone checks only the "American Indian/Alaska Native" box, there is no way to discern if they're identifying as American Indian or Alaska Native or both. Alicia tells me that, very often, respondents will check the AI/AN box and then, for Tribal affiliation, write in "American Indian." They do the same for Alaska Native—in 2020, the census received almost 70,000 such results.

Alicia helps me piece together the story these data tell: The total number of nonspecific AI/AN responses is 3.56 million. Because some of the categories are not mutually exclusive, somewhere in the ballpark of 3.45 million people self-identified as American Indian and/or Alaska Native without providing any meaningful Tribal affiliation. Those 3.45 million people represent just over one-third of the 9.7 million people who self-identified as Native.

Of course, it's impossible to know why so many people self-identifying as Native didn't also write in the name of a Tribe. The options rattling around in my head include (from most to least innocuous): they forgot, they refused, they didn't understand, they don't know, there isn't one.

The year Chase turned twelve, she asked her mother if she could speak with the detective who'd overseen her father's case. His death had been ruled an accident—according to the detective's report, he had fallen into a lake and drowned. But Chase's mother and her Canadian relatives—and, well, everyone else, it seemed—knew there'd been foul play.

Once the detective got permission to speak with Chase, he did. In retrospect, Chase thinks he probably shared information that shouldn't have been shared with a twelve-year-old, much less the twelve-year-old daughter of the deceased. In addition to details about the state of her father's body that she sometimes wishes she didn't know, the detective told her that his death definitely wasn't an accident. There was no water in his lungs, which would have suggested he drowned, the wounds on his body suggested he'd been beaten, and he had a hole in his skull.

But the detectives didn't have proof. There was no DNA evidence. No eyewitnesses who'd come forward. Investigators were stuck.

Despite their conversation's happening nearly thirty years ago, when she was only twelve, Chase vividly remembers the detective speaking with both passion and sadness. She could see he really wanted to bring her father's killer to justice. "He wanted me to know that he tried," she says.

For years—her entire childhood—people told Chase how great her father was. She grew up in his mysterious shadow. From old photos, she knew she sort of looked like him. From stories, she knew she sort of acted like him. All these years later, she realizes that the comments made her angry—angry because she felt wholly out of place where she was. Not only did she look very different from her mother, but she felt deeply neglected by her. She suspects there were unresolved mental health issues on that side of her family. "I thought my mom hated me," Chase says.

Finally, at age fourteen, Chase was allowed to make the trip to Canada, to her father's reservation. She took the trip alone, riding several hours on a bus to Detroit, boarding a train, and riding twenty-four hours in a direction unknown to her. Alone, she arrived to a community ready to embrace her. For them, she was the one connection they still had to their brother, cousin, son. To Chase Senior.

Chase stayed at her family's reservation for two weeks on that trip. It was the second time she'd been there, but the first time she remembered it. She remembers her grandmother singing to her in the Mi'kmaq language, some of which she remembers her cousins trying to teach her.

I ask Chase if, at fourteen, she felt a clear difference between the U.S. Midwest and Canada, between her hometown and her father's. She tells me that although Canada felt more comfortable to her than the American Midwest did, she still didn't fit in there. She hadn't been raised there; she didn't know the language or much about the traditions. "I felt like maybe I wouldn't belong anywhere," she says.

The next time she visited her father's reservation, Chase had just turned eighteen. By then, she was in what she calls an unhealthy state—among other things, using marijuana and alcohol to cope. Because the drinking age of the Canadian province she was in was eighteen, Chase calls that trip a blur. She does remember that her grandmother was upset about a tattoo Chase had recently gotten and that she'd wanted Chase to stay. She worried what would happen to her if she returned home to the United States. When, after two weeks, Chase did return home, she dropped out of high school. She didn't see it as a particularly important part of her life. "I didn't plan on living past twenty-one," she says.

When she first says this, I misunderstand. I think she means she didn't plan to live *in the Midwest* past the age of twenty-one, that she would eventually pack up and go somewhere else. I ask her where she thought she'd move to. Naturally, the question confuses her. She clarifies, telling me about her many suicide attempts, all the cutting. By that point, she says, she just didn't care.

One night, at a house party, she met a man whom she describes as an "army dude." He'd just been discharged from the military and had moved back to town. Chase felt a connection to the man, but she avoided him out of caution—she was unhappy and didn't plan on being around for long.

I ask her if she'd ever viewed this attitude as the continuation of a family pattern—of her father's reluctance to date her mother out of a concern he wouldn't be good for her. She tells me that, yes, she has definitely considered that. Of course she has. Of course she realizes the pattern. But, she says, the army dude didn't listen. Despite her misgivings, he pursued her.

By this point, the themes of Chase's story, the mood of it all, have created in me a deep feeling of dread. Between her father's murder and her own traumatic upbringing, I've found myself on the very edge of my seat at her festive autumnal table. I am nervously waiting for the other shoe to drop, for the next tragedy to strike.

Chase takes her time. She understands the importance of a denouement, of building a story to a climax.

"His name was Josh," she says. "And we've been married for twenty-one years."

My friend Ryan frames his identity this way: Being a citizen of the Cherokee Nation isn't a racial designation; it's a political one. Ryan tells me he thinks of himself as looking "like a white guy."

The idea of Ryan's Cherokee identity being primarily a political one makes a lot of sense. I've read really smart articles by really smart scholars who have posited that the so-called Indian box shouldn't exist at all. Sovereignty, enrollment, membership—these are all manifestations of a *political* identity, not a racial one.

But let's think of a different example, a different person: Anthony Long, the cousin Tricia Long introduced me to, the Meskwaki historian. Anthony Long is Meskwaki, of course, but because of the rule that only people with Meskwaki fathers can be enrolled in the Tribe, he will never be able to carry that political identity. Anthony will never be in possession of an enrollment card; nor will his children. Does that make Anthony Long's Meskwaki identity, or that of his children, primarily a racial one?

I begin to think about my own Native identity as a series of overlapping circles. A Venn diagram, if you will. In one of these circles exists political identity: membership in the Lumbee Tribe, citizenship through the process of enrollment. From a Native Nations standpoint, this identity seems paramount. Enrollment is the mechanism by which Tribes maintain political sovereignty and the vehicle by which they ensure their continued survival.

In another circle exists my racial identity: I am a Lumbee woman; a Native woman. Of course, the concept of a "Native race" is complicated.[18] Many people would consider their *Tribe* to be their primary identity; they do not feel an inherent sense of belonging to a more global, pan-Indian "race." I'll be honest: it's something I'm still navigating for myself.

Maybe there are more than two circles in the Venn diagram. Maybe we could add a circle called "Tradition." For some people who claim Native identity, elements of cultural practices and teachings have formed an important part of their identity. Maybe we could add a circle called "Geography": for some claiming Native identity, attachment to a place, be it a reservation or otherwise, has become an important part of their identity. Maybe there's a circle called "Family."

My friend Andy considers himself white. If he took a genealogy spit test, the results would probably come back as a mixture of western European places, though Andy thinks the majority of his ancestors hailed from Ireland. Andy is a citizen of the United States. He was born in the Midwest to parents who were also born in the Midwest.

I tell Andy about my identity Venn diagram. We talk about the fact that most people—whether Native or not—could construct for themselves a similar series of overlapping circles. Together, we imagine Andy's Venn diagram: He is a white U.S. citizen with Irish ancestry. He grew up in the Midwest, where his family remains. I ask Andy if he's ever been questioned about any of these identities.

"By who?" he asks. It's not something he's ever really had to think about.

I've lost track of the number of times I've been asked "how much" Indian I am, sometimes by complete strangers. I'm often surprised at the number of people both familiar with the concept of blood quantum and comfortable asking Native people about theirs. As if that's a perfectly reasonable question to ask someone. As if it's anyone else's business. As if there were some mathematical way to quantify an identity that was both meaningful and accurate.

I'd be lying if I said it wasn't a question I'd also asked of myself. As if there were some sort of chart, one of those posters with a picture of a thermometer measuring progress toward a goal. As if, at the top, in big bubble script, is written, "100% Indian!" Sometimes I feel like I've spent my whole life trying to color in more of the thermometer, trying to advance to the top.

As if, at some point, I might finally be able to say I've done it. I've become Indian enough.

When Chase refills her coffee, I decide to stretch my legs. We've been sitting at her dining table for a couple of hours by this point. I wander over to a hall off the entryway, where I spot a large portrait of the family on canvas. Chase and a man I now know as Josh are flanked by two teenage girls and a small boy. The family members are color-coordinated in light blues and whites. They look genuinely happy.

At nineteen, Chase became pregnant with her eldest daughter. She describes her life then as a "fucking mess," but she glosses over the specifics. The part of the story she chooses to elaborate on is the fact that when Josh learned she was expecting, he was incredibly supportive, and together, they survived. They got married when she was six months along and allowed their families to throw them a small wedding. (They had wanted to elope.) They managed to build a life for themselves with what they now know was very little.

It was during her first pregnancy, Chase says, that she "started to give a shit." She earned her GED and signed up for writing classes at a local community college. One professor encouraged her to keep writing. She thinks it was the first time anyone had told her she was good at anything. She earned an associate's degree and transferred to a university, where she earned her bachelor's. She tells me she's currently pursuing her master's. "It turns out I'm not dumb," she says.

In describing how she and her husband inched themselves out of an objectively bad situation, Chase gives a lot of credit to circumstance. The two qualified for a Veterans Administration home loan. They didn't need to pay for childcare because they each worked a different shift. They had family close by.

I suspect there are other factors at play. During a brief house tour, Chase shows me the kitchen she and Josh renovated themselves, by hand; she tells me about laying the flooring and putting in the tile. When she got an internship with a great company, she says, she immediately began figuring out where there were gaps in processes and filling them. Eventually, she worked her way up to director of the organization. Her self-deprecating version of the story doesn't include the word *driven*, but that's exactly what she is: she has done difficult things in the face of even more difficult realities.

I ask Chase what it's been like to live as a Native woman in a place that doesn't have a lot of racial diversity, and to raise Native children in that same place. Instead of talking about herself, she chooses to tell me about her best friend while growing up, who was Black. Chase heard people call the girl "the N-word" in the hallways at school. She talks about how isolated her friend felt; like Chase, she didn't have many other friends.

When I press her on her own experience, Chase pauses to consider the question. "My daughter has been told by people that she looks Asian," she says. "When she tells them she's Native, they call her a liar." Chase tells me she's always thought of herself as looking somewhat racially ambiguous. She's fielded guesses of Korean, Mexican, and Latina, among others. Plus, her First Nations community, the Mi'kmaq, is one that most people in the United States have not heard of. While growing up, and even now occasionally, Chase has had people tell her the Tribe isn't real.

Recently, Chase was able to take her entire family up to Canada for the first time. She calls the trip a game changer. After the first day, her husband seemed to have an epiphany: "You never belonged in the Midwest," he told her. "You belong here." She thinks her younger daughter— whom she describes as never having fit in back home—was also deeply impacted by the visit. "Her whole demeanor changed." She suddenly felt she'd found a community.

Though it wouldn't surprise her to see that daughter end up in Canada, Chase has built a life for herself in the Midwest. It's where her husband's family lives, where she has found work she cares about. And Chase's strained relationship with her notwithstanding, it is where her mother lives, too.

Chase tells me that, a few years ago, her midwestern town asked her to accept a proclamation for Indigenous Peoples' Day. It's a trend we see in more and more places across the United States, as non-Native folks come to terms with the fact that Columbus was not the hero they'd like him to be: the celebration, in mid-October, of an Indigenous Peoples' Day, to acknowledge and honor the Native communities that existed long before colonists and other settlers set foot on the continent. To honor indigenous communities, Chase's town would hold a small ceremony. The mayor would make the announcement, there would be applause, a ceremonial piece of paper would change hands.

Chase was unsure about accepting. In addition to being a part of a First Nations community not located in the United States, she always felt weird about claiming her heritage. Not growing up in her Native community—even if it was the result of her father's displacement and murder—has led to deep insecurity. But when she called her family in Canada and asked them about it, they encouraged her to accept. "They were proud," she says.

But what Chase thought would be a relatively ceremonial event—accepting the town's proclamation—turned into a bit of a nightmare. There was a huge backlash against the idea, with people targeting Chase, the honorary recipient. They emailed her, phoned her, and posted on Facebook that she was trying to change history; some made explicit threats. Chase says that what surprised her most was the lack of support she received. "Even the people who asked me to do it weren't coming to my aid," she says.

As I'm packing up to leave, Chase tells me that, a few years ago, there was an update to her father's case. An article in a local paper had urged detectives to reexamine it, even calling the death a murder. Chase says she tried to reach out to the folks mentioned in the article, including members of law enforcement, but was met with almost unanimous pushback. According to one person she spoke with, the case would never go any farther; she should quit wasting her time, she was told, and move on with her life.

"They told me that the facts of the case didn't matter," she says. "My father was just another dead Indian."

It is in January 2023—while I was writing this book—that I begin to notice an uptick in the number of people who have claimed Native identity who are exposed as liars. As frauds. Sure, some of these exposés appear in—how should I say this?—less-than-reputable media. Some I'd liken to tabloids with all the markers of gotcha journalism. But many of the claims of fraud feel legitimate, like true instances of people knowingly making false claims to profit somehow.

In some ways, Native identity is relatively easy to forge. Native people have no particular "look," despite what their portrayals on television and film might lead us to believe. Removal, assimilation, relocation—all these have made the situation even more convoluted. A person can easily claim to have been disconnected from their Tribe because of any number of federal policies. Plus, with more than five hundred federally recognized Tribes in the United States, it's likely the average American—and, therefore, the average onlooker—wouldn't know the complexities of any one Tribe. Hell, if they don't mind strangers asking personal questions about their fraction of Indian blood or their relationship to famous Indians throughout history, an imposter could probably live as an "Indian" for some time.

It was this way for the woman I read about in January 2023, who deceived an entire community into believing her lies. Some of her methods were pretty appalling. In addition to tanning her skin and dying her hair darker, she purchased Native-made art from websites and sold them as her own.

Another case of fraud involved a professor who routinely spoke on conference panels about her Native identity. When she was sent a cease-and-desist letter by the Tribe to which she claimed to be a member, she eliminated all references to that heritage from her website. Yet another instance involved three men, all professors at the same university. All three men's Native identities were precarious at best. None was enrolled in a Tribe or possessed any "evidence" of their connection to one.

These stories are like train wrecks we can't look away from. It's no surprise. American society is fascinated by imposter narratives, particularly when they involve people living identities that are not their own: the cases of Rachel Dolezal and Jessica Krug (two white women exposed as passing as Black) and of H. G. Carrillo (a Detroit-born African American writer who falsely claimed to be a Cuban immigrant) have taught us to take interest in such stories. They are ones that feature in documentaries, on podcasts, and in segments on the nightly news.

My observation, though, is that, while stories like these have some shock value, many of them are not so clear-cut. Identity is rarely a well-marked line that a person is on either one side of or the other. This ambiguity feels especially true for people who claim Native identity. Often, such claimants are relying on stories passed down by family members or genealogy going back centuries. They may have been told that their great-great-great-grandparent was Cherokee, and so they have internalized this not only as historical truth but as their modern-day reality.

I think about a student I once met. He believed himself to be Native—he'd been told so by a grandparent—but he wasn't sure from which distant relative his Native ancestry came. He believed he was connected to a particular Tribe, but he was not enrolled in the Tribe. Nor had he ever visited its reservation; he didn't know anyone there. Still, he spent a lot of his time fighting for what we might call indigenous causes. He attended protests against the Dakota Access Pipeline, he was active in the Missing and Murdered Indigenous Women movement, and he wore buttons with slogans like "#LandBack."

Certainly, there's a big difference between people who profit from possessing a particular Native identity and those who don't. Certainly, private citizens are free to claim any identity they want. They could conceive of themselves as Native, whether falsely or not, and live that way their entire life. They could assume that identity at dinner parties, church gatherings, basketball games. They could check any box they wanted on the U.S. Census. Sure, their doing so would be head-scratching; wrong, even. But I'm not sure that private instances of such claims warrant much action on the part of Tribes.

It is when a person begins to profit from their precarious Native identity, though, that we must have a real conversation about recourse. Cases of Native identity fraud have become particularly problematic in academia and the arts. Universities seem especially prone to hiring people untruthfully claiming Native identity, whether because of mismanagement during the hiring process, a desire on the part of institutions to beef up their diversity numbers, or something else. Maybe it's that our society values lived experience so much that we're willing to ignore certain red flags and continue to believe a person's backstory and well-crafted ideologies. Maybe it's that people who falsely claim Native identity often embody what are considered stereotypes, such as poverty, substance addiction, marginalization—as if being Native means those things and nothing else.

A logical answer might go something like this: Native Nations are sovereign entities, and anyone claiming affiliation to one is making not a racial statement but, rather, a political one. For this reason, it is up to the Tribes themselves to confirm or deny that person's claim. No one else has the right or authority to do so.

The challenge, of course, is that Tribes have a lot of other stuff to do. They're busy providing education and health care and housing and employment opportunities for their members; they're busy advocating for #LandBack and water justice and Missing and Murdered Indigenous Women; they're busy mourning the children whose bodies are buried on the grounds of old Indian boarding schools; they're busy fighting for their continued survival. Adjudicating individual identity claims is simply not a priority.

I suppose a straightforward way that industries—academia and the arts, among others—could take the initial step in verifying Native identity would be to require a Tribal enrollment card. That, to abide by a Tribe's own processes is to respect its sovereignty. Even in that paradigm, though, there will be those who legitimately claim Native identity and are nonetheless left out.

The more I research history, interview thoughtful Native scholars, and contemplate my own story, the more I think about Native identity as, among other things, deeply relational. As professor and writer Jimmy Beason, a member of the Osage Nation of Oklahoma, has said, Native identity "is not so much who you claim; it's who claims you."[19]

On the flip side, I'm sure no one disagrees that people who are both objectively lying about their Native identity and profiting from it must be checked. The problem is that what has emerged to counteract the fraud are individuals and small groups who operate under the non-rules of vigilante justice. Social media takedowns, internet trolling, harassment both online and in the real world—all are among their frustrating and terrifying tactics. Tactics, I should mention, they also use on people whose Native identity should never be questioned.

Many times, this work is done under the pretext of exposing "pretendians"—as in "pretend Indians." Every time a new pretendian is unmasked to the public, I feel a little gurgle in my stomach. Will I be next? And which part of my identity will serve as the tipping point? The fact that I've never danced in a powwow? The fact that my Tribe, thanks to a combination of racism and political injustice, has yet to be fully federally recognized? That my eyes are this mix of green and brown that my dad always called dirty hazel? That, recently, when a friend mentioned the use of a "cradleboard," I blanked; I had no idea what she was talking about?

I've been told there's a list of "pretendians" floating around on the internet. I've never looked for it. After spending almost three years digging through lists—lists of "Indians About to Emigrate West of the Mississippi River," of slaves, of mulattos, of Tribes that received tiny "presents" for gigantic swaths of land, of full-bloods and half-breeds, of Indians "voluntarily relocating"—I can't stomach the idea of seeing it.

Return

In the weeks leading up to my family's trip to North Carolina, I distracted myself with preparations. I spent my days assembling sets of matching outfits for my kids because, while growing up, I never got to wear matching clothes with a sibling and I now live vicariously through my children. I refreshed the weather app in the hope that the "96 degrees and sunny" would magically change to "75 and breezy." I printed copies of birth certificates in triplicate because maybe this would be the one time in my life I'd need something printed in triplicate.

My husband mostly just stood back and let the freight train power through. His usual packing technique is to wait until roughly two hours before boarding time and throw miscellaneous socks and shorts into a duffel. He refuses to check a bag, on principle. He will never forgive airlines for charging for luggage.

We had decided to time our trip with Lumbee Homecoming, an annual event around the Fourth of July. This was partly because my mom and I had never been. The week promised a Lumbee market with works by local artists, a powwow, a film festival, and other events. Also, we knew that some of our more distant relatives would be making the trip into town, too.

When the day arrived for our family to pile into the car and drive the twenty minutes to the airport, we woke the kids up when it was still dark, dressed them in matching jammies, and made sure we had enough snacks. We paid our daily homage to the inventors of handheld applesauce pouches.

In the chaos of packing our things and schlepping my family through the airport to our boarding gate, I had temporarily forgotten about the importance of what was to come. Thanks to Covid-19, this would be the first time I'd be back in North Carolina in a few years, the first time most of my relatives would get to meet my husband. The first time my kids, both born in the throes of the pandemic, would set foot in Lumbee country.

O n any given summer day, you'll find a gaggle of kids eagerly waiting their turn to take the plunge into the Lumbee River off the overpass at Chicken Road.[1] Some wear T-shirts and shorts; others don swimming suits. The spot is about two miles outside the small town of Pembroke (home to the Lumbee Tribe headquarters). Children from the area walk or bike here; older kids drive cars borrowed from relatives. They all seek refuge from the heavy North Carolina heat.

If you consider that the Mississippi River, the second longest in the United States, runs over 2,350 miles from the top of the country to the bottom, the Lumbee River seems short in comparison. It begins in Hoke County, North Carolina, in the coastal plains of the state, and runs 130 miles southeast, just past the border with South Carolina. It curves and winds in a pattern that is no pattern at all. In most places, the river is just a few feet deep; at its widest point, it is just 75 feet, less than the length of a regulation basketball court.

Yet, for the Lumbee people, the Lumbee River defies measurement. Its importance spans generations and centuries. It would be impossible to count all the children who have jumped, screaming with delight, from that overpass on Chicken Road. It would be impossible to count the number of babies washed in the river's waters, the number of ailments treated with the flowering swamp rose mallow growing along its banks. It was in the areas along this river, then called Drowning Creek, that early accounts of our Lumbee ancestors were recorded by European settlers. The earliest of those was a map prepared by John Herbert, commissioner of Indian trade, in 1725.[2]

According to archeological records, successive cultures of Native people have inhabited the area around the Lumbee River for nearly fourteen thousand years.[3] This includes Native people who are known to have lived there continuously from at least 930 C.E., the radio-carbon date of a dugout canoe found eleven miles upriver from the swimming spot at Chicken Road.[4]

Most of the archeological digs around the Lumbee River Basin have taken place in Robeson County, whose population is nearly 40 percent Native American, the vast majority of them Lumbee. A total of 429 archeological sites have been recorded in the area, spanning from the Paleo-Indian period in B.C.E. 7000 to more recent times, after contact with Europeans settlers.[5]

In the language of anthropologists, the historic Tribes who lived in the area around the Lumbee River were Iroquoian-, Siouan-, and Algonquian-speaking people.[6] Some have labeled the groups who traditionally called this place home the Tuscarora, Hatteras, Keyauwee, Catawba, Saponi, Weyanoke, and Cheraw.[7] In Herbert's 1725 map, he identified the Indian communities as Pedee, Scavanos, Wacomas, and "Saraws."

As in most records, the spelling of these names varies considerably. The accuracy is subject to the ways English-speaking colonists would have transcribed words unknown to them. It's subject to misguided record keepers with Europeanized views of what Indians should do or be, of what they should look like, how they should dress. After all, by the time most of these records were written, our Lumbee ancestors would have shed the individual languages and practices of the Tribes from which they originated, opting instead to create a more universal set of traditions.[8]

In a word, the Lumbee people are an amalgamation.[9]

We originate from a diverse array of Indian people who found themselves living together out of circumstance—or, rather, *circumstances* plural, for the circumstances were as many as there were families themselves.

Some of the earliest colonization of the place we now call the United States happened in and around what we today call North Carolina. We know that as early as 1585, settlers docked on land that has become famous as the Lost Colony of Roanoke—"lost" because in 1590, when John White, the expedition's leader, returned from England after sailing there for more supplies, he found all traces of the original colonists gone, including his own family members. All that remained was the message "Croatoan" carved into a tree.[10]

Some historians posit that the Lumbee people are, at least in part, descendants of that lost colony. After the settlers were left on the shores of North Carolina to fend for themselves while awaiting White's return, they are believed to have taken up residence with the local Native people and, eventually, made their way south with them, toward Drowning Creek.[11]

What we know from the historical record is that European contact was the start of a long journey for Indian people that included, but was not limited to, disease, enslavement, warfare, and the imposition of rules that didn't make sense.[12] Among those rules was the idea of paying for the land (including in annual taxes) that Indian families had lived on for generations. And if they did not keep up with those payments, they could be fined or jailed or run out of town. They could accumulate insurmountable debts that would be passed on to their children in the form of indentured servitude.[13]

To escape this carousel of trauma, Indian families took refuge in the dense swampland of the coastal plains of North Carolina, in the areas around Drowning Creek, along what we today call the Lumbee River. There, they sought freedom from colonization and found community among a diverse group of people, themselves a diverse mix of Tribes.

When such an amalgamation of diverse communities comes together, they must find a common language. This was the case for our Lumbee ancestors, who adopted English as their lingua franca. They would have used English to communicate with settlers—who we know were the primary record keepers of the day—using English names for places like Drowning Creek, Cape Fear, New Hope.[14] According to scholar Malinda Maynor Lowery, it's likely our Lumbee ancestors wouldn't have spoken the names of their ancestral Tribes, as those names were in languages they no longer used.[15] This would have led some record keepers to consider these Indian people not Indian at all.

Our Lumbee ancestors probably confused the hell out of early colonists, including a large colony of Scottish settlers who descended upon an area along the Lumbee River in the mid-1700s.[16] Our Lumbee ancestors would likely have worn European clothing and lived in log cabins. They would have spoken English. And they would have done all this out of pragmatism.[17] If several families from several different Tribes form an egalitarian community, it makes sense to blend their individual practices, to create a shared sense of tradition.

Over the years, the Lumbees have continued to confuse the hell out of everyone but themselves. It was this way with my great-great-grandmother Annie Pearl, whose race changed in every U.S. Census in which she appeared. And not because Annie Pearl changed races or identities but because the people counting her had different opinions about what she should be called.

It is also this way with the series of names that folks have called the Lumbee Tribe over the years, a list that includes the Cherokee Indians of Robeson County, Croatan Indians, Indians of Robeson County, and Cheraw Indians. These names were bestowed upon the Lumbee by a graduate student, in an unpublished master's thesis; a state legislator named Hamilton McMillan; the North Carolina General Assembly; and a civil servant named Orland McPherson.[18]

The use of the name "Lumbee" was the first instance of the Tribe itself deciding what it wanted to be called. In 1952, its members voted on the name, which was meant as a tribute to the river, the source of so much of the Tribe's history and tradition. It was a name to honor a place rather than a particular Tribe of origin, to acknowledge that our Lumbee ancestors originated from a diverse set of Tribes.[19]

To say that the Lumbee are merely misunderstood would do a disservice to everyone involved. Certainly, the ways that the Lumbee present are not always in line with stereotypes we in the United States have cultivated about what an Indian should look like. As Lowery and others have reflected, our Lumbee ancestors formed tight-knit communities and intermarried with white settlers, escaped slaves, and free persons of color.[20]

The problem—whether or not we care to admit it—is that we treat Nativeness differently depending on what a person looks like. In the United States, we generally accept claims of Native American ancestry by people who present as white.[21] We believe that it's possible to *look* white but also *be* Indian. What with assimilation and intermarriage and the giant melting pot of urban centers, it's only natural that there are now generations of Native people who do not fit the stereotypical Indian "look."[22] As someone who usually presents as white, I can say I have never had my claim of Native identity challenged by a stranger. Aside from asking me inappropriate questions about my blood quantum, no one has ever told me that because I look white, I cannot also be Native.

Some of the most romanticized portrayals of Native Americans have centered on this idea. In *Pocahontas*, a Powhatan woman marries the white English settler John Rolfe. In the 1992 film version of *The Last of the Mohicans*, Mohawk warrior Uncas falls in love with the white daughter of a British colonel. Hell, even *Dances with Wolves* features a white woman adopted by the Lakota Tribe. Our society has been trained to see these relationships as desirable, something we should cheer as we eat our popcorn and swoon.

Yet we do not as willingly give this same benefit of the doubt to people presenting as Black. It was this way for my grandfather, my cousins, and it's this way for many Lumbee people when they travel outside Robeson County. Their skin matches the color swatch to which society has assigned the category "Black," and so, therefore, they are Black. If they claim Native identity, it's seen as hoax, a fanciful tale they've spun out of a desire to accrue privileges of some sort.[23]

Partly, I imagine, this is a result of the contradictory ways the United States has dictated Nativeness and Blackness throughout history. For Native people, the federal project has long been to dilute their Native blood, to assimilate them into the larger society, to root out their Native traditions and force Europeanization (and whiteness) upon them. In official documents—like the regulations around the Dawes Act and the Indian Reorganization Act—those goals would be achieved once a person had one-half or less Indian blood.[24] It was at that point that a person would cease being Indian and would reach the assigned goal of becoming white.

In the United States, Blackness has long been governed by the idea of "one drop"—that even a single drop of Black blood made a person Black and, thus, stripped them of any privileges or freedoms granted to white people. It was this way in the Jim Crow South, where interracial marriages were prohibited, the idea being that Black people should be separated from white people and that any amount of Black blood was sufficient for that cause.[25]

When I talk to Mikaëla Adams, a scholar who has written extensively on race and Native citizenship, she tells me that in the nineteenth century, as slavery became more important to the U.S. economy, the goal was to increase the number of potential slaves. It was therefore the project of the dominant (white) society to ensure that anyone with Black ancestry could be enslaved. Hence, anyone with any amount of Black blood would have been considered Black.

"White people weren't as much after Native bodies as land," Adams tells me. "So, instead, the goal was to decrease the number of Native people to eventually make them disappear."

Lumbee Homecoming is a tradition, but a relatively recent one. It was established in 1968, one year after the inaugural Miss Lumbee pageant. Some credit the American civil rights movement as a big motivating factor in the birth of Lumbee Homecoming—the 1960s saw Tribes across the country taking pride in showcasing their art and culture, something akin to a renaissance. Today, the Miss Lumbee pageant—which has been expanded to include categories for nearly every age, from small children through seniors—still serves as one of the week's most anticipated events.

I can say with confidence that I've never seen, nor do I ever expect to see, as many golf carts as there are at Lumbee Homecoming. Golf carts in all configurations (two-seaters, four-seaters, six-seaters; roofed and unroofed) and colors (black, green, orange) line the streets of Pembroke each year in the week surrounding the Fourth of July. The golf carts are part of the tradition. For forty dollars, you can receive a permit to drive one on the streets of town. They're a handy tool in the hot and sweaty crowds of Lumbee Homecoming, when walking feels like swimming through hot air and parking spaces for full-size vehicles are at a premium.

I had always avoided Lumbee Homecoming, for a variety of reasons that included the heat and the crowds. I'm a fan of neither. According to estimates from event organizers, anywhere from 30,000 to 35,000 folks descend upon Pembroke (population 2,800) for the week's festivities. Around the Fourth of July, North Carolina temperatures can easily climb into the upper nineties, and the heat index can soar fifteen degrees past that.

I took stock of every single one of those degrees on the Saturday morning of Lumbee Homecoming 2023 as I sat with my two children on a curb along East Third, waiting for the parade to start. Some kind soul had given us paper fans, and I tried to direct as much warm wind as I could onto my babies' red faces. A few floats arrived, their riders prepared to toss ice pops at parade goers, but by the time they reached us, the treats had devolved into colorful tubes of lukewarm sugar water.

If it were possible to bestow upon oneself the title of Lumbee class president, the woman sitting on a lawn chair behind us would have done just that. She knew everyone, and shouted the names of every single float participant as they slowly rode past our spot. To some, she'd add things like "Got you out of the house today, huh?" or "Good to see you, girl!" Every so often, she'd turn to the guy next to her and say, "Those are your people!"

I sat on that curb, my knees bent at an angle that defied geometry, deep in a thought exercise. Say I'd grown up in Pembroke. Say I'd gone to school here, graduated from UNC Pembroke, even. Say my entire family, including my parents and siblings and nieces and nephews, still lived here, too. How would this experience have been different? Would I, too, have known the names of all the people on the parade floats? Would I have shared inside jokes about my Lumbeeness with the people sitting in lawn chairs around me? Hell, would I have known to bring a lawn chair in the first place?

These were, after all, the things that had always made me feel so deeply out of place, so awkward and uncomfortable in a space where I assumed I should fit in, so envious of my younger cousins who'd grown up on Lowry Circle and other small neighborhoods in town, surrounded by their Lumbee kin.

Earlier that morning, after my husband and I had parked our car, unfurled our double stroller, and convinced our children they'd have so much fun—and then, when that didn't work, promised them cookies—we'd begun walking toward a destination unknown. The streets were already lined with thousands of people, even two hours before the parade was to begin. Lost and a little bit flustered, I called my cousin Joan and asked her where we were supposed to go. She told us to meet her in front of Old Main and then quickly hung up.

My husband decided to move the car—he wanted to park nearer to wherever the hell we were going. I stood in the driveway of a fast-food chain feeling very, very alone. I took a calculated guess about the direction to walk and pushed on. Because the sidewalks were packed with people and tents, I pushed the stroller carrying my two increasingly whiny kids along the street. I tried to steer as close to the curb as I could, because I was sharing the narrow lane with golf carts and vehicles. Every so often, I'd pass a police officer directing traffic who'd have to wait for me to walk by. I tried my best to ignore the stares, which came from every direction.

When I was finally able to navigate the stroller off the street, I walked up to the nearest group of people, women in their fifties, and asked them for directions to Old Main.

"Where you from?" one of them asked.

I launched into my routine, the shortened version that included my grandpa and his military service and my family's connection to Pembroke. I'm not sure why I felt the need to do the dance—it was hot, I was hot, my kids were hot. No one was questioning my identity—besides, well, me.

"I used to live in Iowa," one of the women said.

When I arrived at the brick building I now know as Old Main, I spotted my mother and Joan, who led us to a small tent along the parade route. I parked the stroller, unbuckled my soggy children, and took off the backpack I'd been carrying, which seemed to weigh more than when I began. I peeked inside the tent but didn't see anyone I recognized.

My kids began to climb a golf cart, whose owner looked on without much interest. I was considering trying to corral them when I felt a soft tap on my shoulder. I turned to see my cousin Leo, Joan's brother. Leo was one of the first North Carolina relatives I remember ever meeting; he and Cousin Calvin had visited us in Iowa when I was about nine. Leo had always been a quiet man, something I chalked up to both DNA and a history of significant trauma. He'd lost two of his children by the time they were grown.

It'd been several years since I'd seen Leo, and seeing him there at the Lumbee Homecoming Parade took my breath away. He looked just like my grandpa. Or, at least, what I remember my grandpa to have looked like all those years ago, before he passed away when I was twelve. We gave each other a gentle hug, and Leo asked me how I'd been. I pointed to my babies, both now running the narrow aisles between chairs under the tent. Leo invited me in, motioning to a few empty seats.

My midwestern politeness kicked in, and I assured him we were fine—we'd stand or find another place to sit. I worried that the tent was for people who'd shown up early, or maybe for a specific group or family.

But then an older woman, probably in her eighties or more, motioned to me, moving her handbag from one of the chairs. "Sit right here, baby," she said.

One of the first times I visited Robeson County, North Carolina, I remember sitting on the floor of our motel room in Lumberton, holding the spine of the phonebook in one hand while carefully flipping through the pages and pages of *L*s with the other. I was showing my dad how many people shared my mother's surname, "Lowry."

Anytime we stayed in a hotel while I was growing up, the first thing my dad would do was lift the phonebook from the nightstand drawer and flip to the end, to the *S* section. As surnames go, his is an uncommon one; he'd always been told that everyone named Schuettpelz was related to one another. My dad would sit on the edge of the bed and run his finger down the list of esses, carefully, slowly, looking for a match. Most often, there weren't any. But every once in a while—especially in larger cities in the Midwest, in a place like Chicago or Milwaukee or Minneapolis—he'd find a Schuettpelz in town. Sometimes, he'd call them, introduce himself and name his relatives, in the hope the person on the other end of the line would, too.

It wasn't until I was in my twenties—on a road trip with friends, when I pulled out the hotel phonebook and repeated my father's ritual—that I realized it was unusual. That not everyone had such a fascination with names.

Sitting in that motel room in Lumberton, I was excited to see so many people with my mother's name. Sure, I'd heard the name "Lowry" before—I had been particularly fond of the writer Lois Lowry while growing up. But seeing the hundreds of other Lowrys in that phonebook in that place gave me a sense of deep belonging—of validity, even.

What I learned from perusing the Robeson County phonebook all those years ago was that there were a few very common last names. "Lowry" was certainly one; I found pages and pages of them in the area. Some spelled the name like we did, with a *y*; sometimes, it was "Lowrie," or "Lowery." In the years since then, I have learned that even within the same family, folks will spell it differently.

Other common names in that phonebook were "Chavis," "Hunt," "Locklear," "Maynor," "Oxendine," "Bullard," and about a dozen more. I thought especially about my cousin whose wedding had brought us into town that week: she was marrying a man with the same last name as hers, though the two were unrelated by blood. The name they shared was common to many others in the area. I thought about the joke my dad was preparing to tell when he walked into the church and asked to sit "on the Bullard side."

In some ways, my early interest in finding Lowrys was fitting. As scholars like Malinda Maynor Lowery have written, knowledge of kinship and place is critical to Lumbee identity. "Who's your people" is common shorthand for this, often asked in the context of belonging.[26] It's not a measure of purity, but of roots. It's a question not of how Lumbee a person is but, rather, how a person is Lumbee.

I suppose it's fitting, too, that a major inflection point of our Lumbee origin story was the coming together of multi-Tribal and multiracial settlements along the winding Lumbee River of Robeson County. There, the Lowrys, Chavises, Locklears, Wilkinses, Braveboys, and others formed a community they hoped would be free from colonial rule, where they could raise their babies and steward the land in ways that would sustain their families for generations. These ancestors of today's Lumbees eventually migrated to the marshy backwoods of places we still call Drowning Creek and Burnt Swamp.[27]

Today, driving down Pembroke's main drag—alternately called East Third and Highway 711—we see that those original Lumbee names are still omnipresent. Eating lunch at McDonald's requires turning onto Lowry Street; Revels Body Shop sits at the corner of West Fifth and Maynor Streets. Along the neatly maintained walkways lining the campus of UNC Pembroke are buildings emblazoned with names like "Locklear," "Jacobs," and "Oxendine." The school, part of the University of North Carolina system, was originally opened in 1888 as the Croatan Normal School, to train Native American teachers.[28]

According to Lowery, one of the earliest written records we have of Lumbee ancestors is from a letter written to colonial authorities in 1773 by white settlers in the area of Robeson County. In the letter, they called their neighbors a "mob of Negroes and Indians, riotously assembled."[29] The names of the so-called rogue families are familiar to anyone who's ever flipped through a Robeson County phonebook—"Chavis," "Lock-lear," "Grooms," "Ivey," "Sweat," "Kearsey," "Dial."

Later, in the nineteenth century, a report by a white settler described an Indian settlement in the same area composed of about two hundred Indian families along with a small number of free Black and white families and enslaved people.[30] Another observer of the time wrote, "The whole race is more or less connected by blood, and some five or six names constitute the majority of the inhabitants, the Lowerys, the Oxendines, and the Chavises being the largest in number."[31]

Of the names the Lumbee are called, none of them includes "federally recognized."

Growing up, I knew this fact like I knew my home phone number. I could recite it on command. Of course, at ages six or seven or eight, I had no earthly idea what federal recognition meant, but I'd refer to the injustice of our not having it just the same. Over the years, I learned the history behind our lack of recognition and various editorialized versions of its causes and implications. My aunt Diana, an attorney and former judge, had a particularly lengthy set of explanations.

Still, all these years later—after nearly thirty-five years of being in possession of my own Indian card—I still can't say for certain why it remains true. Over the course of the last 130 years, twenty-nine congressional bills calling for Lumbee federal recognition, authored by a variety of members of Congress, mostly from the state of North Carolina, have been introduced. The first bill to recognize the Lumbee Tribe was introduced in 1899.[32] Like all those that came after, it failed.

The truth is that the Lumbee struggle is complicated.

In an act signed on June 7, 1956, known as the Lumbee Act, Congress designated Indians "residing in Robeson and adjoining counties of North Carolina" as the "Lumbee Indians of North Carolina,"[33] adding that "Nothing in this Act shall make such Indians eligible for any services performed by the United States for Indians because of their status as Indians, and none of the statutes of the United States which affect Indians because of their status as Indians shall be applicable to the Lumbee Indians."[34]

Technically speaking, the Lumbee *are* recognized by the federal government; we are recognized as being Indian. What we are *not* recognized as is qualifying for certain federal funding from the Bureau of Indian Affairs or the Indian Health Service. As being entitled to the same level of sovereignty or self-government as other Tribes or to the repatriation of ancestral remains or lands in trust.

From a historical standpoint, the passage of the Lumbee Act wasn't particularly surprising. In the 1950s, we know that Congress was taking a new approach to the so-called "Indian Problem," one aptly referred to as termination. We know that, besides assimilation, one of the key goals of this approach was to eliminate federal support for Tribes, to reduce federal spending and federal obligation. Congress terminated a lot of Tribes during this period, including Tribes it had spent decades putting on short fiscal leashes for land it had stolen from them or, at the very least, cheated them out of.

But there's something else going on, too.

For a long time—as long as anyone alive can remember—the Lumbee people have found their Native identity constantly questioned. It was this way in 1936, when the Lumbee sought recognition under the Indian Reorganization Act. One key stipulation in that Act was that individuals possess one-half or more Indian blood to be recognized as Indian by the U.S. government.[35] Over the next two years, 209 people identifying as Indians of Robeson County—out of a population of nearly 36,000—volunteered to undergo testing.[36] Reporting to a makeshift office set up in Pembroke, they were subjected to inhumane experiments conducted by anthropologists hired by the federal government. To quantify the applicants' Indian blood, agents measured heads, hair, teeth, noses, and lips.[37] They scratched at skin, the thinking being that a reddish mark indicated mixed blood. They stuck pencils into hair, the thinking being that if the pencil fell out, it indicated "real" Indian hair.[38]

Eula Jacobs was eighteen when she underwent these tests. In her file, on the first page, is the transcript of her interview. In it, she lists in great detail her family tree and each member's approximated Indian blood.

Both her parents were three-quarters Indian. Farther into Eula's file is her "Racial Diagnosis," as conducted by a team of anthropologists.[39] Her hair is described as the "deep wave variety and presents clear frizzling at the ends." It is called "highly suggestive of Negroidal origin." The prominence of her chin was deemed "definitely non-Indian." Anthropologist Carl Seltzer diagnosed Eula Jacobs as "an individual of about equal parts of White and Negroid blood plus a dash of Indian." A dash. On the next page, on U.S. Department of the Interior letterhead it states that Eula Jacobs is not eligible for registration as an Indian.

In the end, out of the 209 total people subjected to racist tests, 22 passed. An additional 11 were classified as "borderline," and 7 as "near borderline." In several cases, full siblings were put into different categories.[40] These so-called Original 22 attempted to gain federal recognition, but were ultimately denied. According to Arlinda Locklear, an enrolled member of the Lumbee Tribe and a lawyer who has argued cases in front of the Supreme Court, "the Department of Interior was concerned that if those 22 Indians, tested and proved Indian by Carl Seltzer, became recognized[,] then they would create a Tribe of 36,000."[41]

In 1989, the Department of the Interior's Office of the Solicitor determined that the Lumbee Tribe could not seek federal recognition through an administrative process—that is, by submitting an application to the Bureau of Indian Affairs the way every other Tribe could. Rather, they could receive federal recognition only through a vote in Congress, through the machinations that happen on Capitol Hill.[42]

A few facts have made this development deeply problematic for the Lumbee federal recognition plight. For one thing, the Lumbee Tribe is very large. Were it to receive full federal recognition, it would be the fifth largest Tribe in the country. As a result, its share of the federal funding pie would be big. In years when the total size of the pie stayed the same, the addition of the Lumbee Tribe would result in every other Tribe's share shrinking considerably. This has created a zero-sum situation in which some Tribes actively oppose recognition for others.

In addition, were the Lumbee Tribe to receive full federal recognition, it would very likely build a casino on its land. And thanks to its land's strategic location, off Interstate 95—which connects northern cities like Boston, New York, and Washington, D.C., to Florida—that facility would very likely draw traffic away from nearby gaming facilities.

Last, but perhaps most important, is a factor that's not as easy to categorize or quantify. As a Tribe whose ancestors were themselves a mix of Native people, white settlers, and freed and escaped slaves, Lumbee people do not possess a stereotypical Indian "look." This includes a large proportion of Lumbee who present as Black. And as for other Tribes in this situation, the road to recognition has been fraught with racism.[43]

Initially, the requirements for federal recognition seem straightforward. According to the Bureau of Indian Affairs, in order to be federally recognized, a Tribe must:[44]

1. Identify as an American Indian entity on a substantially continuous basis since 1900;
2. Comprise a distinct community and demonstrate that it existed as a community from 1900 until the present;
3. Maintain political influence or authority over its members as an autonomous entity from 1900 until the present;
4. Have governing documents;
5. Consist of individuals who descend from a historical Indian Tribe (or from historical Indian Tribes that combined and functioned as a single autonomous political entity); and
6. Consist principally of persons who are not members of any federally recognized Tribe.

When I read the fine print, I'm struck by what counts as evidence to support these ideas. That, even after the Dawes Act and other legislation to rid Tribes' leaders of their power, a Tribe must demonstrate that it "is able to mobilize significant numbers of members and significant resources from its members for group purposes." Despite children having been stolen and murdered at boarding schools designed to rid them of their cultural traditions, Tribes must demonstrate that "at least 50 percent of the entity members maintain distinct cultural patterns such as, but not limited to, language, kinship system, religious beliefs and practices, or ceremonies." Even in the face of the Indian Relocation Act, Tribes must demonstrate that "more than 50 percent of the members reside in a geographical area exclusively or almost exclusively composed of members of the entity."[45]

The building's setup had changed a bit since I last visited in 2014, but the general idea was the same. After we parked in the parking lot of the turtle-shaped Lumbee Headquarters, my husband and children and I dutifully made our way up the sidewalk. Of course, on the way inside, my son fell on the pavement and scraped his knee because those gray sandals never fit quite right.

We walked into the lobby area, a space considerably different from how it looked the last time I visited—smaller, more intimate. We'd aimed to arrive by 8:30 a.m., when it opened, and had almost gotten there by then. We checked in with a woman behind a glass window and took our seats in a waiting area that reminded me of a doctor's office.

When the enrollment officer pushed open the door and called our names, we followed her into a small room that somehow felt like a basement, despite its being on the ground floor. The woman took her seat behind a boxy computer. There was no chitchat, no particular conversation, just a clicking of keys interrupted only by a request for my children's birth certificates. When it came time to take their pictures, the woman motioned for them to sit in an upholstered navy chair against the wall. She took out a digital camera and snapped a few photos of my three-year-old son. For my infant daughter, I was instructed to hold her in my lap and hide my face behind hers.

If asked ten years ago if I'd enroll my hypothetical children in the Lumbee Tribe, my answer would have been a resounding "Hell, yes." There would have be no pause. It would have been an absolute certainty.

That's because, ten years ago, I didn't stop to consider what Tribal enrollment was, where it came from, why it existed at all.

After years of research and interviews and staring at the walls of my
living room, lost in thought, I suppose my ideas about enrollment have
become more complicated. Yes, Tribal membership and enrollment were
imposed on Native communities. Yes, often the processes behind enrollment were racist and fraught with misunderstanding and mismanagement. Yes, even today, some policies around enrollment do not serve the
very people they are intended to serve.

But I've also come to see Tribal enrollment as protective. Having a robust membership is protective of Tribal survival; it means we are alive. Despite centuries of federal policies meant to eradicate us altogether, Indians
have not disappeared. I wish I didn't have to think about it this way, but
Tribal enrollment is personally protective, too. I think about enrollment as
a shield that might protect my children from identity policing, from the
constant questions about whether they are Indian *enough*.

When she was done taking my children's pictures, the enrollment
officer plugged the camera into her computer, and together, we waited.
My children were growing increasingly antsy by this point, having been
promised snacks once we were done. My husband chased my daughter
into the next room, another enrollment office, while I busied myself
entertaining our son with my phone, showing him photos from our trip.

Finally, a small machine in the corner made a gentle whirring noise
and spat out two wallet-size plastic cards.

Epilogue

A friend of mine who works in Washington, D.C., tells me the federal government might begin to require people to return to their offices. It's 2024, and after four years of Covid-19 recovery, the city is beginning to see the negative impacts of having allowed federal employees to work remotely. Downtown D.C. is suffering. Coffee shops, restaurants, barbers—all once patronized by federal workers commuting into the city—are going out of business. A policy meant to keep people home and away from gatherings, to keep them safe, has caused harm.

A student in my class does a research project on "universal pre-K." It's an idea that's been thrown around for a while: that the United States should implement a system of required subsidized preschool for kids ages three to five. In general, it seems like the right thing to do. Parents are drowning in childcare costs; children from lower-income households are suffering from lack of access to quality care; measures of educational achievement in the United States are failing to keep pace with those in other developed countries. What my student learns is that, in communities that have implemented universal pre-K, daycares have struggled. In-home daycares in particular are finding it difficult to stay in business as the kids are transferred to universal pre-K.

I've worked in the policy field long enough to understand that with every law passed and every program implemented, there will be unintended consequences. No matter how lovingly or passionately a policy is created, no matter how much good a policy is meant to do, there will always be people who suffer as a result.

It feels this way with Native American Tribal enrollment. As sovereign entities, Tribes define their own membership; that is their right. They should always have that right. No one should deny them that right. And there are good reasons that the Tribal enrollment process involves lists.

Because Tribal enrollment is relational—that is, it's based on how people are connected to earlier generations—lists are an important mechanism for making those determinations. Plus, the existence of an established list reduces the element of subjectivity. No, it does not eliminate questionable decisions or motives. It doesn't prevent cases of unethical disenrollment. But it certainly reduces the likelihood that personal vendettas, political subversions, or resource commandeering will target people for non-inclusion.

At the same time, some people are not well served by lists. Certainly, there's a valid case to be made against static, historic Tribal rolls—particularly those created by the federal government to allot land. Certainly, from the historical record and from research by a lot of very smart scholars, we know that the ways those rolls were assembled were often problematic. They included people who shouldn't have been included and left a lot of people out.

The challenge is that Tribes are limited to using what exists. It's not like there are a lot of other, high-quality lists floating around, lists being ignored in favor of historic federal rolls. And because federal recognition and continued self-determination require that processes be in place around membership, historic federal rolls are often the best available option.

And, yes, sure, Tribes could make new lists. They could spend a great deal of time and money conducting new censuses and dealing with questionable claims of Native identity. They could attempt to track down every person with a legitimate claim to Tribal affiliation, even those who do not come forward independently or who live very far away. But would that produce a better count? Would it be so significantly better as to warrant the costs? Would it be worth it in the end?

I'll be honest: it's nerve-racking to write about Tribal enrollment, particularly the non-process process of the Dawes Rolls. In addition to not wanting to undermine the inherent right of Tribal sovereignty—the right of Tribes to choose which rolls they use and how they use them—I'm also deeply aware of the abundance of precarious ancestry claims, to the Five Tribes in particular. I know, for example, there are people who claim (and profit from) Native identity without any supporting evidence or connection and who use the inaccuracy of the Dawes Rolls to do so. My intent is not to provide people with the ammunition needed to make such questionable claims.

Which brings me to blood quantum.

As a historical construct, blood quantum is egregious. It's one of those ideas we reflect on with dismay. With disgust. Blood quantum was a federal project to quantify Indians and Indianness, to measure individuals' degree of proximity to full, unsalvageable Indians with the hope that, eventually, they would cease to exist.

It's fair, then, to look at Tribes' policies involving blood quantum with some suspicion. It's a legitimate question to ask why, after so many centuries of injustice and violence and persecution over Native blood, are we using it to measure and determine *ourselves*?

I wonder if, for those Tribes that use it, blood quantum has become a proxy of sorts. Because it was already recorded on some historic rolls, perhaps blood quantum has become the path of least resistance for determining kinship. Determining whose claim of belonging is (albeit, subjectively) legitimate versus whose is so distant and abstract that it shouldn't be considered.

I think back to the U.S. Census, to the sudden explosion in the number of people claiming Native identity. I wonder if blood quantum has become the shield Tribes have decided to use to defend themselves against what they perceive as precarious claims. Still, it's difficult to square this with the fact that blood quantum has become a blunt tool of exclusion. I think about Darlene Wind and her grandchildren and others whose (at least formal) Tribal membership will end with them. I fear that, particularly with increased rates of urbanity and intermarriage, blood quantum will become a tool of extinction.

For better or for worse, Tribal membership and enrollment, lists and rolls, Native identity and belonging—all have become wrapped up together in a tangled ball of yarn. Sure, there are people for whom this is not the case. There are those, like my friend Lee, who claim that an enrollment card doesn't change the way they feel about themselves or their inherent sense of belonging. But for a lot of people, it does and it will.

For me, Tribal enrollment has become not just a source of protection but also of pride. My enrollment is a piece of Lumbee history just as much as of my own personal history. Frankly, being enrolled has also started to feel like an act of political dissent, of speaking truth to power. Despite historical injustices and federal rejection and attempts to claim that Lumbees aren't really Indian at all, we are still fighting this fight. We are still here.

About This Project

O ne of the first lessons I learned about storytelling was the importance of a throughline.

A throughline is the strand you weave from the beginning of the story all the way through to the end. It's a thread that should secure itself through the entire story. Everything in the story should, in some way, be connected to the throughline.

When you think about the sheer number of Native American Tribes and, therefore, the sheer number of Native American stories, you realize very quickly that there is no one simple throughline. Certainly, big federal policies eventually led to other policies in a way that might resemble a throughline. But the impacts of those policies—the ways they created winners and losers, perverse incentives; the ways they were both destructive and good—complicate any tidy throughline.

My MFA mentor, Judy Mitchell, introduced me to a metaphor that writers use to adhere to their story's throughline. Writing, Judy told me, is like strapping a backpack onto the reader and sending them up a mountain. Every piece of the story, every detail, is something you're asking the reader to put into that backpack. Each item should have some utility to the reader as they make their journey. When, at last, they reach the top of that mountain—when they finish the story—they are going to empty that backpack. And if there are items in it that weren't relevant, items they didn't need along that journey, they're going to be angry they were asked to carry those things up the mountain.

In this book, I have tried my best to construct a throughline, giving readers only the items in their backpack that they will need. As a consequence, I have undoubtedly left important things out, sometimes intentionally, sometimes not. I have also, very likely, left important scholars out of the discussion. This project was not meant to be exhaustive but, rather, illustrative.

Speaking of illustrative—from the very beginning of my writing process, I knew how important it was going to be to conduct interviews. My story is just one story, and I knew it would be helpful for the reader *and* for me to understand the different ways that issues of Native identity and enrollment and belonging play out.

There is a long and problematic history of Native American stories, experiences, and wisdom being taken advantage of by researchers. This has led to a lot of distrust—which particularly manifests itself when Native people are contacted by random researchers and asked to recount their experiences.

The interviews in this book are primarily with people with whom I had a prior relationship, and they are almost entirely with women—a conscious decision on my part. Many of my interview subjects were women I consider friends. Every person who was the subject of a long-form interview was given the opportunity to read and revise their interview for clarity and comfort. In certain places, the interviews are written in a way that is vague on details, and that decision was made out of respect. I have shared only as much as each person was comfortable sharing. Where possible, I have tried to include a diverse array of voices in terms of Tribes. Still, the women I interviewed do not represent the entire Native experience. It is my hope, though, that their stories resonate more broadly.

One of my biggest hopes for future work on Native identity and enrollment is around Tribes from the southwest, particularly those that straddle the border between the U.S. and Mexico. Unfortunately, that work was beyond the scope of this book.

I have tried to distance myself from the murky waters of "What do Native people prefer to be called?" by choosing consistency. In this book, I have mostly used "Native" to describe contemporary people and issues and "Native American" in instances where I wanted to avoid confusion (to differentiate between Native American Tribes and Canadian First Nations communities, for example). For each long-form interview, I used the language the interviewee used to describe themselves. For historical records and discussions that included the word "Indian," my language reflects that choice. I have also used that term to describe functions and policies related to departments that describe themselves in that way. "Indigenous" seems to be used more often, but I have reserved it for describing issues or movements that are international in scope.

I have also tried to best reflect the language of communities by using the names and adjectives they use to describe themselves. This includes whether they use "Tribe" or "Nation" in their official name. For sections involving treaties or a formal relationship with the U.S. government, I have tried to use "Nation." As a general descriptor, I have used "Tribe," both to maintain consistency and because "national enrollment" is not in line with how most Tribes would describe that process.

I'll admit that there are places in the book where my word choice was guided by the rhythm of the language or by a desire to avoid repetition, but never in the case of a specific person or community. I will also admit that I have used "Indian" to describe myself in scenes where that's what I would say. Its use is not intended to convey some blanket form of acceptance or condonation for that term. In my experience, "Indian" is being reclaimed in some Native American spaces, and I find myself reclaiming it, too.

In instances where I am describing modern Lumbee tradition or reality, I have chosen to use the word "we." Some early readers of my manuscript wondered why I chose "they," as opposed to "we," in many instances in which I describe Native American culture, policies, histories. The reason is that no one person can possibly represent all those things. Yes, I am Native American; and yes, I have had some of the same experiences of other Native people, and some of those historical decisions and federal policies have impacted me, too. But I am one small star in a very, very large cosmos, and I prefer to frame the overarching story as not necessarily my own.

I am not a historian, and I do not think of myself as an academic. The research in this book was driven by personal stakes and my own curiosity.

I am 100 percent confident that I have made mistakes along the way. My hope is that I have modeled here what I try to teach my own students: a healthy sense of persistence and determination. Of trying to find answers to questions that are really, really hard.

Acknowledgments

I owe a great deal of gratitude to the two people without whom this project would not exist: my agent, Ayesha Pande, and my editor, Lee Oglesby. I do not believe it to be a coincidence that they, both women of color, have fought tirelessly to champion and support the work of women whose stories aren't what we might consider "mainstream." Thanks to Flatiron Books for what has felt like limitless support, particularly to Megan Lynch, Claire McLaughlin, Maris Tasaka, Maxine Charles, Elishia Merricks, Mary Retta, Ryan T. Jenkins.

Although this book was not peer-reviewed in the strictest, academic sense, I am very grateful to the brilliant scholars who've helped me think through ideas and read early drafts: Robert Miller (Eastern Shawnee), Kevin Washburn (Chickasaw), Libby Washburn (Chickasaw), Eva Marie Garroutte (Cherokee), Elizabeth Rule (Chickasaw), Gabe Galanda (Round Valley), Matthew Fletcher (Grand Traverse Band), Chris Houk (Wyandotte), Kyle Key (Chickasaw). Kendra Taira Field, Kirsty Gover, Christopher Haveman, Rose Buchanan, Dan Littlefield, Robert Cargill, Jane Ferguson, Katherine Ellinghaus, Alexandra Harmon, Paul Spruhan, Stephen Pevar, Mikaela Adams. A special thanks to David Wilkins and Malinda Maynor Lowery, both Lumbee scholars who I've come to consider mentors.

An enormous amount of gratitude to the people who've allowed me to share their stories: Tricia Long (Meskwaki), Anthony Long (Meskwaki), Kayla Dennis (Wyandotte), Taylor Beyal (Navajo), Deb Beyal (Navajo), Darlene Wind (Leech Lake), Marilyn Vann (Cherokee), Karen Diver (Fond du Lac), Don Diver (Fond du Lac), Chase Timmons (Mi'kmaq).

Thanks to Cole Redhorse Taylor (Mdewakanton Dakota) for the beautiful cover art. Thanks to my research assistants: Laura Carpenter, Andrew Parr, Clara Tang, Katie Herbert.

Thank you to the Whiting Foundation for its generous support.

In a lot of ways, I learned how to write by reading the writing of others, particularly those I studied from and with: Judy Mitchell, Jesse Lee Kercheval, and Danielle Evans; Maddy Court, Dantiel Moniz, Rodrigo Restrepo Montoya, Jack Ortiz, and Jennie Seidewand. A special thanks to Emily Shetler for her careful review of the manuscript.

There are very few truths I know with absolute certainty, but one is the love of my dearest friends, some of whom read early chapters and drafts: Kristin Sellers, Abbi Castle, Amy Hager, Chris Martin, Marty Gross, Carrie Teahen, Alix Edwards, Evi Harmon, Polly Parrent, Virginia Flores, Sydney Hoyle, Kristy DiIanni, Nicole McCormick, Andy Lewis, Ashley Jennings, Lauren Andrews, Niki Villanueva, Sam Zuhlke, Travis Kraus, Chloe Angyal, Deanna Dano, Eiren Caffall, Kelly Clougher. To Becky Parks, friend and fact-checker extraordinaire. To my sixth grade forevers: Alicia Ambler and John Shean. To Lucie Laurian and Melissa Febos for unwavering support. To my public policy peers and mentors: Jennifer Ho, Ann Oliva, Shaun Donovan, Julián Castro, Margot Wallström, Sarah Hunter, Kevin Solarte, Todd Shenk, Zach Wahls, Farah Ahmad, Carlyn Reichel, Emily Cadik.

Thank you to my Lumbee family, who've served me endless amounts of food and love: JL, BB, LB, JL, MB, PB, LB, TB, VB, CL, WVL.

To my parents, Carl Schuettpelz and Dawn Lowry Schuettpelz, who never once balked at the idea of me "becoming a writer." To my brothers Eran and Jamie and their families, to my aunts and uncles and cousins. To my second parents, Jim and Michelle. To my bonus family: Rose, Rich, David, Phillip, and Sara.

To my beautiful Lumbee children, GCW and ORW. To my husband, Matt. The words on this page could never do justice to the love I have for you. To Pluto and back.

Notes

Introduction

1. Andrew Van Dam, "The Native American Population Exploded, the Census Shows. Here's Why," *Washington Post*, October 27, 2023, https://www.washingtonpost.com/business/2023/10/27/native-americans-2020-census; Nicole Chavez and Harmeet Kaur, "Why the Jump in the Native American Population May Be One of the Hardest to Explain," CNN, August 19, 2021, https://www.cnn.com/2021/08/19/us/census-native-americans-rise-population/index.html.

2. Nicholas A. Jones and Amy Symens Smith, "The Two or More Races Population: 2000," Report Number C2KBR/01-6, Census 2000 Brief, November 2001, https://www.census.gov/library/publications/2001/dec/c2kbr01-06.html.

3. Mike Schneider, "Some Minority Groups Missed at Higher Rate in 2020 US Census," Associated Press, March 11, 2022, https://apnews.com/article/us-census-bureau-hispanics-census-2020-d284cdbe32fd9ad1a1ad3794cd4d0362.

4. Nesreen Khashan, "Tribes Form Complete Count Committees to Promote Census Participation," U.S. Census Bureau, June 25, 2019, https://www.census.gov/library/stories/2019/06/complete-2020-census-count-vital-for-tribal-areas.html.

5. As of 2024, the U.S. Bureau of Indian Affairs estimates there to be "approximately 1.9 million" members of federally recognized Tribes in the United States. It is difficult to put that number in direct conversation with the 9.7 million people checking the Indian box, because the 9.7 million count includes people who self-identify as having indigenous roots outside the United States (Aztec heritage from Mexico, for example).

6. "Osiyo!" Cherokee Nation website, https://www.cherokee.org.

7. Eastern Band of Cherokee Indians, *Comprehensive Economic Development Strategy 2018–2022*, Department of Commerce, June 2018, https://ebci.com/wp-content/uploads/2018/05/2018-CEDS-Document-For-Public-Comment.pdf.

8. "'Ani-gi-du-wa-gi' Is Our Original Name," The United Keetoowah Band of Cherokee Indians in Oklahoma, n.d., https://www.ukb-nsn.gov/about-us.

9. The U.S. Census tabulated a total of seventeen different Cherokee categories in 2020, including seven state-recognized Cherokee Tribes. A total of 16,429 tabulated responses of "Cherokee" were not part of the four categories I specifically named. Their inclusion would not change the overarching statistics. I have chosen not to include them because, for the purposes of my research, I have limited the scope to federally recognized Tribes.

10. Circe Sturm, *Becoming Indian: The Struggle over Cherokee Identity in the Twenty-First Century*, 1st ed. (Santa Fe, N.M.: SAR Press, 2011), muse.jhu.edu/book/82409.

11. Other instances of notable differences between the number of people who self-identified in the 2020 U.S. Census and the Tribe's enrolled population (in parentheses): Blackfeet, 297,899 (17,321); Navajo, 423,412 (399,494); Muscogee Creek, 121,581 (100,766); Chickasaw, 85,511 (73,000).

12. *See especially* Joel W. Martin, "My Grandmother Was a Cherokee Princess": Representations of Indians in Southern History," in S. Elizabeth Bird, ed., *Dressing in Feathers: The Construction of the Indian in American Popular Culture* (Boulder, Colo.: Westview Press, 1996).

13. I will refer to the Lumbee Tribe of North Carolina as "the Lumbee Tribe" for the remainder of the book.

14. The comedian Mel Brooks is often quoted as having said that "Humor is just another defense against the universe."

Chapter 1: Membership

1. David E. Wilkins and K. Tsianina Lomawaima, *Uneven Grounds: American Indian Sovereignty and Federal Law* (Norman: University of Oklahoma Press, 2001).

2. Bureau of Indian Affairs, "Frequently Asked Questions," U.S. Department of Interior, n.d., https://www.bia.gov/frequently-asked-questions.

3. Terri Hansen, "How the Iroquois Great Law of Peace Shaped U.S. Democracy," Native America, n.d., PBS, https://www.pbs.org/native-america/blog/how-the-iroquois-great-law-of-peace-shaped-us-democracy.

4. Jennifer Davis, "The Haudenosaunee Confederacy and the Constitution," *In Custodia Legis*, Library of Congress Blogs, September 21, 2023, https://blogs.loc.gov/law/2023/09/the-haudenosaunee-confederacy-and-the-constitution/.

5. Bureau of Indian Affairs, "Frequently Asked Questions."

6. Registration Form, NPS Form 10–900, National Register of Historic Places National Park Service, October 1990, PDF, https://files.nc.gov/ncdcr/nr/RB0479.pdf.

7. Maggie Walter and Michele Suina, "Indigenous Data, Indigenous Methodologies and Indigenous Data Sovereignty," *International Journal of Social Research Methodology* 22, No. 3 (2019): 233–43.

8. Susan Shain, "The Unapologetic 'Auntie' of Indigenous Data," *New York Times*, December 12, 2023, https://www.nytimes.com/2023/12/12/health/indigenous-data-abigail-echo-hawk.html.

9. *See especially* Walt Wolfram and Clare Dannenberg, "Dialect Identity in a Tri-ethnic Context: The Case of Lumbee American Indian English," *English World-Wide* 20, No. 2 (1999): 179–216.

10. Thanks to Professor Kirsty Gover, who provided us with her constitution research to cross-reference our own. Her research was compiled for her by Cate Read (trial division researcher, Supreme Court of Victoria) on behalf of the Melbourne Law School Academic Research Service.

11. I have not included in this number Tribes that operate under a code of laws or regulations, only those that have passed a document officially called a constitution.

12. Kiowa Indian Tribe of Oklahoma and U.S. Office of Indian Affairs, Amendment A (New Constitution), Kiowa Tribe of Oklahoma, ratified April 17, 2017, PDF, https://www.kiowatribe.org/sites/default/files/inline-files/Kiowa%20 Tribe%20Constitution%20April%2017%202017.pdf.

13. Choctaw Nation of Oklahoma, Constitution of the Choctaw Nation of Oklahoma, ratified July 25, 1983, PDF, https://www.choctawnation.com/wp -content/uploads/2022/03/constitution.pdf.

14. Of the Tribes for which we do not believe a constitution exists, 66 percent have enrolled populations estimated to be under one thousand people.

15. Lawrence C. Kelly, "The Indian Reorganization Act: The Dream and the Reality," *Pacific Historical Review* 44, No. 3 (1975): 291–312, doi:10.2307/3638029.

16. Kelly, "The Indian Reorganization Act."

17. Daniel Kraker, "Navajo Seeks Support for Tribal Constitution," *Day to Day*, NPR, December 20, 2007, https://www.npr.org/2007/12/20/17452654/navajo -seeks-support-for-tribal-constitution.

18. Diné Policy Institute, *Navajo Nation Constitutional Feasibility and Government Reform Project*, Diné Policy Institute, October 20, 2008, PDF, https://www .dinecollege.edu/wp-content/uploads/2020/10/dpiStudyReport.pdf.

19. "Navajo Nation Code," Navajo Nation Office of Legislative Services, n.d., https:// www.nnols.org/navajo-nation-code/.

20. Kirsty Gover, *Tribal Constitutionalism: States, Tribes, and the Governance of Membership* (Oxford; New York: Oxford University Press, 2010).

21. Oneida Nation, Constitution and By-Laws of the Oneida Nation, Amended, ratified June 16, 2015, https://oneida-nsn.gov/wp-content/uploads/2018/05 /2015-06-16-Tribal-Constitution.pdf.

22. Bureau of Indian Affairs. "Tracing American Indian and Alaska Native Ancestry," U.S. Department of the Interior, https://www.bia.gov/guide/tracing -american-indian-and-alaska-native-aian-ancestry.

23. Congressional Budget Office, *The Foreign-Born Population, the U.S. Economy, and the Federal Budget*, Congressional Budget Office, April 5, 2023, https:// www.cbo.gov/publication/58939.

24. U.S. Global Legal Research Directorate, Issuing Body, *Birthright Citizenship Around the World* (Washington, D.C.: The Law Library of Congress, Global Legal Research Directorate, 2018), PDF, https://www.loc.gov/item /2018655070/.

25. Gover, *Tribal Constitutionalism*.

Chapter 2: Belonging

1. Alan Menken and Stephen Laurence Schwartz, "Colors of the Wind," Genius, n.d., https://genius.com/Vanessa-williams-colors-of-the-wind-lyrics.

2. "Native American Agriculture," (online) Encyclopedia of the Great Plains, ed. David J. Wishart, http://plainshumanities.unl.edu/encyclopedia/doc/egp.ag.052.

3. André Le Dressay, Normand Lavallee, and Jason Reeves, "First Nations Trade, Specialization, and Market Institutions: A Historical Survey of First Nation

Market Culture," Aboriginal Policy Research Consortium International (APRCi), 72 (2010), https://ir.lib.uwo.ca/cgi/viewcontent.cgi?article=1372&context=aprci.

4. Le Dressay, Lavallee, and Reeves, "First Nations Trade, Specialization, and Market Institutions."

5. Phillip Drucker, "The Northern and Central Nootkan Tribes," *Smithsonian Institute Bureau of American Ethnology Bulletin* 144 (1951): 248.

6. Francis Haines, *The Nez Percés: Tribesmen of the Columbia Plateau*, 1st ed. (Norman: University of Oklahoma Press, 1955), p. 15.

7. Haines, *The Nez Percés*, p. 15.

8. Haines, *The Nez Percés*, pp. 15–16.

9. Jeff Zucker, Kay Hummel, and Bob Hogfoss, *Oregon Indians: Culture, History and Current Affairs, an Atlas and Introduction* (Portland, Ore.: Western Imprints, the Press of the Oregon Historical Society, 1983).

10. Gregory D. Smithers, *Reclaiming Two-Spirits: Sexuality, Spiritual Renewal and Sovereignty in Native America* (Boston: Beacon Press, 2022).

11. Garrick Alan Bailey, ed., *Traditions of the Osage: Stories Collected and Translated by Francis La Flesche* (Albuquerque: University of New Mexico Press, 2010), p. 16.

12. Earl Boyd Pierce and Rennard Strickland, *The Cherokee People*, Indian Tribal Series (Phoenix, Ariz.: Indian Tribal Series, 1973), pp. 13–14.

13. W. David Baird, *The Choctaw People*, Indian Tribal Series (Phoenix, Ariz.: Indian Tribal Series, 1973), p. 6.

14. Harry C. James, *The Hopi Indians: Their History and Their Culture* (Caldwell, Ida.: Caxton, 1956), p. 39.

15. James, *The Hopi Indians*, p. 40.

16. Baird, *The Choctaw People*, p. 6.

17. Donna Akers, "Social Customs, Gender Roles, Family Life and Children," in *Culture and Customs of the Choctaw Indians* (New York: Greenwood/Bloomsbury, 2013), chap. 4, https://www.bloomsbury.com/us/culture-and-customs-of-the-choctaw-indians-9780313364013/.

18. Brent Richards Weisman, *Unconquered People: Florida's Seminole and Miccosukee Indians* (Gainesville: University Press of Florida, 1999), p. 30.

19. Anthony F. C. Wallace and Sheila C. Steen, *The Death and Rebirth of the Seneca* (New York: Alfred A. Knopf, 1970), pp. 22–23.

20. Office of Minority Health, "Diabetes and American Indians/Alaska Natives," U.S. Department of Health and Human Services, n.d., https://minorityhealth.hhs.gov/diabetes-and-american-indiansalaska-natives.

21. "National Museum of the American Indian," Smithsonian Institution Archives, n.d., https://siarchives.si.edu/history/national-museum-american-indian.

22. "The Meskwaki Nation's History," The Meskwaki Nation, n.d., https://www.meskwaki.org/history/.

23. Eric Steven Zimmer, "Settlement Sovereignty: The Meskwaki Fight for Self-Governance, 1856–1937," *The Annals of Iowa* 73, No. 4 (2014).

24. Zimmer, "Settlement Sovereignty."

25. Cris Barrish, "Joining Forces to Restore Ancestral Lands to Nanticoke and Lenape Tribes," WHYY, PBS, December 6, 2021, https://whyy.org/articles/joining-forces-to-restore-ancestral-lands-to-nanticoke-and-lenape-tribes/.

26. See especially Nick Estes, Melanie Yazzie, Jennifer Nez Denetdale, and David Correia, *Red Nation Rising: From Bordertown Violence to Native Liberation* (Oakland, Calif.: PM Press, 2021).

27. Elise Hansen, "The Forgotten Minority in Police Shootings," CNN, November 13, 2017, https://www.cnn.com/2017/11/10/us/native-lives-matter/index.html.

28. Vimal Patel, "Hotelier's Post Barring Native Americans Prompts Outrage in South Dakota," *New York Times*, March 26, 2022, https://www.nytimes.com/2022/03/26/us/grand-gateway-hotel-native-americans.html.

29. Dan O'Brien, *Wild Idea: Buffalo and Family in a Difficult Land* (Lincoln, Neb.: Bison Books, 2014), p. 74.

30. André B. Rosay, "Violence Against American Indian and Alaska Native Women and Men," *NIJ Journal* 277 (2016), PDF, https://www.ojp.gov/pdffiles1/nij/249822.pdf.

31. Rosay, "Violence Against American Indian and Alaska Native Women and Men."

32. M. A. Jaimes Guerrero, "'Patriarchal Colonialism' and Indigenism: Implications for Native Feminist Spirituality and Native Womanism," *Hypatia* 18, No. 2 (2003): 58–69, http://www.jstor.org/stable/3811011.

33. *See especially* Roe Bubar and Pamela Jumper Thurman. "Violence Against Native Women," *Social Justice* 31, No. 4 (98) (2004): 70–86, http://www.jstor.org/stable/29768276; Emma LaRocque, "The Colonization of a Native Woman Scholar," *Women of the First Nations: Power, Wisdom, and Strength* 9, No. 11 (1996): 12–18.

34. National Museum of the American Indian, "Celebrating Native Cultures Through Words: Storytelling and Oral Traditions," https://americanindian.si.edu/nk360/informational/storytelling-and-oral-traditions.

35. Ronald J. Mason, "Archaeology and Native North American Oral Traditions," *American Antiquity* 65, No. 2 (2000): 239–66, https://doi.org/10.2307/2694058.

36. Becky Morgan, "American Indian Veterans Have Highest Record of Military Service," National Indian Council on Aging, November 8, 2019, https://www.nicoa.org/american-indian-veterans-have-highest-record-of-military-service/.

Chapter 3: Counting

1. U.S. Constitution, Art. I, Sec. 2.

2. Samantha Payne, "Congress Counts: History of the U.S. Census," Pieces of History, U.S. National Archives, March 1, 2015, https://prologue.blogs.archives.gov/2015/03/01/congress-counts-history-of-the-us-census/.

3. Judge John Marshall and Supreme Court of the United States, "U.S. Reports: Worcester v. the State of Georgia, 31 U.S. (6 Pet.) 515 (1832)," https://www.loc.gov/item/usrep031515/.

4. An Act Providing for the Enumeration of the Inhabitants of the United States, Mar. 1, 1790, U.S. Statutes at Large, chap. 2, 11 Stat.
5. An Act Providing for the Enumeration of the Inhabitants of the United States, Mar. 1, 1790.
6. "Value of $200 from 1790 to 2023," CPI Inflation Calculator, accessed March 11, 2024, https://www.officialdata.org/us/inflation/1790?endYear=2023&amount=200.
7. "United States Marshals and Their Deputies: 1789–1989," U.S. Marshals Service, https://www.usmarshals.gov/who-we-are/history/historical-reading-room/lawmen-united-states-marshals-and-their-deputies-1789-1989.
8. "United States Marshals and Their Deputies: 1789–1989."
9. An Act Providing for the Enumeration of the Inhabitants of the United States, Mar. 1, 1790.
10. A big thanks to Rose Buchanan for graciously allowing me to build off her work with my own archival research. Her original article is Rose Buchanan, "Stand Up and Be Counted: Native Americans in the Federal Census," U.S. National Archives, April 21, 2022, https://www.archives.gov/news/articles/native-americans-census.
11. Heriberto Dixon and Laurence M. Hauptman, "From West Point to Wahoo Swamp: The Career of Cadet David Moniac, Class of 1822," *American Indian: Magazine of Smithsonian's National Museum of the American Indian* 17, No. 4 (Spring 2016), https://www.americanindianmagazine.org/story/west-point-wahoo-swamp-career-cadet-david-moniac-class-1822.
12. James P. Pate, "LeFlore, Greenwood (1800–1865)," (online) Encyclopedia of Oklahoma History and Culture, Oklahoma Historical Society, n.d., https://www.okhistory.org/publications/enc/entry.php?entry=LE008.
13. Kathryn E. Holland Braund, "Guardians of Tradition and Handmaidens to Change: Women's Roles in Creek Economic and Social Life During the Eighteenth Century," *American Indian Quarterly* 14, No. 3 (1990): 239–58, https://doi.org/10.2307/1185653; "Chiefs, Clans & Kin Exhibit," Choctaw Cultural Center, n.d., https://choctawculturalcenter.com/chiefs-clans-and-kin/.
14. "Milestones and Moments in Global Census History," Projects PACE: Policy, Advocacy, and Communication Enhanced for Population and Reproductive Health, https://www.prb.org/resources/milestones-and-moments-in-global-census-history/.
15. "Milestones and Moments in Global Census History."
16. Robert R. Cargill, *The Cities That Built the Bible*, 1st ed. (New York: HarperOne, an imprint of HarperCollins Publishers, 2016), p. 230.
17. "Milestones and Moments in Global Census History."
18. Thomas Allsen, "Mongol Census Taking in Rus', 1245–1275," *Harvard Ukrainian Studies* 5, No. 1 (1981): 32–53, http://www.jstor.org/stable/41035891.
19. Jean Johnson, "The Mongol Dynasty: When Kublai Khan Ruled China," Asia Society, n.d., https://asiasociety.org/education/mongol-dynasty.

20. Jane Ferguson, "Who's Counting? Ethnicity, Belonging, and the National Census in Burma/Myanmar," *Brill* 171, No. 1 (2015): 2.

21. Ferguson, "Who's Counting?"

22. Charles Hirschman, "The Meaning and Measurement of Ethnicity in Malaysia: An Analysis of Census Classifications," *The Journal of Asian Studies* 46, No. 3 (August 1987).

23. Benedict Anderson, *Imagined Communities: Reflections on the Origin and Spread of Nationalism*, rev. ed. (New York: Verso, 2006), p. 166.

24. "1850 Census Instructions to Enumerators," U.S. Census Bureau, last revised October 8, 2021, https://www.census.gov/programs-surveys/decennial-census/technical-documentation/questionnaires/1850/1850-instructions.html.

25. "1870 Census Instructions to Enumerators," U.S. Census Bureau, last revised October 8, 2021, https://www.census.gov/programs-surveys/decennial-census/technical-documentation/questionnaires/1870/1870-instructions.html.

26. Andrés Reséndez, *The Other Slavery: The Uncovered Story of Indian Enslavement in America* (Boston: Houghton Mifflin Harcourt, 2016).

27. "1880 Census Instructions to Enumerators," U.S. Census Bureau, last revised October 8, 2021, https://www.census.gov/programs-surveys/decennial-census/technical-documentation/questionnaires/1880/1880-instructions.html.

28. "Department of Interior, Census Office, May 1, 1880," U.S. Census Bureau, n.d., PDF, https://www.census.gov/history/pdf/1880enumerator-instructions.pdf.

29. "Department of Interior, Census Office, May 1, 1880."

30. "Unusual Golden Wedding Anniversary," *The Robesonian*, September 11, 1916, https://www.newspapers.com/article/the-robesonian-duncan-buie-daniel-buie-t/5397927/.

31. Malinda Maynor Lowery, *Lumbee Indians in the Jim Crow South: Race, Identity, and the Making of a Nation* (Chapel Hill: University of North Carolina Press, 2010), http://www.jstor.org/stable/10.5149/9780807898284_lowery.

32. "1900 Census Instructions to Enumerators," U.S. Census Bureau, last revised October 8, 2021, https://www.census.gov/programs-surveys/decennial-census/technical-documentation/questionnaires/1900/1900-instructions.html.

33. Wyandotte Nation, Constitution of the Wyandotte Tribe of Oklahoma, ratified September 29, 1999, PDF, https://wyandotte-nation.org/wp-content/uploads/2021/12/Constitution.pdf.

34. Becky Little, "The Most Controversial Census Changes in American History," History.com, updated May 23, 2023, https://www.history.com/news/census-changes-controversy-citizenship.

35. Melissa Nobles, *Shades of Citizenship: Race and the Census in Modern Politics* (Stanford, Calif.: Stanford University Press, 2000).

36. Josiah Clark Nott, "Two Lectures on the Natural History of the Caucasian and Negro Races" (Mobile, Ala.: Dade and Thompson, 1844), p. 35, from Reginald Horsman, "Scientific Racism and the American Indian in the Mid-Nineteenth Century," *American Quarterly* 27, No. 2 (May 1975): 152–68.

37. Robert J. Miller, "Nazi Germany's Race Laws, the United States, and American Indians," *St. John's Law Review* 94, No. 3 (2021): 751.

38. Miller, "Nazi Germany's Race Laws, the United States, and American Indians," p. 767.

39. Edwin Black, *IBM and the Holocaust: The Strategic Alliance Between Nazi Germany and America's Most Powerful Corporation*, 1st ed. (New York: Crown, 2001), p. 58.

40. Black, *IBM and the Holocaust*, p. 58.

41. Black, *IBM and the Holocaust*.

42. Black, *IBM and the Holocaust*, p. 26.

43. Black, *IBM and the Holocaust*, p. 21.

44. Black, *IBM and the Holocaust*, p. 21.

Chapter 4: Payment

1. David R. Wrone, "Indian Treaties and the Democratic Idea," *Wisconsin Magazine of History* 70 (Winter 1986).

2. Peter Nabokov, *Native American Testimony: A Chronicle of Indian-White Relations from Prophecy to the Present, 1492–2000* (New York: Penguin Books, 1999), p. 118.

3. Wrone, "Indian Treaties and the Democratic Idea."

4. Wrone, "Indian Treaties and the Democratic Idea."

5. Wrone, "Indian Treaties and the Democratic Idea."

6. Wrone, "Indian Treaties and the Democratic Idea."

7. Ryan P. Smith, "Why the Very First Treaty Between the United States and a Native People Still Resonates Today," *Smithsonian Magazine*, May 24, 2018.

8. Margaret Ball, "1778 Treaty of Fort Pitt: U.S. Treaty-Making with the Lenape Nation," National Museum of American Diplomacy, July 29, 2022, https://diplomacy.state.gov/stories/treaty-of-fort-pitt/.

9. C. A. Weslager, *The Delaware Indians: A History* (New Brunswick, N.J.: Rutgers University Press, 1972), pp. 304–6.

10. Smith, "Why the Very First Treaty Between the United States and a Native People Still Resonates Today."

11. A. G. Roeber and Max Kade, *Ethnographies and Exchanges: Native Americans, Moravians, and Catholics in Early North America* (University Park: Pennsylvania State University Press, 2008), p. 34.

12. Ned Blackhawk, *The Rediscovery of America: Native Peoples and the Unmaking of U.S. History* (New Haven, Conn.: Yale University Press, 2023), p. 339.

13. Sammy Matsaw, Dylan Hedden-Nicely, and Barbara Cosens, "Cultural Linguistics and Treaty Language: Modernized Approach to Interpreting Treaty Language to Capture the Tribe's Understanding," *Environmental Law* 50, No. 2 (2020): 415–46, https://www.jstor.org/stable/26939864.

14. U.S. Bureau of Statistics, "Farm Prices in Two Centuries," U.S Department of Agriculture, Washington, D.C., 1892, p. 332, https://hdl.handle.net/2027/mdp.39015035798035.

15. Black Hawk (Sauk chief), *Life of Ma-ka-tai-me-she-kia-kiak, or Black Hawk*, ed. John Barton Patterson (Boston: Russell, Odiorne and Metcalf, 1834), digitized October 31, 2007.

16. Nabokov, *Native American Testimony*, p. 120.

17. Treaty with the Creeks, 1790, n.d., https://treaties.okstate.edu/treaties/treaty -with-the-creeks-1796-0046. The description of the land's location is my own, based on information from Native Land Digital, https://native-land.ca/maps /treaties/cession-7/.

18. Matsaw, Hedden-Nicely, and Cosens, "Cultural Linguistics and Treaty Language."

19. "From George Washington to the United States Senate, 23 March 1792," Founders Online, National Archives, https://founders.archives.gov/documents /Washington/05-10-02-0090; original source: *The Papers of George Washington*, Presidential Series, vol. 10: *1 March 1792–15 August 1792*, ed. Robert F. Haggard and Mark A. Mastromarino (Charlottesville: University of Virginia Press, 2002), pp. 151–52.

20. "Treaty with the Wyandot, etc., 1805," Tribal Treaties Database, n.d., https: //treaties.okstate.edu/treaties/treaty-with-the-wyandot-etc-1805-0077; William Barrow, "Western Reserve," (online) Encyclopedia of Cleveland History, Case Western University, n.d., https://case.edu/ech/articles/w/western-reserve.

21. "Treaty with the Quapaw, 1818," Tribal Treaties Database, n.d., https://treaties .okstate.edu/treaties/treaty-with-the-quapaw-1818-0160; "Quapaw Treaty, 1824 November 15," Arkansas Digital Archives, n.d., https://digitalheritage.arkansas .gov/quapaw-treaty/.

22. "Treaty with the Chippewa, 1819," Tribal Treaties Database, n.d., John Fierst, "The 1819 Treaty of Saginaw," Central Michigan University, November 26, 2019, https://blogs.cmich.edu/library/2019/11/26/the-1819-treaty-of-saginaw/.

23. Norman B. Wilkinson, "Robert Morris and the Treaty of Big Tree," *The Mississippi Valley Historical Review* 40, No. 2 (1953): 276, https://doi.org/10.2307 /1888927.

24. U.S. Congress, House, Committee on Indian Affairs, Regulating the Indian Department (to Accompany Bills H.R. Nos. 488 489, & 490), 23rd Cong., 1st Sess., 1834, H. Rep. 474, 9, https://www.govinfo.gov/app/details/SERIALSET -00263_00_00-029-0474-0000.

25. There are many records in the U.S. Archives that testify to this fact. *See especially*, "Records of Treaties 1851–1860—Ledger," United States Archives, RG 75, NAID: 245236229, https://catalog.archives.gov/id/245236229.

26. U.S. Congress, House, Committee on Indian Affairs, "Regulating the Indian Department" (to Accompany Bills H.R. Nos. 488 489, & 490).

27. U.S. Congress, House, Committee on Indian Affairs, "Regulating the Indian Department" (to Accompany Bills H.R. Nos. 488 489, & 490).

28. U.S. Congress, House, Committee on Indian Affairs, "Regulating the Indian Department" (to Accompany Bills H.R. Nos. 488 489, & 490.

29. U.S. Congress, Senate, To Amend an Act Titled, "An Act to Provide for the

Better Organization of the Department of Indian Affairs" and an Act Titled "An Act to Regulate Trade and Intercourse with the Indian Tribes, and to Preserve Peace on the Frontiers" Act of 1847, HR 649, 29th Cong., 2d Sess., introduced in Senate February 26, 1847, https://www.congress.gov/bill/29th-congress /house-bill/649/text?s=1&r=42.

30. "American Indian Annuity Rolls," FamilySearch, last updated December 8, 2022, https://www.familysearch.org/en/wiki/American_Indian_Annuity_Rolls.

31. "Treaty with the Creeks, 1832," Opened for signature March 24, 1832. Tribal Treaties Database, https://treaties.okstate.edu/treaties/treaty-with-the-creeks -1833-0388.

32. "Treaty with the Creeks, 1832."

33. Ocmulgee Mounds NHP, "Ocmulgee Mounds: Muscogee (Creek) Removal," National Park Service, U.S. Department of Interior, n.d., PDF, https://www.nps .gov/ocmu/learn/historyculture/upload/Accessible-Muscogee-Creek-Removal .pdf.

34. Roberta Estes, "Parsons and Abbott Roll—1832 Creek Census," Native Heritage Project, July 14, 2014, https://nativeheritageproject.com/2014/07/14 /parsons-and-abbott-roll-1832-creek-census/.

35. Christopher D. Haveman, "The Removal of the Creek Indians from the Southeast, 1825–1838" (PhD diss., Auburn University, 2009), p. 147. Referencing 1832 Census of Creek Indians Taken by Parsons and Abbott, RG-75, M-275, reel-1, 113–196, NA and John J. Abert to Lewis Cass, 15 October 1834, RG-75, Letters Received by the OIA, Creek Agency Reserves, M-234, reel-241, 465–476, NA.

36. Larry S. Watson, Senate Document #512, 23rd Cong., 1st Sess., Volume IV, Part 2, p. 24 (Yuma, Ariz.: Histree, 2007), https://books.google.com/books?id =0PKdIeHu0U8C&pg.

37. Quoted in Watson, Senate Document #512.

38. U.S. Congress, Senate, Emigration of Indians Between the 30th of November 1831 and December 27th 1833 with Abstracts of Expenditures by Disbursing Agents, in the Removal and Subsistence of Indians, Furnished in Answer to a Resolution of the Senate of 27th December 1832 by Commissary General of Subsistence, 23rd Cong., 1st Sess., 1833, S. Doc. 512, No. 245. 851, https: //memory.loc.gov/cgi-bin/ampage?collId=llss&fileName=0200/0245/llss0245 .db&recNum=0.

39. U.S. Congress, Senate, "Emigration of Indians Between the 30th of November 1831 and December 27th 1833."

40. U.S. Congress, Senate, "Emigration of Indians Between the 30th of November 1831 and December 27th 1833."

41. Haveman, "The Removal of the Creek Indians from the Southeast, 1825–1838," p. 151.

42. Christopher D. Haveman, *Rivers of Sand: Creek Indian Emigration, Relocation, and Ethnic Cleansing in the American South* (Lincoln: University of Nebraska Press, 2016).

43. Kristin T. Ruppel, *Unearthing Indian Land: Living with the Legacies of Allotment* (Tucson: University of Arizona Press, 2008).

44. David Wilkins, interview by author, January 21, 2024.

45. UN Human Rights Experts, "USA: Evictions of Indigenous Nooksack Must Stop," press release, OHCHR, February 3, 2022, https://www.ohchr.org/en /press-releases/2022/02/usa-evictions-indigenous-nooksack-must-stop-un -experts.

46. Mike Baker, "A Tribe's Bitter Purge Brings an Unusual Request: Federal Inter- vention," *New York Times*, January 2, 2022, https://www.nytimes.com/2022/01 /02/us/nooksack-306-evictions-tribal-sovereignty.html?searchResultPosition=1.

47. Baker, "A Tribe's Bitter Purge Brings an Unusual Request."

48. David E. Wilkins and Shelly Hulse Wilkins, *Dismembered: Native Disenrollment and the Battle for Human Rights* (Seattle: University of Washington Press, 2017), p. 150.

49. Wilkins and Wilkins, *Dismembered*, p. 67.

50. Author's own analysis, based on National Indian Gaming Commission's December 2023 Gaming Tribe Report, https://www.nigc.gov/images/uploads /12182023_TribesbyABCOrder.pdf.

51. Author's own analysis, based on National Indian Gaming Commission's Decem- ber 2023 Gaming Tribe Report, accessed March 11, 2024. https://www.nigc .gov/images/uploads/12182023_TribesbyABCOrder.pdf.

52. "Indian Gaming Regulatory Act," National Indian Gaming Commission, https: //www.nigc.gov/general-counsel/indian-gaming-regulatory-act.

53. Dan Haar, "Making Sense of Foxwoods' Casino Upgrade Amid Flat Gambling Revenue," *CT Insider*, August 31, 2023, https://www.ctinsider.com/columnist /article/foxwoods-upgrade-gambling-expansion-18339378.php.

54. Robert J. Miller, *Reservation Capitalism* (Lincoln, Neb.: Bison Books, 2013), p. 84.

55. "The Commission: FAQs," National Indian Gaming Commission, https://www .nigc.gov/commission/faqs.

56. Laurel Wheeler, "More than Chance: The Local Labor Market Effects of Tribal Gaming," Center for Indian Country Development, Federal Reserve Bank of Minneapolis, March 2023, https://www.minneapolisfed.org/research/cicd -working-paper-series/more-than-chance-the-local-labor-market-effects-of-tribal -gaming.

57. Ana Radelat, "When It Comes to American Indian Gaming, Some, but Not All, Tribes Come Up Big Winners," *MinnPost*, August 29, 2023, https://www .minnpost.com/economy/2023/08/when-there-comes-to-american-indian -gaming-some-but-not-all-Tribes-come-up-big-winners/.

58. A. Malinovskaya, "Per Capita Distribution of Gaming Revenues and Gaming Compact First BIA Approval Dates," Per caps dataset, 2020, https://sites.google .com/cornell.edu/datarepository-nativeamericans/per-caps, as cited by Adam Crepelle, Paasha Mahdavi, and Dominic Parker, "Effects of Per Capita Payments on Governance: Evidence from Tribal Casinos," *Public Choice* (2022): 1–22, doi:10.1007/s11127-022-01012-1.

59. Mavis Harris, "FY 2022 Indian Gaming Revenue Breaks Records at $40.9 Billion," National Indian Gaming Commission, July 2019, https://www.nigc.gov /news/detail/fy-2022-indian-gaming-revenue-breaks-records-at-40.9-billion.

60. Bill Donovan, "50 Years Ago: Navajo Rejects Idea of Per-Capita Payments," *Navajo Times*, May 28, 2015, https://navajotimes.com/50years/50-years-ago -navajo-rejects-idea-of-per-capita-payments/.

61. ICT Staff, "Disenrollments Boost Pechanga Per Capita Monthly Payments to $30K," News, ICT, September 12, 2018, https://ictnews.org/archive /disenrollments-boost-pechanga-per-capita-monthly-payments-to-30k.

62. ICT Staff, "Disenrollments Boost Pechanga Per Capita Monthly Payments to $30K."

63. Marc Cooper, "Tribal Flush: Pechanga People 'Disenrolled' en Masse," *LA Weekly*, January 2, 2008, https://www.laweekly.com/Tribal-flush-pechanga -people-disenrolled-en-masse/.

64. Cooper, "Tribal Flush."

Chapter 5: Remove

1. Office of the Historian, "Milestones: 1830–1860—Indian Treaties and the Removal Act of 1830," https://history.state.gov/milestones/1830-1860/indian -treaties.

2. President Jackson's Message to Congress "On Indian Removal," December 6, 1830, Record Group 46, Records of the United States Senate, 1789–1990, National Archives and Records Administration.

3. "Indian Removal, 1814–1858," People and Events, PBS, https://www.pbs.org /wgbh/aia/part4/4p2959.html.

4. Office of the Historian, "Milestones: 1830–1860—Indian Treaties and the Removal Act of 1830."

5. President Jackson's Message to Congress "On Indian Removal."

6. Daniel F. Littlefield and James W. Parins, eds., *Encyclopedia of American Indian Removal* (Santa Barbara, Calif.: Greenwood, 2011).

7. History.com editors, "Trail of Tears," History.com, September 26, 2023, https: //www.history.com/topics/native-american-history/trail-of-tears.

8. History.com editors, "Trail of Tears."

9. John Ehle, *Trail of Tears: The Rise and Fall of the Cherokee Nation* (New York City: Anchor Books, 2011), p. 392.

10. Nicky Michael and Beverly Jean Smith, "Reclaiming Social Justice and Human Rights: The 1830 Indian Removal Act and the Ethnic Cleansing of Native American Tribes," *Journal of Health and Human Experience* 7, No. 1 (Spring 2021): 125.

11. *See especially* Patrick Minges, "Beneath the Underdog: Race, Religion, and the Trail of Tears," *American Indian Quarterly* 25, No. 3 (2001): 453–79.

12. *See especially* "Indian Removal Muster Rolls," National Archives Catalog, Record Group 75, NAID: 231930716, https://catalog.archives.gov/id/231930716.

13. "Annual Report of the Commissioner of Indian Affairs, for the Years 1826–

1839 [1826–1839]," University of Wisconsin Libraries, p. 152, https://digital
.library.wisc.edu/1711.dl/3YVW4ZRARQT7J8S.

14. "Indian Removal Muster Rolls."

15. This quote has been widely (and inaccurately) attributed to Zora Neale Hurston. It was first published in: Walker, Alice. *Possessing the Secret of Joy.* Vol. 3. Open Road Media, 2011.

16. "History of White Earth," White Earth Nation, n.d., https://whiteearth.com /history.

17. Calvin Bartholomew et al., "The Brotherton Indians of New Jersey, 1780," The Gilder Lehrman Institute of American History, History Resources, https: //www.gilderlehrman.org/history-resources/spotlight-primary-source/brotherton -indians-new-jersey-1780.

18. Bartholomew et al., "The Brotherton Indians of New Jersey, 1780."

19. Bartholomew et al., "The Brotherton Indians of New Jersey, 1780."

20. "Tribal Property Interests in Executive-Order Reservations: A Compensable Indian Right Source," *The Yale Law Journal* 69, No. 4 (March 1960): 627–42.

21. *See especially* Ronald Spores, "Too Small a Place: The Removal of the Willamette Valley Indians, 1850–1856," *American Indian Quarterly* 17, No. 2 (1993): 171–91, https://doi.org/10.2307/1185526.

22. "The U.S. Congress Passes the Indian Removal Act," National Library of Medicine's Native Voices Timeline, https://www.nlm.nih.gov/nativevoices/timeline /317.html.

23. *See especially* Brian Howard and Traci Morris, *Tribal Technology Assessment: The State of Internet Service on Tribal Lands*, ASU American Indian Policy Institute, Fall 2019, PDF, https://aipi.asu.edu/sites/default/files/tribal_tech_assessment _compressed.pdf.

24. Ana Hernández Kent and Lowell R. Ricketts, "The State of U.S. Wealth Inequality," Federal Reserve Bank of St. Louis, October 18, 2023, https://www .stlouisfed.org/institute-for-economic-equity/the-state-of-us-wealth-inequality.

25. Kent and Ricketts, "The State of U.S. Wealth Inequality."

26. Kent and Ricketts, "The State of U.S. Wealth Inequality."

27. National Association of Realtors Research Group, "Wealth Gains by Income and Racial/Ethnic Group," April 2023, PDF, https://cdn.nar.realtor//sites/ default/files/documents/2023-04-wealth-gains-by-income-and-racial-ethnic-group-04-18-2023.pdf.

28. *See especially* Richard Rothstein, *The Color of Law: A Forgotten History of How Our Government Segregated America*, 1st ed. (New York: Liveright Publishing Corporation, 2017).

29. Larry Rothman, "Analyzing 100 Years of Real Estate Price History in Manhattan," Elika Real Estate, October 18, 2020, https://www.elikarealestate.com/blog /tracing-buying-real-estate-new-york-past-100-years/.

30. *See especially* Claudio Saunt, *Unworthy Republic: The Dispossession of Native Americans and the Road to Indian Territory*, 1st ed. (New York: W. W. Norton, 2020). Note that the 1.5 billion is based primarily on a series of maps developed

by Claudio Saunt and others showing the patterns of land cessation by the U.S. government. Those maps can be found at https://usg.maps.arcgis.com/apps /webappviewer/index.html?id=eb6ca76e008543a89349ff2517db47e6.

31. *See especially* Vine Deloria Jr., *Behind the Trail of Broken Treaties: An Indian Declaration of Independence* (New York: Delacorte Press, 1974).

32. "Treaty with the Sauk and Foxes, 1804," Treaties Portal, Oklahoma State University, https://treaties.okstate.edu/treaties/treaty-with-the-sauk-and-foxes -1804-0074.

33. "Harrison Land Act 1800," Indiana Historical Bureau, https://www.in.gov /history/about-indiana-history-and-trivia/explore-indiana-history-by-topic /indiana-documents-leading-to-statehood/harrison-land-act-1800.

34. National Agricultural Statistics Service, "Land Values 2022 Summary," Department of Agriculture, August 2022, PDF, https://www.nass.usda.gov /Publications/Todays_Reports/reports/land0822.pdf.

35. "Indian Census Rolls, 1885–1940," U.S. National Archives and Records Administration, https://www.archives.gov/research/census/native-americans /1885-1940.html.

36. Historic Fort Snelling, "The US Indian Agency (1820–1853)," Historic Fort Snelling, https://www.mnhs.org/fortsnelling/learn/native-americans/us-indian -agency.

37. Historic Fort Snelling. "The US Indian Agency (1820–1853)."

38. Bryan Todd Newland and U.S. Bureau of Indian Affairs, issuing body, *Federal Indian Boarding School Initiative Investigative Report*, Office of the Secretary, U.S. Department of the Interior, Washington, D.C., May 2022.

39. Newland and U.S. Bureau of Indian Affairs, *Federal Indian Boarding School Initiative Investigative Report*.

40. Eric Margolis, "Looking at Discipline, Looking at Labour: Photographic Representations of Indian Boarding Schools," *Visual Studies* 19, No. 1 (2004): 72–96.

41. *See especially* Hilary A. Rose, "'I Didn't Get to Say Good-Bye . . . Didn't Get to Pet My Dogs or Nothing': Bioecological Theory and the Indian Residential School Experience in Canada," *Journal of Family Theory and Review* 10, No. 2 (2018): 348–66. Although written specifically about Canadian First Nations boarding schools, the experiences were often quite similar to those in the United States.

42. Act of July 1, 1898, Chap. 545, Sess. 1, 30 Stat. 571, 573.

43. Quoted in Newland, "*Federal Indian Boarding School Initiative Investigative Report.*"

44. "Cheyenne and Arapaho, 1928–1935," *M1011-Superintendent's Annual Narrative and Statistical Reports from Field Jurisdictions of the Bureau of Indian Affairs*, p. 994, National Archives Catalog, RG 75, NAID: 155862354, https://catalog .archives.gov/id/155862354?object.

45. "Indian Census Rolls, 1885–1940."

46. "Indian Census Rolls, 1885–1940."

47. "Indian Census Rolls, 1885–1940."

48. "Indian Census Rolls, 1885–1940."

49. Cherokee (North Carolina), 1930–1932, Indian Census Rolls, 1885–1941, Microfilm Publication M595, roll 25, pp. 5–128, Office of the Commissioner, Office of Indian Affairs, Records of the Department of the Interior, 1849–9/17/1947, Record Group 75, National Archives and Records Administration, NAID: 595276, National Archives Building, Washington, D.C.

50. Cherokee (North Carolina) 1930–1932.

51. Deloria Vine Jr., "Laws Founded in Justice and Humanity: Reflections on the Content and Character of Federal Indian Law," *Arizona Law Review* 31, No. 2 (1989): 203–24.

52. "Enrollment Office," Leech Lake Band of Ojibwe, n.d., https://www.llojibwe .org/admin/enrollment.html.

53. Nicole MartinRogers, Anna Granias, and Carolyn Liebler, "Red Lake Nation: Population Projects," Amherst H. Wilder Foundation, September 2022, https: //www.wilder.org/wilder-research/research-library/red-lake-nation-population -projections.

Interlude

1. "Declaration of Independence: A Transcription," America's Founding Documents, U.S. National Archives and Records Administration, n.d., https://www .archives.gov/founding-docs/declaration-transcript.

2. Tony Tekaroniake Evans, "Abraham Lincoln's Uneasy Relationship with Native Americans," History.com, updated July 12, 2023, https://www.history.com /news/abraham-lincoln-native-americans.

3. Alysa Landry, "Theodore Roosevelt: 'The Only Good Indians Are the Dead Indians,'" News, ICT, September 13, 2018, https://ictnews.org/archive/theodore -roosevelt-the-only-good-indians-are-the-dead-indians.

4. "George Washington Owned Slaves, Ordered Indians Killed. Will Mural of That History Be Hidden?" *Washington Post*, August 25, 2019, https://www .washingtonpost.com/history/2019/08/25/george-washington-owned-slaves -ordered-indians-killed-will-mural-that-history-be-hidden/.

5. Clint Smith, "Transcript: Race in America—'History Matters' with 'How the Word Is Passed,'" *Washington Post*, July 8, 2021, https://www.washingtonpost .com/washington-post-live/2021/07/08/transcript-race-america-history-matters -with-how-word-is-passed-author-clint-smith/.

Chapter 6: Separate

1. Pope Alexander VI, "Demarcation Bull Granting Spain Possession of Lands Discovered by Columbus," May 4, 1493, PDF, https://www.gilderlehrman.org /sites/default/files/inline-pdfs/T-04093.pdf.

2. Richard Edwards, "African Americans and the Southern Homestead Act," *Great Plains Quarterly* 39, No. 2 (2019): 103–30, https://www.jstor.org/stable /26643068.

3. National Archives, "Homestead Act (1862)," National Archives, last updated June 7, 2022, https://www.archives.gov/milestone-documents/homestead-act.

4. Lee Ann Potter, "The Homestead Act of 1862," *Cobblestone* 20, No. 2 (1999): 4, http://login.proxy.lib.uiowa.edu/login?url=https://www.proquest .com/trade-journals/homestead-act-1862/docview/210616459/se-2 ?accountid=14663.

5. Edwards, "African Americans and the Southern Homestead Act."

6. National Archives, "Homestead Act (1862)."

7. For a fuller discussion of how "the Indian Problem" was understood, see Robert G. Hays, *A Race at Bay: New York Times Editorials on "the Indian Problem," 1860–1900* (Carbondale: Southern Illinois University Press, 1997).

8. Blackhawk, *The Rediscovery of America*, p. 334.

9. An Act to Provide for the Allotment of Lands in Severalty to Indians on the Various Reservations (General Allotment Act or Dawes Act), Statutes at Large 24, 388–91, NADP Document A1887.

10. D. S. Otis and House Committee on Indian Affairs, *The Dawes Act and the Allotment of Indian Land* (Norman: University of Oklahoma Press, 1973).

11. Nabokov, *Native American Testimony*, pp. 238–39.

12. Quote from a passage in Dave Roos, "How the Dawes Act Stole 90 Million Acres of Native American Land," HowStuffWorks, January 26, 2021, https: //history.howstuffworks.com/american-history/dawes-act.htm.

13. Kenneth H. Bobroff, "Retelling Allotment: Indian Property Rights and the Myth of Common Ownership," *Vanderbilt Law Review* 54, No. 4 (May 2001), https://scholarship.law.vanderbilt.edu/cgi/viewcontent.cgi?article=1879 &context=vlr.

14. Lewis Meriam, "General Summary of Findings and Recommendations," chap. 1 of *Meriam Report: The Problem of Indian Administration*, National Indian Law Library (NILL), PDF, https://narf.org/nill/documents/merriam/d_meriam _chapter1_summary_of_findings.pdf.

15. Quoted in Grant Foreman, Superintendent for Five Civilized Tribes, *Dawes Commission*, Vol. 20, Oklahoma Historical Society, p. 9, PDF, https://www .okhistory.org/research/digital/foremantrans/foreman.sup20.pdf.

16. Nabokov, *Native American Testimony*, p. 236.

17. Addison Kliewer and Miranda Mahmud, "Cherokee Trail of Tears Just One of Many Forced Removals of Eastern Tribes to Oklahoma," Cronkite News, January 5, 2021. https://cronkitenews.azpbs.org/2021/01/05/cherokee-trail-of-tears -just-one-of-many-forced-removals-of-eastern-tribes-to-oklahoma/.

18. Vine Deloria Jr., *Behind the Trail of Broken Treaties* (Austin: University of Texas Press, 1985), p. 9.

19. Blackhawk, *The Rediscovery of America*, p. 334.

20. In the 2020 U.S. Census, 9.7 million people self-identified as Native American and/or Alaska Native, compared with a total estimated U.S. population of 329.5 million.

21. "How a Court Answered a Forgotten Question of Slavery's Legacy," *Time*, September 11, 2017, https://time.com/4935802/cherokee-slavery-court-decision/.

22. Kendra Taira Field, *Growing up with the Country: Family, Race, and Nation After the Civil War* (New Haven, Conn.: Yale University Press, 2018), p. ix.

23. "How a Court Answered a Forgotten Question of Slavery's Legacy."

24. Kent Carter, *The Dawes Commission and the Allotment of the Five Civilized Tribes, 1893–1914* (Orem, Utah: Ancestry.com, 1999), pp. 106–7.

25. "History," Cherokee Nation History, https://www.cherokee.org/about-the -nation/history.

26. Tiya Miles, *Ties That Bind: The Story of an Afro-Cherokee Family in Slavery and Freedom* (Berkeley: University of California Press, 2005), p. 189.

27. From this point forward, any reference to the Dawes Act includes the Curtis Act as well.

28. *See especially* Sharon O'Brien, "Tribes and Indians: With Whom Does the United States Maintain a Relationship," *Notre Dame Law Review* 66, No. 5 (1990–1991): 1461–94; Janet A. McDonnell, *The Dispossession of the American Indian, 1887–1934* (Bloomington: Indiana University Press, 1991); Vine Deloria Jr., *Custer Died for Your Sins: An Indian Manifesto* (New York: Macmillan, 1969); Leonard A. Carlson and American Council of Learned Societies, *Indians, Bureaucrats, and Land: The Dawes Act and the Decline of Indian Farming / Leonard A. Carlson* (Westport, Conn.: Greenwood Press, 1981).

29. John H. Oberly, *57th Annual Report of the Commissioner of Indian Affairs to the Secretary of the Interior, for the Year 1888* (p. xxxiii), University of Wisconsin–Madison Libraries, https://digital.library.wisc.edu/1711.dl /ZPN6BOUAZOCIV8P.

30. Actions for Allotments, U.S. Code 25 (2015), Sess. 345, https://www.govinfo.gov /app/details/USCODE-2015-title25/USCODE-2015-title25-chap9-sec345.

31. An Act for the Protection of the People of Indian Territory, 3728 S. Doc. No. 33, 55th Cong., 3rd Sess. (1898), Pub. L. No. 55–517, 30 Stat. 495.

32. "Arch McKennon (1841–1920)," (online) Encyclopedia of Arkansas, June 16, 2023, https://encyclopediaofarkansas.net/entries/arch-mckennon-4560/.

33. Quoted in Carter, *The Dawes Commission and the Allotment of the Five Civilized Tribes, 1893–1914*, p. 48.

34. Office of the Commissioner to the Five Civilized Tribes, 1893–1914, Dawes Enrollment Jacket for Creek Enrollment, Card #782, Office of Indian Affairs, Department of the Interior, at Digital Public Library of America, https://catalog .archives.gov/id/45165561.

35. "Pannell, Caroline," Indian-Pioneer Papers, University of Oklahoma Libraries Western History Collection, 1937, PDF, http://digital.libraries.ou.edu/cdm/ref /collection/indianpp/id/1232.

36. "Pannell, Caroline."

37. Kat Chow, "So What Exactly Is 'Blood Quantum'?" *Code Switch* (podcast), NPR, February 9, 2018, https://www.npr.org/sections/codeswitch/2018/02/09 /583987261/so-what-exactly-is-blood-quantum.

38. Chow, "So What Exactly is 'Blood Quantum'?"

39. Katherine M. B. Osburn, "'Any Sane Person': Race, Rights, and Tribal Sovereignty in the Construction of the Dawes Rolls for the Choctaw Nation," *The Journal of the Gilded Age and Progressive Era* 9, No. 4 (2010): 451–71, doi:10.1017/S1537781400004217.

40. Osburn, "'Any Sane Person': Race, Rights, and Tribal Sovereignty in the Construction of the Dawes Rolls for the Choctaw Nation."

41. "No Hair Cut [*sic*] for Cherokees. They Go to Jail and Finally Enroll Before the Dawes Commission Rather than Submit to It," *Charlotte Observer* (Charlotte, N.C.), March 17, 1902.

42. "No Hair Cut [*sic*] for Cherokees."

43. Office of the Commissioner to the Five Civilized Tribes, 1893–1914, Dawes Enrollment Jacket for Creek Enrollment.

44. "Treaty with the Cherokee, 1866," Tribal Treaties Database, Treaties.okstate .edu, n.d., https://treaties.okstate.edu/treaties/treaty-with-the-cherokee -1866-0942.

45. Circe Sturm, "Blood Politics, Racial Classification, and Cherokee National Identity: The Trials and Tribulations of the Cherokee Freedmen," *American Indian Quarterly* 22, No. 1/2 (1998): 235, http://www.jstor.org/stable /1185118.

46. Evelyn Nieves, "Putting to a Vote the Question 'Who Is Cherokee?'" *New York Times*, March 3, 2007, https://www.nytimes.com/2007/03/03/us/03cherokee.html

47. For the full time line of the court cases involved, see Cherokee Nation v. Nash, 267 F. Supp. 3d 86 (D.D.C. 2017), https://casetext.com/case/cherokee-nation-v -nash-4.

48. Cherokee Nation v. Nash.

49. Cherokee Nation v. Nash.

50. My searches of the Dawes Rolls were conducted via Ancestry.com.

51. William Waller Hening, ed., The Statutes at Large, Vol. 12, p. 184, https: //vagenweb.org/hening/.

52. Abi Fain and Mary Nagle, "The Reliance on Minimum Blood Quantum Close to Zero," *Mitchell Hamline Law Review* 43, No. 4 (2017), https://open .mitchellhamline.edu/cgi/viewcontent.cgi?article=1086&context=mhlr.

53. Paul Spruhan, "A Legal History of Blood Quantum in Federal Indian Law to 1935," *South Dakota Law Review* 51, No. 1 (2006): 1.

54. Kenneth H. Bobroff, "Retelling Allotment: Indian Property Rights and the Myth of Common Ownership," *Vanderbilt Law Review* 54, No. 4 (2001): 1559–626.

55. Katherine Ellinghaus, *Blood Will Tell: Native Americans and Assimilation Policy* (Lincoln: University of Nebraska Press, 2022), p. 54.

56. Ellinghaus, *Blood Will Tell*, p. 40.

57. "Stubs of Certificates of Competency, 1911—ca. 1916," U.S. National Archives, NAID: 2103189. Scans of several of the files (which are not digitized) are in the author's possession.

58. Janet McDonnell, "Competency Commissions and Indian Land Policy, 1913–1920," *South Dakota History* 11, No. 1 (1980): 21–34.

59. Ellinghaus, *Blood Will Tell*, p. 49.
60. Janet A. McDonnell, *The Dispossession of the American Indian, 1887–1934* (Bloomington: Indiana University Press, 1991), p. 121.

Chapter 7: Disconnect

1. Jennifer Biess, "Homelessness in Indian Country Is a Hidden, but Critical, Problem," Urban Institute, April 11, 2017, https://www.urban.org/urban-wire /homelessness-indian-country-hidden-critical-problem.
2. Adam Crepelle, "Federal Policies Trap Tribes in Poverty," American Bar Association, January 6, 2023, https://www.americanbar.org/groups/crsj/publications /human_rights_magazine_home/wealth-disparities-in-civil-rights/federal -policies-trap-tribes-in-poverty.
3. Mical Raz, *Abusive Policies: How the American Child Welfare System Lost Its Way* (Chapel Hill: UNC Press Books, 2020), p. 79.
4. "Disproportionate Representation of Native Americans in Foster Care Across United States," Potawatomi.org, April 6, 2021, https://www.potawatomi.org /blog/2021/04/06/disproportionate-representation-of-native-americans-in-foster -care-across-united-states/.
5. Crepelle, "Federal Policies Trap Tribes in Poverty."
6. Dedrick Asante-Muhammad et al., "Racial Wealth Snapshot: Native Americans," National Community Reinvestment Coalition, February 14, 2022, https: //ncrc.org/racial-wealth-snapshot-native-americans/.
7. Lewis Meriam and Hubert Work, *The Problem of Indian Administration: Report of a Survey Made at the Request of Honourable Hubert Work, Secretary of the Interior, and Submitted to Him, February 21, 1928* (Baltimore, Md.: Johns Hopkins University Press, 1928).
8. Blackhawk, *The Rediscovery of America*, pp. 406–7.
9. Act of June 18, 1934 (Indian Reorganization Act), Pub. L. No. 73–383, § 479, 48 Stat. 984, PDF, https://www.govinfo.gov/content/pkg/COMPS-5299/pdf /COMPS-5299.pdf.
10. Curtis Berkey, "John Collier and the Indian Reorganization Act," *American Indian Journal* 2, No. 7 (1976): 2.
11. E. A. Schwartz, "Red Atlantis Revisited: Community and Culture in the Writings of John Collier," *American Indian Quarterly* 18, No. 4 (1994): 507–31, https://doi.org/10.2307/1185395.
12. Vine Deloria Jr. and Clifford M. Lytle, *The Nations Within: The Past and Future of American Indian Sovereignty*, 1st ed. (New York: Pantheon Books, 1984), 186–88.
13. Randall Akee and Miriam Jorgensen. "Property Institutions and Business Investment on American Indian Reservations," *Regional Science and Urban Economics* 46 (2014): 116–25, doi:10.1016/j.regsciurbeco.2014.04.001.
14. Kelly, "The Indian Reorganization Act."
15. Blackhawk, *The Rediscovery of America*, pp. 406–7.
16. Richmond L. Clow, "The Indian Reorganization Act and the Loss of Tribal

Sovereignty: Constitutions on the Rosebud and Pine Ridge Reservations," *Great Plains Quarterly* 7, No. 2 (1987): 125–34.

17. Kelly, "The Indian Reorganization Act," p. 299.

18. Felix S. Cohen, *On the Drafting of Tribal Constitutions* (Norman: University of Oklahoma Press, 2006), 1:xxiii.

19. Cohen, *On the Drafting of Tribal Constitutions*, 1:xxvii.

20. Cohen, *On the Drafting of Tribal Constitutions*, 1:14.

21. Theodore H. Haas and U.S. Bureau of Indian Affairs, issuing body, "Ten Years of Tribal Government Under I.R.A." U.S. Indian Service, Chicago, 1947.

22. The author's own research shows that as of January 1, 2024, 69 of the 110 Tribes Haas listed in his 1947 paper use some sort of blood quantum requirement for enrollment.

23. "Sample Constitution of the Example Tribe," U.S. Department of Interior Bureau of Indian Affairs, n.d., https://www.bia.gov/sites/default/files/dup/assets/bia/ois/pdf/idc-001884.pdf.

24. U.S. Congress, House, *Indians*, H.R. Con. Res. 108, 83rd Cong., 1st Sess., 67 Stat. B132. (enacted), https://www.govinfo.gov/content/pkg/STATUTE-67/pdf/STATUTE-67-PgB132.pdf.

25. Deloria and Lytle, *The Nations Within*.

26. Stephen L. Pevar, *The Rights of Indians and Tribes: The Authoritative ACLU Guide to Indian and Tribal Rights*, 3rd ed. (Carbondale: Southern Illinois University Press, 2002).

27. Roberta Ulrich, *American Indian Nations from Termination to Restoration, 1953–2006* (Lincoln: University of Nebraska Press, 2010), p. xiv.

28. Stephen J. Herzberg, "The Menominee Indians: Termination to Restoration," *American Indian Law Review* 6, No. 1 (1978): 143–86, https://doi.org/10.2307/20068052.

29. Nancy Oestreich Lurie, "Menominee Termination: From Reservation to Colony," *Human Organization* 31, No. 3 (1972): 268, http://www.jstor.org/stable/44115125.

30. Nicholas C. Peroff, *Menominee Drums: Tribal Termination and Restoration, 1954–1974* (Norman: University of Oklahoma Press, 2006), 83.

31. Charles F. Wilkinson and Eric R. Biggs, "The Evolution of the Termination Policy," *American Indian Law Review* 5, No. 1 (1977): 139–84, https://doi.org/10.2307/20068014.

32. Office of the Secretary, "Legislation Terminating Federal Controls over Eight Indian Groups Submitted to Congress," Information Service, U.S. Department of Interior, January 21, 1954, https://web.archive.org/web/20140610043006/http://www.bia.gov/cs/groups/public/documents/text/idc012737.pdf.

33. Carole Goldberg and Duane Champagne, "Status and Needs of Unrecognized and Terminated California Indian Tribes," chap. XI in *A Second Century of Dishonor: Federal Inequities and California Tribes*, Report prepared by the UCLA Native American Studies Center for the Advisory Council on California Indian Policy (Community Service/Governance/Census Task Force Report) (1996).

Note that while this article is from 1996, no additional Tribes in California have been granted federal recognition since this date.

34. House Committee on Interior and Insular Affairs, *Report with Respect to the House Resolution Authorizing the Committee on Interior and Insular Affairs to Conduct an Investigation of the Bureau of Indian Affairs*, 82nd Cong., 2nd Sess., 1952, H. Rep. 2503, 158–61, https://www.govinfo.gov/app/details /SERIALSET-11582_00_00-002-2503-0000.

35. House Committee on Interior and Insular Affairs, *Report with Respect to the House Resolution Authorizing the Committee on Interior and Insular Affairs to Conduct an Investigation of the Bureau of Indian Affairs*.

36. Commission on Organization of the Executive Branch of the Government, *Social Security and Education, Indian Affairs: A Report to the Congress by the Commission on Organization of the Executive Branch of the Government, March 1949* (Washington, D.C.: U.S. Government Printing Office, 1949), p. 67.

37. An Act Relative to Employment for Certain Adult Indians on or Near Indian Reservations, Public Law 959, U.S. Statutes at Large 70 (1956): 986, https: //www.govinfo.gov/app/details/STATUTE-70/STATUTE-70-Pg986.

38. Kenneth R. Philp, "Stride Toward Freedom: The Relocation of Indians to Cities, 1952–1960," *The Western Historical Quarterly* 16, No. 2 (1985): 175–90, https://doi.org/10.2307/969660.

39. Philp, "Stride Toward Freedom."

40. Quoted in Robert L. Bennett et al., "Relocation," in *Indian Self Rule: First-Hand Accounts of Indian-White Relations from Roosevelt to Reagan*, ed. Kenneth R. Philp (Louisville: University Press of Colorado, 1986), 166, https://doi.org /10.2307/j.ctt46nr85.18.

41. Ned Blackhawk, "I Can Carry on from Here: The Relocation of American Indians to Los Angeles," *Wicazo Sa Review* 11, No. 2 (1995): 18, https://doi.org /10.2307/1409093.

42. Kenneth R. Philp, "Dillon S. Myer and the Advent of Termination: 1950–1953," *The Western Historical Quarterly* 19, No. 1 (1988): 37–59, https://doi.org /10.2307/969792.

43. Ickes quoted in Donald R. McCoy and Richard T. Ruetten, *Quest and Response* (Lawrence: University Press of Kansas, 1973), 304.

44. Ayanna Yonemura, *Race, Nation, War*, 1st ed. (London: Routledge, 2019), pp. 25–48, doi:10.4324/9780429467691.

45. *See especially*, Bennett et al., "Relocation," p. 164.

46. Blackhawk, "I Can Carry on from Here."

47. Philp, "Stride Toward Freedom," p. 186.

48. Bennett et al., "Relocation," p. 163.

49. Bennett et al., "Relocation," p. 163.

50. Larry W. Burt, "Roots of the Native American Urban Experience: Relocation Policy in the 1950s," *American Indian Quarterly* 10, No. 2 (1986): 85–99, doi:10.2307/1183982.

51. *See especially* Donald L. Fixico, *Termination and Relocation: Federal Indian Policy,*

1945–1960 (Albuquerque: University of New Mexico Press, 1986), p. 71; "American Indian Urban Relocation," U.S. National Archives, last reviewed March 3, 2023, https://www.archives.gov/education/lessons/indian-relocation.html.

52. Donald L. Fixico, "The Federal Indian Relocation Programme of the 1950s and the Urbanization of Indian Identity," in Richard Bessel and Claudia Haakes, eds., *Removing Peoples: Forced Removal in the Modern World* (London: Oxford University Press, 2009), p. 122.

53. Deloria, *Custer Died for Your Sins*, p. 157.

54. Chicago Field Office, Employment Assistance Case Files, 1952–1960, Record Group 75, Records of the Bureau of Indian Affairs, author's personal collection.

55. U.S. Bureau of Indian Affairs, "Bureau of Indian Affairs Indian Relocation Records 1936–1975," Exhibition Catalog, Edward E. Ayer Manuscript Collection, Newberry Library Digital Collections, https://collections.newberry.org/asset-management/2KXJ8Z9XL08K.

56. Chicago Field Office Employment Assistance Case Files, 1952–1960.

57. "S.1017–93rd Congress (1973–1974): An Act to Provide Maximum Indian Participation in the Government and Education of the Indian People; to Provide for the Full Participation of Indian Tribes in Programs and Services Conducted by the Federal Government for Indians and to Encourage the Development of Human Resources of the Indian People; to Establish a Program of Assistance to Upgrade Indian Education; to Support the Right of Indian Citizens to Control Their Own Educational Activities; and for Other Purposes," January 4, 1975, Congress.gov. https://www.congress.gov/bill/93rd-congress/senate-bill/1017.

58. Stephen Cornell and Joseph P. Kalt, "American Indian Self-Determination," Working Paper 1 (2010): 2117090916–1577391906, Joint Occasional Papers on Native Affairs.

59. "Native Americans Had a Surprising Ally: Richard Nixon," History.com, October 31, 2023, https://www.history.com/news/richard-nixon-native-american-policies.

60. Erin Blakemore, "The Radical History of the Red Power Movement's Fight for Native American Sovereignty," National Geographic, November 25, 2020, https://www.nationalgeographic.com/history/article/red-power-movement-radical-fight-native-american-sovereignty.

61. S.1017–93rd Congress (1973–1974): An Act to Provide Maximum Indian Participation.

62. Ulrich, *American Indian Nations from Termination to Restoration, 1953–2006*, p. 247.

63. Ulrich, *American Indian Nations from Termination to Restoration, 1953–2006*, p. 238.

64. Bureau of Indian Affairs, "Frequently Asked Questions."

65. Faith Roessel, "Federal Recognition—A Historical Twist of Fate," 1989, PDF, https://narf.org/nill/documents/nlr/nlr14–3.pdf.

66. Carmen Rojas and Jesse Beason, "Stolen Justice: Reinstate Federal Recognition of the Chinook Indian Nation," *Seattle Times*, April 29, 2022, https://www

.seattletimes.com/opinion/stolen-justice-reinstate-federal-recognition-of-the
-chinook-indian-nation/.

67. Debbie Elliott, "Virginia's Monacan Indian Nation Seeks Recognition," NPR, March 25, 2007, https://www.npr.org/transcripts/9124174?storyId=9124174 ?storyId=9124174.

68. Jenna Portnoy, "Trump Signs Bill Recognizing Virginia Indian Tribes," *Washington Post*, January 30, 2018, https://www.washingtonpost.com/local/virginia -politics/trump-signs-bill-recognizing-virginia-indian-tribes/2018/01/30 /8a46b038-05d4-11e8-94e8-e8b8600ade23_story.html.

69. K. Alexa Koenig and Jonathan Stein, "State Recognition of American Indian Tribes: A Survey of State-Recognized Tribes and State Recognition Processes, in *Recognition, Sovereignty, Struggles, and Indigenous Rights in the United States*, eds. Amy E. Den Ouden and Jean M. O'Brien (Chapel Hill: The University of North Carolina Press, 2013), 116.

70. "State Recognition of American Indian Tribes."

71. Other scholars have written far more eloquently about this phenomenon than I ever could, including Amanda J. Cobb, "Understanding Tribal Sovereignty: Definitions, Conceptualizations, and Interpretations," *American Studies (Lawrence)* 46, No. 3/4 (2005): 115–32; Vine Deloria Jr., "Self-Determination and the Concept of Sovereignty," in *Native American Sovereignty* (Taylor & Francis e-Library, 2005), pp. 107–14.

Interlude

1. "Record Group 75—Records of the Bureau of Indian Affairs," National Archives, n.d., https://www.archives.gov/findingaid/stat/discovery/75.

Chapter 8: Identity

1. *Longmire*, Season 1, Episode 9, "Dogs, Horses, and Indians," directed by Steve Robin, written by Craig Johnson, Hunt Baldwin, John Coveny, featuring Robert Taylor, Katee Sackhoff, and Lou Diamond Phillips, aired August 5, 2012, Netflix, https://www.netflix.com/watch/70268884.

2. Paul Spruhan, "CDIB: The Role of the Certificate of Degree of Indian Blood in Defining Native American Legal Identity," *American Indian Law Journal* 6, Issue 2, Article 4 (2017): 169.

3. Spruhan, "CDIB," 169.

4. "Enrollment," *Bureau of Indian Affairs Manual* 83, Supplement 2, Section 7.7, PDF, https://www.bia.gov/sites/bia.gov/files/assets/public/raca/pdf/idc012024.pdf.

5. "Enrollment."

6. Gover, *Tribal Constitutionalism*.

7. Act of June 18, 1934 (Indian Reorganization Act).

8. "Enrollment as a Member of an Indian Tribe," Section 3.1, 83 BIAM Supplement 2, accessed March 11, 2024. https://www.bia.gov/sites/default/files/dup /assets/public/raca/pdf/idc012024.pdf.

9. 42 U.S.C. § 136.12, https://www.ihs.gov/prc/eligibility/requirements-eligibility/.

10. R. Glen Melville, "Tribal Government Services," September 10, 2018, in author's possession.

11. Paul Spruhan, interview by author, February 8, 2023.

12. Cathy Purvis Lively, "Covid-19 in the Navajo Nation Without Access to Running Water: The Lasting Effects of Settler Colonialism," *Voices in Bioethics* 7 (March 2021), https://doi.org/10.7916/vib.v7i.7889.

13. "Chickasaw Citizenship."

14. "Certificate of Degree of Indian or Alaska Native Blood," Bureau of Indian Affairs, OMB Control No. 1076–0153, https://www.bia.gov/sites/default/files/dup/assets/public/raca/online_forms/pdf/1076-0153_CDIB%20Form_Expires%2011.30.2024_508.pdf.

15. "Determining Degree of Indian Blood," Section 7.2, 83 BIAM Supplement 2, accessed March 11, 2024. https://www.bia.gov/sites/default/files/dup/assets/public/raca/pdf/idc012024.pdf.

16. Nicholas Jones et al., "2020 Census Illuminates Racial and Ethnic Composition of the Country," U.S. Census Bureau, August 12, 2021, https://www.census.gov/library/stories/2021/08/improved-race-ethnicity-measures-reveal-united-states-population-much-more-multiracial.html.

17. Sturm, *Becoming Indian*, p. 5. *See also* Philip Joseph Deloria, *Playing Indian* (New Haven, Conn.: Yale University Press, 1998).

18. Robert Maxim, Gabriel R. Sanchez, and Kimberly R. Huyser, "Why the Federal Government Needs to Change How It Collects Data on Native Americans," The Brookings Institution, March 30, 2023, https://www.brookings.edu/articles/why-the-federal-government-needs-to-change-how-it-collects-data-on-native-americans/.

19. Anna Spoerre, "3 KU Professors Are Accused of Faking Native American Ancestry. But It's Complicated," *Kansas City Star*, July 25, 2023, https://www.kansascity.com/news/article277464123.html.

Chapter 9: Return

1. The Lumbee River is also known as the Lumber River.

2. "History and Culture," Lumbee Tribe of North Carolina, n.d., https://www.lumbeetribe.com/history-and-culture.

3. Robesonian, "Lumbee Homecoming Serves as Celebration of Culture and Look at a Community in Need," Robesonian, July 6, 2021, https://www.robesonian.com/news/147688/lumbee-homecoming-serves-as-celebration-of-culture-and-look-at-a-community-in-need/amp.

4. "Historic Dugout Canoe," University of North Carolina at Pembroke, n.d., https://www.uncp.edu/resources/museum-southeast-american-indian/museum-exhibits/historic-dugout-canoe.

5. "History," City of Lumberton North Carolina, n.d., www.lumbertonnc.gov, https://www.lumbertonnc.gov/238/History.

6. "History and Culture," Lumbee Tribe of North Carolina.

7. Malinda Maynor Lowery, *The Lumbee Indians.* 1st ed. Chapel Hill: The University of North Carolina Press, 2018. doi:10.5149/9781469646398_Lowery.

8. Lowery, *The Lumbee Indians*.

9. Adolph L. Dial and David K. Eliades, *The Only Land I Know: A History of the Lumbee Indians* (Syracuse, N.Y.: Syracuse University Press, 1996).

10. "What Happened to the 'Lost Colony' of Roanoke?" History.com, June 20, 2023, https://www.history.com/news/what-happened-to-the-lost-colony-of-roanoke.

11. Lowery, *The Lumbee Indians*.

12. Lowery, *The Lumbee Indians*.

13. Lowery, *The Lumbee Indians*.

14. Lowery, *The Lumbee Indians*.

15. Lowery, *The Lumbee Indians*.

16. "The Curious Story of the Croatans of Bulloch County," *Statesboro Herald*, last updated June 18, 2020, https://www.statesboroherald.com/life/curious-story-croatans-bulloch-county/.

17. Lowery, *The Lumbee Indians*.

18. "The Lumbee Indians Of North Carolina," Historical Timeline, Do You Speak American?, PBS, n.d., https://www.pbs.org/speak/seatosea/americanvarieties/lumbee/timeline/; and "From Sea to Shining Sea," Do You Speak American?, PBS, n.d., https://www.pbs.org/speak/seatosea/.

19. "Testimony of Principal Chief Richard Sneed Eastern Band of Cherokee Indians a Hearing on H.R. 1964, the 'Lumbee Recognition Act' Before the House Subcommittee for Indigenous Peoples of the United States," December 4, 2019, PDF, https://www.congress.gov/116/meeting/house/110282/witnesses/HHRG-116-II24-Wstate-SneedR-20191204.pdf.

20. Lowery, *The Lumbee Indians*.

21. D'Vera Cohn, "American Indian and White, but Not 'Multiracial,'" Pew Research Center, June 11, 2015, https://www.pewresearch.org/short-reads/2015/06/11/american-indian-and-white-but-not-multiracial/.

22. Sturm, *Becoming Indian*.

23. Philip Deloria, "When Tribal Nations Expel Their Black Members," *The New Yorker*, July 14, 2022, https://www.newyorker.com/magazine/2022/07/25/when-tribal-nations-expel-their-black-members-caleb-gayle-we-refuse-to-forget-alaina-e-roberts-ive-been-here-all-the-while.

24. "Act of June 18, 1934 (Indian Reorganization Act)."

25. Christine B. Hickman, "The Devil and the One Drop Rule: Racial Categories, African Americans, and the U.S. Census," *Michigan Law Review* 95, No. 1161 (1997).

26. Lowery, *Lumbee Indians in the Jim Crow South*.

27. Lowery, *Lumbee Indians in the Jim Crow South*.

28. "The Croatan Normal School," The Carolina Story: A Virtual Museum of University History, n.d., https://museum.unc.edu/exhibits/show/american-indians-and-chapel-hi/the-croatan-normal-school--pem.

29. Morris F. Britt, *Implosion: The Secret History of the Lumbee Indians of Robeson County North Carolina* (Lulu.com, 2017), p. 569; Lowery, *The Lumbee Indians*, p. 42.

30. Lowery, *The Lumbee Indians*, p. 44.
31. Lowery, *Lumbee Indians in the Jim Crow South*, pp. 44–45.
32. "H. Rept. 111–103—Lumbee Recognition Act," Congress.gov, https://www .congress.gov/congressional-report/111th-congress/house-report/103/1.
33. "H. Rept. 111–103—Lumbee Recognition Act."
34. Act of June 7, 1956 (70 Stat. 254).
35. "Act of June 18, 1934 (Indian Reorganization Act)."
36. Arlinda Locklear, "Part 5: Reflections on the Battle for Lumbee Recognition," YouTube video, April 28, 2010, https://dsi.appstate.edu/projects/lumbee /blog032.
37. Lowery, *Lumbee Indians in the Jim Crow South*.
38. Sidney Levy, "A Fight for Recognition: The Lumbee Tribe in Maryland," Maryland Center for History and Culture, August 4, 2016, https://www.mdhistory .org/a-fight-for-recognition-the-lumbee-tribe-in-maryland/.
39. "Case No: 20: Eula Jane Jacobs," Applications for Registration as an Indian, United States Archives, June 8, 1936, RG 75, entry 616, National Archives Catalog, https://catalog.archives.gov/id/2124510.
40. Lowery, *Lumbee Indians in the Jim Crow South*.
41. Locklear, "Part 5: Reflections on the Battle for Lumbee Recognition."
42. 103rd Cong., Lumbee Recognition Act, Report Together with Dissenting Views to Accompany H.R. 334, House Report No. 130–290, House Committee on Natural Resources, dated October 14, 1993, approximately 194 pages.
43. Chandelis Duster, "A Virginia Tribe Says Racism Wiped Their Native Identity from Historic Records. Nearly a Century Later, They're Still Fighting for Recognition," CNN, January 20, 2024, https://www.cnn.com/2024/01/20/us /patawomeck-tribe-federal-recognition/index.html.
44. Bureau of Indian Affairs, "25 CFR Part 83—Procedures for Federal Acknowledgment of Indian Tribes," U.S. Department of Interior, PDF, https://www .bia.gov/sites/default/files/dup/assets/as-ia/ofa/admindocs/25CFRPart83_2015 _abbrev.pdf.
45. Bureau of Indian Affairs, "25 CFR Part 83—PROCEDURES FOR ESTABLISHING THAT AN AMERICAN INDIAN GROUP EXISTS AS AN INDIAN TRIBE," U.S. Department of Interior, PDF, https://www.doi.gov/sites /doi.gov/files/uploads/25cfr83.pdf.

Index

Abbott, Thomas J., 87–88
acculturation, 116, 156–57
Adams, Mikaëla, 201
adoption, by non-Native families, 105, 106, 115
African Americans, 75, 110–11, 145, 200–201, 208–9
African ancestry, 145, 208–9
agriculture, 38
Alabama, 87
Alaska, 155
Alaska Natives, 1, 17
Albuquerque, New Mexico, 118
Alexander VI, Pope, 126
Algonquian-speaking people, 197
allotments, 88–89, 94–95, 118, 130–33, 136, 137, 152, 155
   allotment policy, 152–53
   Burke Act and, 146
   eligibility for, 137
   exclusions from, 88–89
   non-Native people receiving, 89–90
American Indian Defense Association, 153
American Indian Movement, 114–15, 118, 167
Amish, 80, 91–92
ancestry, verification of, 25
ancestry claims, precarious, 214–15
Anderson, Benedict, 63
Anishinaabe, 104. See also Ojibwe
annuity payments, 82–84, 86–90
Apache, 61
Arikara, 38
Arikara War, 77
Arizona, 39
Arkansas, removal of Creeks to, 88
assimilation, 14, 47, 59, 153, 154, 160–61, 169, 200, 208
   "assimilation" phase, 77, 160–61, 169, 191
   forced, 155
Atlanta, Georgia, 82
autonomy, loss of, 153–54

Babylonian Empire, 62
Baldwin, Alabama, 57, 59
Battle of Wahoo Swamp, 59

Bear Clan, 112
Beason, Jimmy, 194
belonging, 14–15, 32–52, 84, 120, 170, 205, 215. See also membership; Tribal enrollment
Bemidji, Minnesota, 106, 107–8, 119, 121
Bennet, Robert L., 163
Berry, Charles, 116–17
birth certificates, 24, 26, 48–49, 61, 69, 70, 119, 211
Black, Edwin, 74
Black Bear Casino Resort, 149, 151
Blackduck, Minnestoa, 107
Blackfeet, 224n11
Black Hawk (Mahkatêwe-meshi- kêhkêhkwa), 79
Black Hills, 45
"Black Natives," 134–35
Blackness, 200–201
Blacks. See African Americans; free Blacks
blood quantum, 3–4, 15, 30, 117–18, 121, 142, 144–46, 155, 187, 200
   as tool of exclusion or extinction, 215
   Tribal enrollment and, 11, 23–24, 27, 154
   weaponized by federal government, 145–46
boarding schools, 44, 152, 160, 161, 165–66, 169, 179, 193
   abuses at, 116
   children abducted and taken to, 116–17, 210–11
   children murdered at, 210–11
   unmarked graves at, 116
border towns, crime in, 45–46
Britain, 78
Brotherton Indians of New Jersey, 108
Browning, D. M., 132
Buie, D. A., 66
Bureau of Indian Affairs (BIA), 14, 101, 116, 132, 137, 141, 209, 210
   Bureau of Indian Affairs Manual (BIAM), 175, 176, 177–78
   Chicago Relocation Office, 164
   dataset maintained by, 16–17
   funding from, 208
   model constitution sent to, 153–54
   Nixon and, 167
   recognition and, 168

Bureau of Indian Affairs (BIA) (*continued*)
  relocation and, 162, 163
  termination and, 156, 157
  website of, 17
Burke Act, 145–46, 147
Burnt Swamp, North Carolina, 65, 66, 67,
    206
Bush administration, 168

Calhoun, John C., 116
California, 12, 39, 97, 145, 155, 156
Canada, First Nations in, 179, 184, 190,
    218
Cape Fear, 198
casinos, 95, 96–97. *See also* gaming operations
Cass, Lewis, 88
Cass Lake Indian Hospital, 104
Catawba people, 197
Catholic Church, 126
Cedar Rapids, Iowa, 7, 19, 157
census enumerators, 56–57, 65, 66
censuses, 22–23, 95. *See also* U.S. Census
  history of, 62–63
  imperialism and, 63
  Indian census rolls from 1930s, 117–18
  in Nazi Germany, 73–74
  taken by Indian agents, 117
census machines, 74
Certificate of Degree of Indian Blood (CDIB),
    174–78
Checotah, Oklahoma, 140
Cheraw, 197, 199
Cherokee, 2, 3–4, 22, 26, 39, 48, 133, 135–36,
    140–44, 192
  "by blood," 134
  Cherokee Freedmen, 128–29, 135, 140,
    142–44
  Cherokee National Council, 135
  Dawes Rolls and, 135
  Delaware Cherokee, 144
  Eastern Band of, 2
  enrollment in, 128–29
  removal of, 100–101
  of Robeson County, 199
  slavery and, 134–35
  United Keetoowah Band of Cherokee in
    Oklahoma, 2
  U.S. Census and, 223n9
Cheyenne River Reservation, 45
Chicago, Illinois, 164
Chickahominy, Eastern, 168
Chickasaw, 26, 133, 177, 224n11
  Chickasaw Freedmen, 136

  of Oklahoma, 14
  removal of, 100–101
children
  abduction of, 152, 165–66, 210–11
  in foster care, 104–8, 150
  murdered at boarding schools, 210–11
  sent to boarding schools, 161
China, 62
Chinook, 168
Chippewa, 83, 104, 119, 120, 149, 150–51, 158,
    169–70, 172. *See also* Ojibwe
  Fond du Lac Band of Lake Superior, 149,
    150–51, 158, 169–70
  Lake Superior Chippewa, 149, 158, 169–70
  Minnesota Chippewa, 119, 120, 121
Choctaw, 21, 39–40, 58, 133, 140, 144
  Mississippi Choctaw, 140, 144
  of Oklahoma, 26
  removal of, 101
Church Rock, New Mexico, 84
citizenship, geographical vs. relational, 25
civil rights movement, 158
Civil War, 135
Clark, William, 126
Cleveland, Grover, 133
Cleveland, Ohio, 158, 159, 161, 164–65, 169,
    171, 172
Clinton administration, 168
Cloquet, Minnesota, 151
"coexistence" phase, 77
Collier, John, 153
colonization, 46, 48, 63, 77–78, 101, 112,
    198
  first contact, 39
  of gender roles, 46
  imagining world free of, 31, 54
  settler colonialism, 17–18
Columbus, Christopher, 125
communal land rights, 38
competency
  assessment of, 145–46, 155
  certificates of, 146
  "Competency Commissions," 146
Connecticut, 23, 96
constitutions, Tribal, 21–22, 224n11
  "sample," 153–54
consultation rights, 167
containment, 115–18
counting, 55–74, 101. *See also* censuses; list
    making
Covid-19 pandemic, 27–28, 60, 196, 213
Cowart, Fletcher J., 116
creation stories, 47

Creek, 58, 82, 87, 94–95, 139, 140, 141.
    See also Muscogee (Creek)
    allotments to, 88–90
    Creek Census, 1832, 87–90, 94
    Creek Freedmen, 141
    matrilineality and, 90
    removal to Arkansas, 88
    Treaty with, 87
Creek War of 1836, 90
crime, in border towns, 45–46
Croatan, 199
Croatan Normal School, 206
Curtis Act, 133–34, 147

Dakota Access Pipeline, 192
Dances with Wolves, 200
data, 14–17, 22, 30, 69, 75
    BIA dataset, 16–17
    builiding a dataset, 60
    indigenous data sovereignty, 15
    kinship and, 38
    in Nazi Germany, 73–74
    technology and, 74
Dawes, Henry L., 138
Dawes Act, 130–34, 136–41, 145–46, 147, 152,
    154, 155, 161, 172, 200–201, 210
Dawes Commission, 133, 138, 139, 140
Dawes Rolls, 26, 128, 135, 138–41, 144–46,
    214–15
Declaration of Independence, 78, 123, 124
Delaware, 43, 78, 79, 132, 144. *See also* Cherokee
Deloria, Vine, Jr., 118, 133, 163
disconnection, patterns of, 2–3, 148–70
discrimination, 45
disease, 152
disenrollment, 95–98
    motivation for, 97–98
    posthumous, 97
displacement, 169
DNA tests, 24, 187
Doctrine of Discovery, 126
Dolezal, Rachel, 192
Drowning Creek, 196, 198, 206
Duluth, Minnesota, 158

Echo-Hawk, Abigail, 16
education, 153, 166–67
    educational benefits, 11
    educational training, 162
    Native student success, 148
    resources for, 153
educational institutions, on stolen land, 148
Egypt, 62

Ellinghaus, Katherine, 146
employment, 153, 161, 162–64
enrollment. *See* Tribal enrollment
enslaved people, 140, 141, 199, 207

family lore, misrepresentation in, 3, 192
federal benefits, 118
    annuity payments to Native Nations, 82–84,
        86–90
    elimination of, 154–56
federal government, 11, 17, 43, 55, 58, 126.
    *See also specific branches, agencies, and
    departments*
    annuity payments and, 82–84, 86–90
    Blackness and, 200–201
    data and, 15–16
    laws of (*see specific legislation*)
    Native Nations and, 10, 17, 77–98, 99–122,
        115–18, 143–44, 176 (*see also specific
        groups*)
    Nativeness and, 200–201
    Native program offices and, 150
    phases of relations to Native Americans,
        77, 99
    policies of, 47, 137, 152–54, 217 (*see also
        specific policies and legislation*)
    population undercounts and, 94–95
    recognition and, 167–68, 207–9, 210
    recordkeeping and, 101, 102
    reservation system and, 108–10
    "termination" phase and, 154–56, 162
    weaponization of blood quantum by, 145–46
Federal Indian Boarding School Initiative, 116
Ferguson, Jane, 63
Field, Kendra Taira, 135
First Nations, in Canada, 179, 184, 190
First Seminole War, 77
Five Tribes, 133, 143. *See also specific Tribes*
    precarious ancestry claims and, 214–15
    removal of, 100–101
    slavery and, 134–35
Flandreau Indian School, 160, 166
Florida, 40
Floyd, George, 75
Fond du Lac Reservation, 151, 158, 161, 164–65,
    169–70
Fond du Lac Veterans Supportive Housing,
    151
food rations, 109
food sovereignty, 33
Ford, Gerald, 166–67
foster care, 104–8, 150
Foxwoods Resort Casino, 96

France, 78, 126
Franklin, Benjamin, 123
fraud, 83, 87, 112, 127
    self-identification and, 191–93, 194
    Tribal enrollment and, 138
    Tribal recognition and, 168
"Freedmen," 135, 207. *See also* African Americans
    Cherokee Freedmen, 128–29, 135, 140,
        142–44
    Chickasaw Freedmen, 136
    Creek Freedmen, 141
    intermarriage with, 199
    Seminole Nation Freedmen, 142
French and Indian War, 78

Galanda, Gabe, 97
gaming communities, 95–98
gaming operations, 95–97
    Class II facilities, 95, 97–98
    Class III facilities, 96
gaming revenue, per capita payments (per caps),
        96, 97–98
Garner, Eric, 75
Gary, Indiana, 164
gaslighting, 99–100
gender roles, colonization of, 46
genealogy, 47, 53–54, 63–72, 192. *See also*
        kinship
    Dawes Rolls and, 138–39
    U.S. Census and, 64–68
General Allotment Act, 130–33
General Land Office, 127
Genghis Khan, 62
genocide, 101
Georgia, 82
Germany, Nazi, 73–74
Gorman, R. C., 80
Gover, Kirsty, 175, 224n10

Haas, Theodore, 154
Han Dynasty, 62
Harrison Land Act, 111–12
Hatteras people, 197
(Haudenosaunee) Iroquois Confederacy, 10
Haveman, Christopher, 90
health care, 169. *See also* Indian Health Service
    health care benefits, 11
    lack of access to, 150
    resources for, 153
health problems, 109, 149–50
Herbert, John, 196, 197
Herring, Elbert, 88–89
Hidatsa, 38

Hispanics, 110
The History of Lumbee, 13–14
Hogan, Thomas, 143
Hoke County, North Carolina, 196
Hollerith, Herman, 74
Holocaust Museum, 75–76
homelessness, 149–50, 151
Homestead Act, 127–28, 129–30
homesteaders, 127–28, 153
Hopi, 39
housing
    benefits, 11
    issues, 150–51, 162
    market, 149–50

IBM, 74
Ickes, Harold, 162
Idaho, 39
Illinois, 112, 164
imposter syndrome, 114, 115
"in-betweenness," 135
Indiana, 145, 164
Indian agents, 115–17, 160
Indian Appropriations Act, 108–9
"Indian blood" concept, 3–4, 11, 15, 23–24, 67,
        121, 215
    certificates of, 142
    quantification of, 117–18, 121, 144–45,
        174–78, 187, 200 (*see also* blood quantum)
    tests of, 208–9
"Indian box," 1, 3, 27
Indian Child Welfare Act, 105
Indian Citizenship Act of 1924, 158
Indian Commission, 87–88
Indian containment, 115–18
Indian Country, 48–49, 86, 132, 137,
        146, 176
Indian Gaming Regulatory Act, 96
Indian Health Manual, 176
Indian Health Service, 24, 169, 176, 208
Indian law, federal, 59 (*see also specific laws*)
Indianness
    adjudication of, 137
    modernity of, 52
Indian New Deal, 152. *See also* Indian
        Reorganization Act
Indian policy (federal), 47, 137, 152–54, 217. *See
        also specific legislation and policies*
    of containment, 115–18
    post-Jackson era, 115–18
    reservation policy, 115–18
"Indian Problem," 129–30, 208
Indian Recognition Act, 154–57

Indian Relocation Act, 158–64, 166, 169, 171, 211
Indian Relocation Program, 158–61, 169
Indian Removal Act, 42–43, 108, 125, 133, 161, 164
Indian Reorganization Act, 22, 152–54, 161, 200–201, 208
Indian Self-Determination and Education Assistance Act, 166–69
Indians of Robeson County, 199
Indian Termination Act, 161
Indian Territory, 90, 133–34. *See also* removal
Indian Trade Office, 116
indigenous data sovereignty, 15
indigenous land, return of, 125–26
Indigenous Peoples' Day, 190
intermarriage, 200
  cross-tribal, 121
  with escaped slaves, 199
  with free persons of color, 199
  rates of, 215
  with white settlers, 199
Iowa, 32–33, 43, 53, 80–81, 84–85, 92–94, 104–5, 106, 118, 119, 122, 204. *See also specific locations*
Iroquoian-speaking people, 197
Iroquois Confederacy, 10

Jackson, Andrew, 42–43, 88, 90, 99–100, 102, 108, 109, 164
Japanese Americans, internment of, 163
Jefferson, Thomas, 99
Jews, in Nazi Germany, 73–74
Jim Crow, 110, 201

Kalona, Iowa, 80, 91, 93
Kansas, 43, 132, 157
Keetowah Nighthawk Society, 141
Kidd, Meredith H., 138
Krug, Jessica, 192
kinship, 37, 39, 40, 48, 210–11
  data and, 38
  determination of, 215
  genealogy and, 47, 53–54
  kinship bands, 54 (*see also* bands)
  kinship groups, 39
  kinship networks, 40–41
  knowledge of, 206
Kiowa, 21
Koi Nation, 167
Koquethagechton (White Eyes), 79

Lakota, 200
land. *See also* allotments; land ownership

ceding of, 108–12
fraud and, 112, 127–28
land acknowledgments, 33–34
land sovereignty, 34, 125–26
land theft, 155
Native land sovereignty, 129
purchase of, 43
return of surplus lands, 153
#LandBank movement, 125, 155, 192, 193
land ownership, 43
  land ownership rights, 11
  provisional, 129–31
land speculators, 133
language(s), 116, 197, 198, 210–11, 219
  language classes, 85
  Native language loss, 47
Larrabee, C. F., 141
The Last of the Mohicans, 200
leadership, hierarchy of, 10
Leech Lake Reservation, 104, 105, 106, 107, **114**, 118, 119, 120–21, 122
LeFlore, Greenwood, 57, 58, 59
Lenape, 43, 78, 79, 108
Lenni-Lenape. *See* Lenape people
Lewis, Meriwether, 126
Lincoln, Abraham, 124, 127
Lincoln, Nebraska, 118
lineage, 22–23, 24, 54, 69–70, 97, 121. *See also* genealogy; matrilineality; patrilineality
lists, 75–76. *See also* censuses; rolls
  list making, 213–14, 215
  origins of list making, 81–82
Littlefield, Daniel, 48–49
Locklear, Arlinda, 209
Longmire, 174
Los Angeles, California, 97
Lost Colony of Roanoke, 197–98
Louisiana Purchase, 126
Lower Lake Rancheria, 167
Lowery, Malinda Maynor, 198, 199, 206–7
Lowry name, 205–6
Lumbee, 195–212
  as amalgamation, 197–99
  earliest written records of, 206–7
  first use of the name, 199
  history of, 216
  language of, 198
  Lumbee ancestors, 199
  Lumbee country, 157
  Lumbee identity, 206, 208
  Lumbee origin story, 206
  misunderstood, 199
  mixed-race composition of, 208–10

Lumbee (*continued*)
  Native identity questioned, 208
  of North Carolina, 3–4, 7, 9, 12–13, 18–21,
    24, 27–28, 34, 36, 53–54, 65–70, 128, 157,
    194, 195–201, 204–11
  threat of recognition to other tribes,
    209–10
  Tribal enrollment and, 18–21
  unrecognized by the U.S. government, 194,
    207–9
Lumbee Act, 207
Lumbee County, North Carolina, 28, 65
Lumbee dialect, 20
Lumbee Homecoming, 195–96, 201–2
Lumbee River, 196, 197, 198, 199, 206
Lumbee Tribal Council, 10–11
Lumbee Tribe Headquarters, 20, 211
Lumberton, North Carolina, 67, 204–5

mascots, 11–12
Mashantucket Pequot, 96
matrilineality, 39, 40, 46, 54, 58, 90
Mattapoini, 168
McDonnell, Janet, 146
McKennon, Archibald S., 138, 140
McMillan, Hamilton, 199
McPherson, Orland, 199
membership. *See* Tribal enrollment
Mennonites, 80, 93. *See also* Amish
Menominee, 155–56
Meriam Report, 131, 152, 153
Meskwaki, 32–36, 41–44, 47, 49–51
  creation story, 35
  enrollment in, 49–50
  land ownership and, 43
  members vs. descendants, 35–36, 44, 47, 48,
    50–52
  Meskwaki foodways, 35
  Meskwaki health care center, 41
  patrilineal ancestry and, 35–36, 49–51
  removed to reservation in Kansas, 43
Meskwaki Bingo Casino Hotel, 42
Meskwaki Road, 41, 51
Meskwaki Settlement, 32–33, 41–42, 44, 50
Meskwaki Settlement School, 42
Micco, Neah, 89–90
Michigan, 83.156
Mi'kmaq, reserve in Southern Quebec, 179,
    184–85
Mi'kmaq language, 184
Miles, Tiya, 135
military draft cards, 70
Miller, Robert, 73

Minnesota, 104, 105–8, 119, 120–22, 148–52,
    155, 158, 161, 164–65
Missing and Murdered Indigenous Women
    movement, 46, 192, 193
Mississippi, 58, 140, 144
Missouri, 112
Mitchell, Judy, 217
mixed-race individuals, on U.S. Census, 58
Mohawks, 200
Monacan, 168
Mongol Empire, 62–63
Moniac, David A., 59
Moniac, David Tate, 57, 58, 59
Monroe, James, 99
"mulattos," 145
Muscogee (Creek), 26, 101, 133, 224n11.
    See also Creek
Museum of the Southeast American Indian, 20
muster rolls, 102, 108
Myer, Dillon S., 162–63

Nabokov, Peter, 130–31
names, fascination with, 205–6
Nansemond Tribe, 168
Nanticoke, 43
Nash, Philleo, 162–63
National Archives and Records Administration, 2,
    81, 86–87, 171
National Indian Gaming Commission, 96–97
National Museum of the American Indian, 42
Native activism, 167. *See also specific movements*
Native American Nations, 168, 218. *See also* First
    Nations; *specific groups*
  annuity payments to Native Nations, 82–84
  constitutions of, 21–22, 153–54, 224n11
  differences among, 38
  federal government and, 11, 17, 77–98,
    99–122, 115–18, 167–68 (*see also* federal
    government)
  governments of, 10, 15–16, 22, 136, 141–42,
    152, 154–56
  numbers of, 217
  phases of relations to federal government, 77, 99
  restoration of status and, 167–68
  southwestern, 218
  sovereignty of, 9–11, 193–94 (*see also*
    sovereignty)
  treaties with federal government, 176
  unrecognized by the U.S. government, 132,
    156, 167–68, 207–9
Native Americans
  animosity toward, 123–24
  romanticized portrayals of, 200

as slaveholders, 58, 59
southeastern, 99
on U.S. Census, 57, 58–59
U.S. citizenship and, 58
Native homelessness, 149–50
Native identity, 14–15, 28
adjudication of, 193
assessment of, 3–4, 5, 11, 15, 23–24, 145,
   147, 187 (*see also* blood quantum)
benefits of, 120
Dawes Act and, 137
demonstration of, 2
destroyed by termination, 155
enrollment and, 170
fraudulently claimed, 191–93
future work on, 218
genealogy and, 68–72
importance of, 120
misrepresentation in family lore, 3
precarious ancestry claims and,
   214–15
race shifting and, 181–82
as relational, 194
rise in numbers of people claiming, 1–2
self-identification, 1–2, 3, 9–10, 181–83,
   189
skin color and, 145 (*see also* race)
stripped, 168
understanding of, 30, 31
on U.S. Census, 57–59, 65–68
validation of, 2, 4, 5, 120
white privilege and, 14
Nativeness, appearance and, 200–201
Native student associations, 113–14
Native student success, 148
Native tradition, destruction of, 47
Native women, 189
considered heads of families, 46 (*see also*
   matrilineality)
Missing and Murdered Indigenous Women
   movement, 46, 192, 193
sexual violence and, 46
natural resources, return of, 125
Navajo, 10, 22, 80–81, 84–86, 92, 93, 94, 97,
   157, 174, 177, 224n11
Navajo Nation Constitutional Feasibility and
   Government Reform Project, 22
Navajo Nation Division of Economic
   Development, 10
Nazi Germany, 73–74
Nebraska, 79, 155
New Hope, Pennsylvania, 198
New Jersey, 108

New Mexico, 80–81, 84–85, 93, 157
New York, 40
Nez Perce (Nimíipuu), 39
Nixon, Richard, 167
Nobles, Melissa, 72
non-Native adoption, 105, 106, 115
Nooksack, 95
   Canadian bands, 95
   Nooksack 306, 97
Norma, 86, 92
North Carolina, 7, 12–13, 19–20, 36–37, 39,
   53–54, 65–67, 145, 195–201, 202,
   204–11. *See also specific locations*
North Dakota, 38
Nott, Josiah, 73
Nuu-chah-nulth, 38

Obama administration, 14, 41, 151
Oberly, John H., 137
Office of the Superintendent of Indian Trade,
   116
Ohio, 83, 132, 158, 159, 161, 164–65, 169
Ohio Trail of Tears, 132
Ojibwe, 112
   Leech Lake Band of, 104, 119–21, 149
Oklahoma, 39, 40, 48–49, 132, 133, 136, 140,
   194
   statehood granted, 135
   United Keetoowah Band of Cherokee in, 2
Oklahoma City, Oklahoma, 142
Oklahoma Historians Hall of Fame, 48
older adults, assistance to, 11
Olympic Peninsula, 38
Oneida Nation, 23–24, 163
Oregon, 155
Oregon Trail, 126
Original 22, 209
origin stories, 47. *See also* creation stories
Osage, 39, 194
Osburn, Katherine M. B., 140

pan-Indian communities, 159–60, 163
Parsons, Benjamin S., 87–88
Parsons, Enoch, 88
Parsons and Abbott Roll, 87–89, 94–95
Passamaquoddy, 23
patrilineality, 35–36, 39, 47, 49–51
Pawnee, 16
Pechanga, 97–98
Pechanga Resort and Casino, 97–98
Pedee, 197
Pembroke, North Carolina, 7, 12, 19–20, 28,
   36–37, 54, 67, 196, 202–3, 206, 208

Pembroke High School, 12
Pevar, Steven, 131
phases of relations between U.S. government
    and Native American Tribes, 77, 99
Pine Ridge Reservation, 45
Pocahontas, 38, 200
political identity, 11
Ponca, 134, 136
Ponca City, Oklahoma, 134, 136
population undercounts, incentives for, 94–95, 97
poverty, 149, 150, 151, 152, 156, 162
precontact history, 31, 40–41, 48, 54
"pretendians," 194
Principal Chiefs Act, 141
Public Law 280, 154–56
Public Law 959, 161

Quapaw, Treaty with the Delaware, 83
Quebec, Ontario, 179
Quechan, Fort Yuma in Arizona and California,
    39

race. *See also* racism
    classification of, 208–9
    fixation on purity, 73
    quantification of, 72–73 (*see also* blood
        quantum)
    race shifting, 181–82, 199
    recognition of Native American Tribes and,
        208–9
    on U.S. Census, 57, 72–73
racism, 45
    classification and, 208–9
    racial redlining, 110–11
    structural, 109
    Tribal recognition and, 208–10
rancherias, 39, 48
Rapid City, South Dakota, 45, 118
Rappahannock, 168
recognition, federal, rules for, 210
recordkeeping, 48, 84, 102
    federal government and, 101 (*see also* U.S.
        Census)
    Native, 81–82, 84 (*see also* tribal rolls)
Red Lake (Nation), 120–21, 122
Red Lake Reservation, 104, 120–21
Red Power movement, 167
relocation
    Indian Relocation Act, 158–64, 166, 169, 171,
        211
    Indian Relocation Program, 158–61, 169
    patterns of, 2–3
    relocation officers, 159

removal, 99–122, 133, 191
    Indian Removal Act, 42–43, 108, 125, 133,
        161, 164
    "Indian removal agents," 102
    to Indian Territory, 90
    lists of Native people removed, 101–2
    "removal and reservations phase," 77, 99–122,
        133
"reorganization" phase, 77. *See also* Indian
    Reorganization Act
reservation policy
    of containment, 115–18
    post-Jackson era, 115–18
reservations, 45, 108, 168
    elimination of, 154–56, 160–61
    post-Jackson era policy, 115–18
    Public Law 280 and, 155
    "removal and reservations phase," 77, 99–122,
        133
    reservation policy of containment, 115–18
    reservation system, 108–10, 115–16
    vs. settlements, 43
reservation system, 108–9
    federal government and, 108–10
    reservation policy of containment, 115–16
Revolutionary War, 78
Robeson County, North Carolina, 65, 197, 200,
    204–11
Rockefeller Foundation, 131
Rolfe, John, 200
rolls, 11, 54, 215
    base rolls, 121
    Creek Census, 1832, 87–90
    Dawes Rolls, 26, 128, 135, 138–41, 144–46,
        214–15
    Indian census rolls from 1930s, 117–18
    muster rolls, 102, 108
    Parsons and Abbott Roll, 87–89, 94–95
    Tribal rolls, 22–23, 25, 26, 87–90, 94–98, 95,
        214, 215 (*see also* censuses)
Roman Empire, 62
Roosevelt, Franklin Delano, 152–53
Roosevelt, Theodore, 124
Rosebud Reservation, 45, 115
Rosebud Sioux, 115
Round Valley Indian Tribes, 97
Russia, 78

Sac and Fox, 42, 51, 79, 111–12. *See also*
    Meskwaki Nation
sales tax, Tribe-levied, 10
Salina, Oklahoma, 48–49
San Diego, California, 12, 97

Saponi people, 197
Savannah, Georgia, 82
Scavanos, 197
Scottish settlers, 199
Sea of Japan, 62
Second Creek War, 90
Second Seminole War, 58
Seed Savers, 34
self-determination, 15, 77, 166–69, 214
self-government, 208. *See also* Tribal self-
     governance
self-identification, 1–3, 9–10, 181–83, 189,
     224n11
   fraud and, 191–93, 194
   vs. Tribal enrollment, 3, 224n11
Sells, Cato, 146
Seltzer, Carl, 209
Seminole, 40, 133
   of Oklahoma, 26
   removal of, 101
   Seminole Freedmen, 142
Seneca, 40, 102
settlements, 45
   vs. reservations, 43
settlers
   first contact with, 39
   intermarriage with, 199
   settler colonialism, 17–18
   settler violence, 87
   white, 39, 125–26, 199
severalty, 130, 152–53
Shawnee, Eastern, 73
Siouan-speaking people, 197
Sioux, 86, 115
   Dakota Sioux, 124
   Rosebud Sioux, 115
   Yankton Sioux, 86
slavery, 127, 134–35, 140, 199
Smith, Clint, 124
social welfare programs, Tribally operated, 10
South Carolina, 196
South Dakota, 45, 115
sovereignty, 25, 55, 125–26, 129, 155, 167,
     193–94, 208, 213–14
   concept of, 10–11
   definition of, 10–11
   food sovereignty, 33
   indigenous data sovereignty, 15
   land sovereignty, 34
   Native land sovereignty, 34, 125–26, 129
   respecting, 193–94
   Tribal, 9–11
Spruhan, Paul, 145, 174, 177

Standing Rock Reservation, 45
state governments. *See also specific states*
   Public Law 280 and, 155
   recognition by, 168
"States in the Degree of Indian Acculturation.,"
     156–57
stereotypes, 12, 13, 200
storytellers, 47
Sturm, Circe, 181–82

Tama, Iowa, 44–45, 46
Tama public schools, 44
taxation, 55, 59, 131
Teller, Henry M., 132–33
Tennessee, 140
"termination" phase, 77, 154–56, 162, 167,
     208
terminology, 218–19
Texas, 140
Third Treaty of Washington, 87, 90
Three Affiliated Tribes of the Fort Berthold
     Reservation in North Dakota, 38
Tohono O'odham of Arizona, 23
Trail of Tears, 43, 101, 108, 136, 143. *See also*
     Ohio Trail of Tears
treaties, 81–84, 108, 118, 132, 133–34, 145,
     176
   dissolution of, 154–56
   treaty making, 78–79, 145
   Treaty of Dancing Rabbit Creek, 58
   Treaty of Fort Industry, 83
   Treaty of Fort Pitt, 78
   Treaty of New York, 82
   Treaty of Saginaw, 83
   Treaty of St. Louis of 1804, 79, 111–12
   Treaty of Washington of 1866, 135, 142, 143
   treaty rights, 55
   Treaty with the Delaware, 78
Tribal consultation, 1
Tribal disenrollment, 95–98
Tribal enrollment, 2–3, 5, 7–28, 43–44, 49–50,
     77, 94–98, 119–20, 137, 154, 170, 211–12,
     212–16
   as act of political dissent, 216
   bases for, 11, 19–24, 27, 35–36, 154 (*see also*
     blood quantum; kinship)
   benefits of, 11
   at birth, 24
   blood quantum and, 23–24, 27, 154
   CBID and, 177
   conflict between enrolled and unenrolled
     people, 143–44
   data on, 14–15, 60, 69 (*see also* Tribal rolls)

Tribal enrollment (*continued*)
  dual enrollment, 121–22
  fraud and, 138
  future work on, 218
  payments and, 95–97
  phone calls, 24–26
  political identity and, 11
  process, 7–28, 30, 31, 60, 61
  as protective, 212
  records of, 48, 81–82
  rejections of, 141–46
  renewal of, 18–19
  required, 140–41
  respecting, 193–94
  vs. self-identification, 3, 224n11
  skin color and, 140
  tests and classes, 19–21
  Tribal determination of, 14–15
  unintended consequences of, 213–14
Tribal enrollment card, 7–9, 18, 31
Tribal governance, 208. *See also* constitutions,
    Tribal
  provisions for, 153–54
  Tribal council, 51
  Tribal justice systems, 10
Tribal rolls, 22–23, 25, 26, 94–98, 214, 215. *See*
    also censuses; Tribal enrollment
  base rolls, 121
  blood quantum and, 23–24, 27, 154, 215
  census rolls, 22–23
  Creek Census, 1832, 87–90
Tribal self-governance, 22, 136, 155
  data and, 15–16
  dismantling of, 154–56
  Tribal law, 141–42
  Tribal law enforcement, 10
Tribal sovereignty, 9–11
  definition of, 10–11
  respecting, 193–94
Tulalip of Washington, 22–23
Tunkashila, the Great Spirit, 86
Tuscarora, 197

Ulrich, Roberta, 155
UNC Pembroke, 20, 202–3
unemployment, 109, 150, 162
UN Human Rights Council, 95
United Keetoowah Band of Cherokee Indians, 2
University of North Carolina system, 206
Upper Mattaponi, 168
Urban Indian Health Institute, 16
urbanity, rates of, 215
U.S. Army, 87–88

Commissary General of Subsistence, 102
  officers as Indian agents, 116–17
U.S. Bureau of Indian Affairs. *See* Bureau of
    Indian Affairs (BIA)
U.S. Census, 1, 55–74, 87, 102
  1790, 55–56
  1790–1840, 56–58, 64
  1830, 57–58
  1840, 64
  1850, 57, 59, 64–65, 73
  1860, 65
  1870, 64
  1880, 66
  1890, 67
  1900, 65, 67
  1920, 67
  1930, 67
  1940, 67
  1970, 180–81
  1990, 1
  2000, 1, 181
  2010, 181, 182
  2020, 2, 180, 181, 182
  "American Indian or Alaska Native" selection
    on, 181–83, 215
  changes to racial identity choices, 1
  Cherokee and, 223n9
  enslaved people on, 65, 72
  enslavers on, 58, 59
  fixation on racial purity and, 73
  genealogy and, 64–68
  Indian Schedule, 65, 67
  Lumbee recognition question and, 208–9
  mixed-race individuals on, 58
  multiracial boxes in, 181
  Native identity on, 1, 57–59, 65–68, 73,
    181–83, 215
  race on, 57, 59, 64–65, 66, 67, 72–73,
    180–81, 182, 199
  Slave Schedules, 65, 72
U.S. Census Bureau, 74, 180, 182, 183
U.S. citizenship, 58
  Burke Act and, 145–46
  provisional, 129–31, 145–46
U.S. Congress, 55, 56, 79, 108–9, 115, 168
  bills to recognize Lumbee, 207
  Burke Act, 145–46
  Curtis Act, 133–34
  Dawes Commission and, 133, 138
  definition of eligibility for allotments and, 137
  "Indian Problem" and, 208
  Jackson's speech to, 99–100
  Lumbee Act, 207

Public Law 280, 154–56
Public Law 959, 161
"Regulating the Indian Department," 83–84
resolution implementing "termination" phase,
    154–56
restoration of status of Native American Tribes
    and, 167–68
U.S. Constitution, 10, 55
U.S. Department of Education, Office of Indian
    Education, 150
U.S. Department of Health and Human Services,
    Administratoin for Native Americans, 150
U.S. Department of Housing and Urban
    Development, 14, 151
Office of Native American Policy, 150
U.S. Department of Justice, 45
U.S. Department of the Interior, 66, 116–17,
    130, 142–43, 153–54, 156, 176, 209
U.S. Department of Veterans Affairs, 151
U.S. Department of War, Indian Commission,
    87–88
U.S. government. *See* federal government; *specific
    branches, agencies, and departments*
U.S. House of Representatives, committee on
    Indian Affairs, 83–84
U.S. Marshals, 56–57, 66
U.S.-Mexico border, 218
U.S. Navy, 12
U.S. Senate, 82

veterans, 12, 150–51
    assistance to, 11
    home loans for, 188–89
Veteran's Administration, 188–89
vigilante justice, 194

Virginia, 145, 168
    "Racial Integrity Act," 168
Voluntary Relocation Program, 162, 163–64, 166

Wacomas, 197
Wahpeton Indian School, 160, 166
Walker, Alice, 102
War of 1812, 77
War Relocation Authority, 163
Washburn, Kevin, 14–15, 16, 108–9
Washington, George, 82, 124
Washington Post, 13
Washington State, 95
Wa'thishnade, 131
wealth gaps, 110–11
Weyanoke, 197
White, John, 197–98
whites, 39, 125–26, 199, 207
Wilkins, David, 9–10, 95
Wilkins, Shelly, 95
Wilkinson, Norman, 83
Wisakeha, 35
Wisconsin, 112, 155, 156
World War II, 12
Wyandot of Kansas, 132
Wyandotte of Oklahoma, 60–62, 69, 70–71,
    132
    "Census Roll of the Nation," 70
    Constitution of, 70
    membership in, 70
    rolls, 70–71

Yankton Sioux, 86

Zimmerman, William, Jr., 157

About the Author

Carrie Lowry Schuettpelz is an enrolled member of the Lumbee Tribe of North Carolina. She spent seven years working in the Obama administration on issues of homelessness and Native policy. She holds an MFA in creative writing from the University of Wisconsin-Madison and a Master in Public Policy from Harvard's Kennedy School of Government. *The Indian Card* is her first book.